I0810024

IMAGES
of America

LA MESA

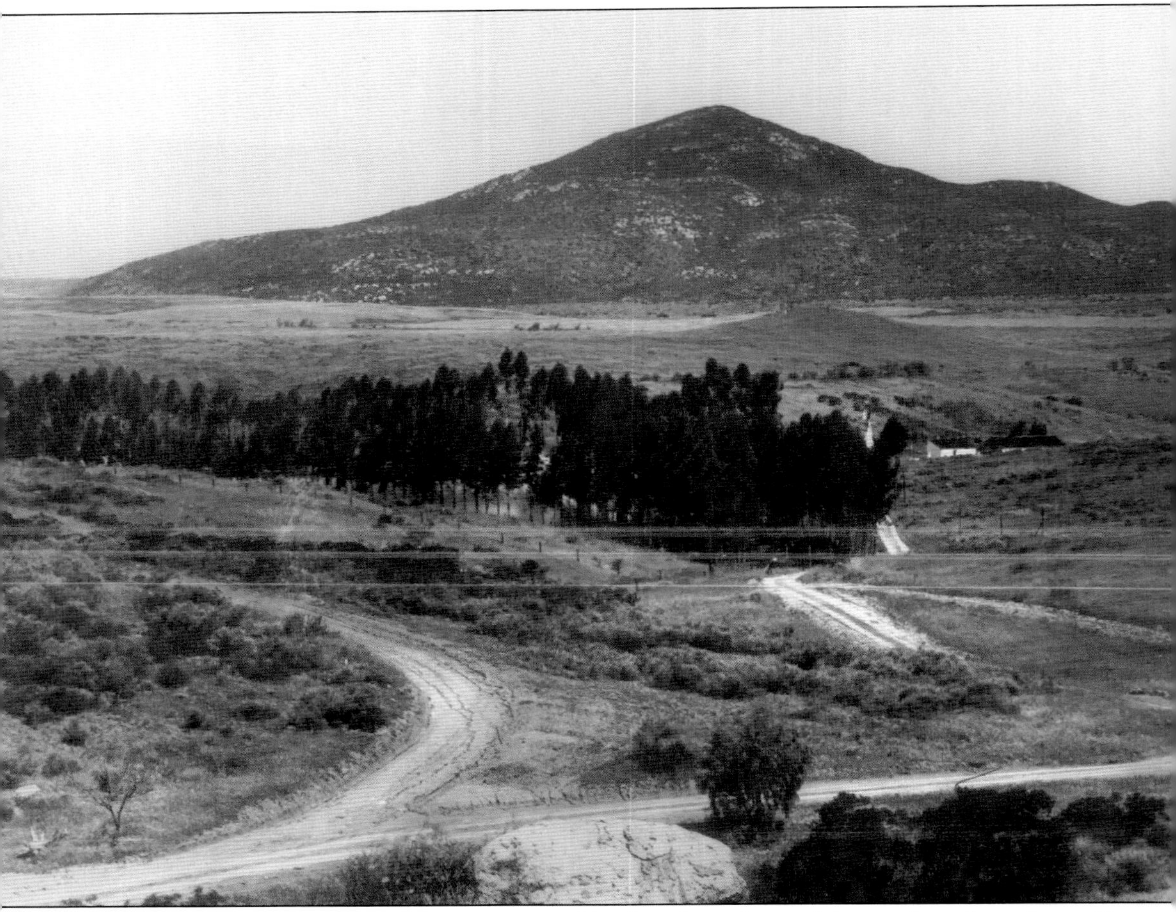

Cowles Mountain, 1910s. An iconic natural landmark just beyond the northern boundary of La Mesa's modern city limits, this distinctive mountain peak, pronounced "Coals" and sometimes known as "Black Mountain," is named for pioneer 19th-century El Cajon Valley rancher/farmer George Cowles. Today it is located within Mission Trails Regional Park, serving millions as a recreational and open space resource. (La Mesa Historical Society.)

On the Cover: La Mesa Springs Fourth of July Parade, 1911. A young La Mesa's community spirit is seen at the corner of Spring Street and Lookout Avenue (now La Mesa Boulevard). Seven months later, the small, mostly rural community of merchants, speculators, entrepreneurs, farmers, and health seekers incorporated the City of La Mesa. (La Mesa Historical Society.)

IMAGES
of America

LA MESA

James D. Newland
La Mesa Historical Society

ARCADIA
PUBLISHING

ISBN 978-0-7385-8043-2

Published by Arcadia Publishing
Charleston, South Carolina

Printed in the United States of America

Library of Congress Control Number: 2009938750

For all general information contact Arcadia Publishing at:
Telephone 843-853-2070
Fax 843-853-0044
E-mail sales@arcadiapublishing.com

Visit us on the Internet at www.arcadiapublishing.com

The book is dedicated to all, past and present, who have helped La Mesa become and continue to be the "Jewel of the Hills."

Contents

ACKNOWLEDGMENTS

This book is the result of the La Mesa Historical Society's wonderful work. First, I must thank past-president Gordon Jones for the opportunity to write this book for the society. Additional thanks to the current board of directors—Ed Blackman, Ruth Contino, Sharon Crockett, Tom Hart, Aaron Landau, Cherie Peacock, Linda Rankin, Pat Stromberg, Kathy Tinsley, and Rod Whitlow—for their enthusiasm and support. Pres. Donna Neimeier deserves special thanks for her leadership, guidance, and access to the La Mesa–Spring Valley School District collections. Previous historical scholarship, including the 1976 City Bicentennial Committee's informative *La Mesa–A Brief History* and the society's own Norrie West, Karna Webster, Pat Kettler, and Carol Lockwood's 2001 *La Mesa Through the Years*, deserve much credit for providing this book with a solid foundation. Society pioneers Pat, Karna, Donna Regan, and many others' significant work to collect and organize the society's archives and photographic collections are admirable and invaluable. This book and the city centennial's upcoming historical undertakings are indebted to the herculean efforts of these dedicated volunteers to preserve and share their community's history. Many other institutions, historians, archivists, and friends have provided assistance and inspiration, including the dedicated and underpaid photo archivists of the San Diego Historical Society, Chris Travers and Carol Myers; UCSD Special Collections; the Helix Water District's Kate Breece and consultant Chris Wray; Lt. Bobby Barrett, La Mesa Police Department, retired; Foothillers-for-life Connie and Lynn Baer and Don Ginn of the Grossmont High School Museum; Rick Hall of the El Cajon Historical Society; 1961 Little-leaguer Chico Leonard; La Mesa bibliophiles Craig Maxwell and Deena While; graphical magician Sandra Farrell; city staffers Yvonne Garrett, Allyson Kinnard, and Kaaren McElroy; and the City Council and Centennial Steering Committee. Additional thanks to Ralph Bowman for sharing his La Mesa postcards and Debbie Seracini for scanning them. Once again, no greater thanks or profession of love can go to my wife, Jennifer, and daughter, Lindsay, for their sacrifices in living with me through another book.

INTRODUCTION

For over 100 years, people have come to the area now known as La Mesa to make a living, build homes, and raise families. Today it is a city of approximately 60,000 citizens, many of who live in the post–World War II–era suburban north and west or in the older neighborhoods surrounding the historic commercial core known as "the Village." Its reputation is that of a small, well-run city that is a bedroom community for Greater San Diego and a gateway to the East County. Others connect it with unincorporated neighboring areas such as Grossmont or Mount Helix and its wonderful and historic open-air Nature Theatre and park. Many, including thousands who do not live here, may associate the city with the regional Grossmont Shopping Center or Grossmont Hospital or with its popular Oktoberfest celebrations, summer car shows, Flag Day parades, or antique shops and restaurants found in the small-town atmosphere of old downtown.

The story of how this small city developed, grew, and prospered while holding off the annexation attempts of its larger and expansion-minded western neighbor San Diego reflects the integral role that this resolute and determined community has played in the overall history of what is now a county of well over 3 million residents. Located between the major metropolitan city of San Diego and the El Cajon Valley and Mount Helix to the east, these table or mesa lands have played a key role in the transportation and urban development history of the region. The city's location at the pass that leads east and its seminal role in the water development of the nearby San Diego River watershed have made it valuable property for those promoting regional agricultural, commercial, and urban growth from the 18th to the 21st century.

Once part of the Mission San Diego de Alcala rancho lands, its documented history can be traced to the Euro-American origins of the region. The natural springs in today's Collier Park, which had served the Kumeyaay and the nearby village of Meti for centuries, were key to providing much-needed water to support the mission's newly imported stock herds. The Spanish colonial missionaries renamed the valley *El Aguaje de San Jorge* (the springs of St. George)—today's Spring Valley. The Spanish colonial system, with its new land uses and social and political systems, forever changed the cultural landscape of the Kumeyaay. These next few decades of rapid change challenged the plans and aspirations of both the Spanish and the Kumeyaay. After the missions' secularization during the Mexican Republic period, the remaining ex-mission rancho lands were sold to former San Diego Presidio commandant Santiago Arguello. After the United States occupied Alta California in 1846 and Arguello died in 1862, the land was caught in decades of litigation between the U.S. government, Arguello's descendants, those who purchased lots from the descendants and land speculators, and squatters. The lengthy and costly litigation would not result in clear title to the future lands of La Mesa until 1884.

One of those early American pioneers to "the Mesa" was Robert Allison, who purchased roughly 4,000 acres surrounding the future Collier Park springs and down into what would become Lemon Grove in 1869. Allison would use the lands for grazing his stock, improving the property only minimally. After the San Diego Flume Company brought San Diego River water to the area and the San Diego, Cuyamaca, and Eastern Railroad (SDCE) came through "Allison's Springs" in the early 1890s, Allison's son Joseph and local rancher/speculator A. S. Crowder platted a small town, La Mesa Springs, around the Allison station and the newly formed La Mesa Lemon Company's packinghouse and store. This small community of mostly citrus farmers would continue to grow, building a school for their children, forming churches and new businesses, and attracting suburban developers shortly after the beginning of the 20th century. The community's concerns for a consistent water supply, economic stability, improved infrastructure, and local control would lead its 700-plus citizens to incorporate La Mesa Springs into the City of La Mesa in February 1912.

La Mesa's reputation as a healthful, prosperous, and convenient place to do business, live, and raise a family quickly became a mantra for its suburban developers and civic and business leaders who subsequently marketed and sold the community as "San Diego's Pasadena," the "Jewel of the Hills," and East County's "Homeland." Steadily the new suburban city continued to grow, along with its outlying neighbors such as Grossmont and Mount Helix, slowly moving the community away from its agricultural roots. With railroad connections to San Diego and points east and with advent of the automobile and motor transport, La Mesa's geographic location also became one of its strongest selling points. Its location on the new state highway (El Cajon Boulevard), later christened U.S. 80 in 1926, strategically positioned the young city for commerce and commuting. With the newest schools, banks, and business opportunities, La Mesa soon became a commercial, civic, and social center not only within the initial city limits but for the then-unincorporated areas west to the boundary of East San Diego and for the eastern and southern communities of Grossmont, Mount Helix, Calavo Gardens, Casa de Oro, Spring Valley, and Lemon Grove. Its growth led to formation of a bevy of voluntary associations and service clubs, an asset that continues to this day.

During the interwar years, the city was buoyed by the local successors to the San Diego Flume Company, Ed Fletcher and James Murray's Cuyamaca Water Company and its 1926 purchaser, the La Mesa, Lemon Grove, and Spring Valley Irrigation District (later the Helix Water District), in its efforts to hold off annexation and disincorporation. The city's steadily growing population reached 3,912 by 1940. Following the region's massive growth during and after World War II, La Mesa became one of the fastest growing suburban communities in San Diego, with its population exponentially tripling in the 1940s and 1950s. Demands on its infrastructure during this postwar boom demanded annexation of lands to the north and west, development of new suburban tracts with thousands of new homes, and the building of many new schools within the city limits, including in 1952 La Mesa Junior High School and Helix High School, a companion to the regional Grossmont High School. By 1980, the city had reached a population of 50,000 and had pressed its geographic limits while challenging the old business district to fully serve the growing population. With the development of freeways such as U.S. 80/Interstate 8 and State Routes 94 and 125, new retail patterns moved toward auto-oriented, suburban shopping centers and regional malls. In 1961, Grossmont Center, only the third regional mall in the county, opened in La Mesa adjacent to the new U.S. 80 freeway bypass, becoming an instant commercial and economic engine for the city.

Civic and business leaders' initial plans for downtown's redevelopment in response to Grossmont Center's opening in the 1960s were delayed but later capitalized on the reactivation of the old SDCE railroad into the Metropolitan Transit Development Board's light-rail trolley system in the 1980s. This triggered transit-oriented, mixed-use redevelopment west of Spring Street that helped reinvigorate and draw attention to the historic Village. Since the 1980s, La Mesa's population growth has subsided, being limited to infill and redevelopment projects—several along the trolley line and a revitalized Fletcher Parkway. As such, the city continues to be a popular location for businesses and families.

Covering such a rich history within the limitations of this book's format presented a challenge. The photographic and archival collections of the La Mesa Historical Society feature several thousand images that provide a fascinating, entertaining, and evocative photographic chronicle of the city and its environs through its key historic periods. With room for just over 200 images, it was necessary to be judicious in the selection of graphics in order not only to present the contextual history but also to do justice to the landmarks, institutions, and events that have shaped the community. As such, I have consciously steered away from large numbers of prominent individuals and family portraits and have attempted to choose photographs of places, buildings, structures, sites, and panoramic images that provide a varied visual chronicle of the city and the area's historical transformation. Therefore many key figures—business, civic, social, and political leaders—whose notable accomplishments warrant their inclusion did not receive individual photographs but are covered in the text, captions, and group images, but in some cases, they are absent. Any individual omissions are my responsibility, and no slight should be inferred from their absence. In addition, I also attempted to avoid using the more recognizable, previously published historical photographs in order to introduce unpublished but similar and informative views when opportunity allowed.

The narrative is organized into six chapters: Historical Origins (Prehistory–1886), Community Beginnings (1886–1912), The Young City (1912–1925), Jewel of the Hills (1925–1945), Postwar Suburban Boomtown (1945–1980), and Hometown for the Next Century (1980–Present). The Historical Origins chapter introduces the Native American, Spanish colonial, Mexican Republic, and Early American groups, individuals, and settlers who set the stage for the community's growth. The Community Beginnings chapter features the story of the foundational infrastructure established via the San Diego Flume Company and San Diego, Cuyamaca, and Eastern Railroad and pioneer individuals, homes, ranches, and subsequent suburban tracts of the fledgling development. The Young City chapter introduces key individuals, families, civic associations and government institutions, landmark businesses, buildings, and homes that served the new city. The Jewel of the Hills chapter chronicles the vibrant interwar years, in which civic promotion built up the community and led it through the challenges of the Great Depression and World War II. Images of civic and promotional events such as the annual Fiesta de los Flores pageant, the long-gone La Mesa Country Club, and community institutions are featured. Postwar Suburban Boomtown chronicles the exponential growth of La Mesa to the north and west, including the regionally significant Grossmont Shopping Center and Grossmont Hospital. New suburban neighborhoods, schools, institutions, and prominent individual accomplishments bringing attention and adulation for the emergent "City of Champions" are included. The final chapter focuses on the recent history of La Mesa—its current institutions and landmarks as well as some of the more well-known and significant La Mesans who have brought leadership, honor, and pride to the city and community.

So, venture back into this city and community's story through the historical images of our little suburban hometown. It is hoped that this brief introduction to the rich heritage of La Mesa will provide residents, neighbors, and visitors with a better understanding of the efforts, accomplishments, challenges, and community spirit that have shaped today's city.

All images are courtesy of the La Mesa Historical Society unless otherwise noted.

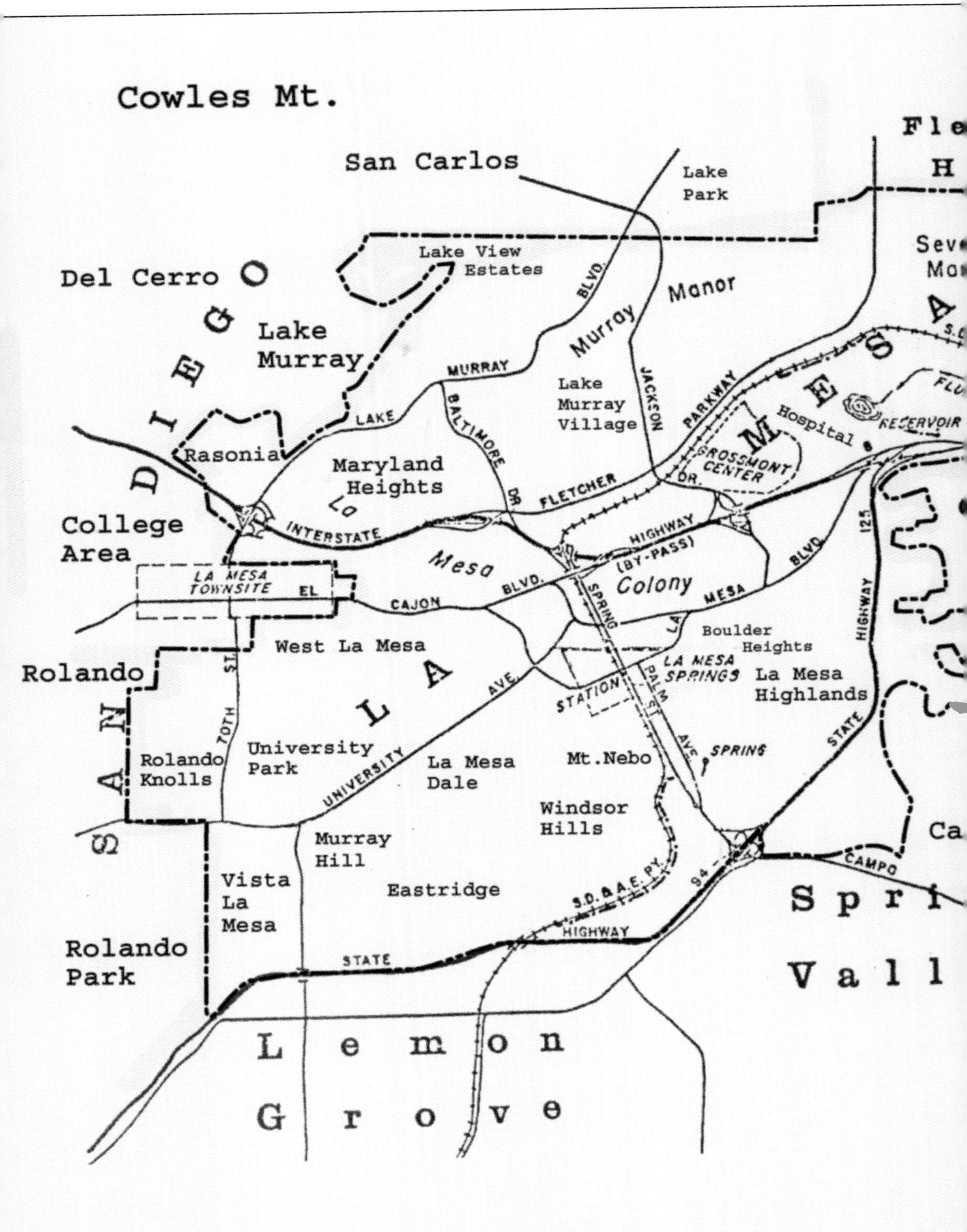
Cowles Mt.
San Carlos
Lake Park
Del Cerro
Lake View Estates
Manor
Murray Blvd.
Lake Murray
Rasonia
Maryland Heights
Lake Murray Village
Hospital
Grossmont Center
Reservoir
College Area
La Mesa Townsite
Colony
Interstate
Fletcher
Highway (By-Pass)
Parkway
Jackson
Baltimore Dr.
Lake Murray
El Cajon Blvd.
La Mesa Blvd.
West La Mesa
Boulder Heights
La Mesa Springs
La Mesa Highlands
Station
Spring St
Palm Ave.
Rolando
Rolando Knolls
University Park
University Ave.
70th St.
La Mesa Dale
Mt. Nebo
Spring
Windsor Hills
Murray Hill
Eastridge
Vista La Mesa
Rolando Park
S.D. & A.E. Ry.
State Highway 94
Highway 125
Campo
San Diego
La Mesa
Lemon Grove
Spri
Vall

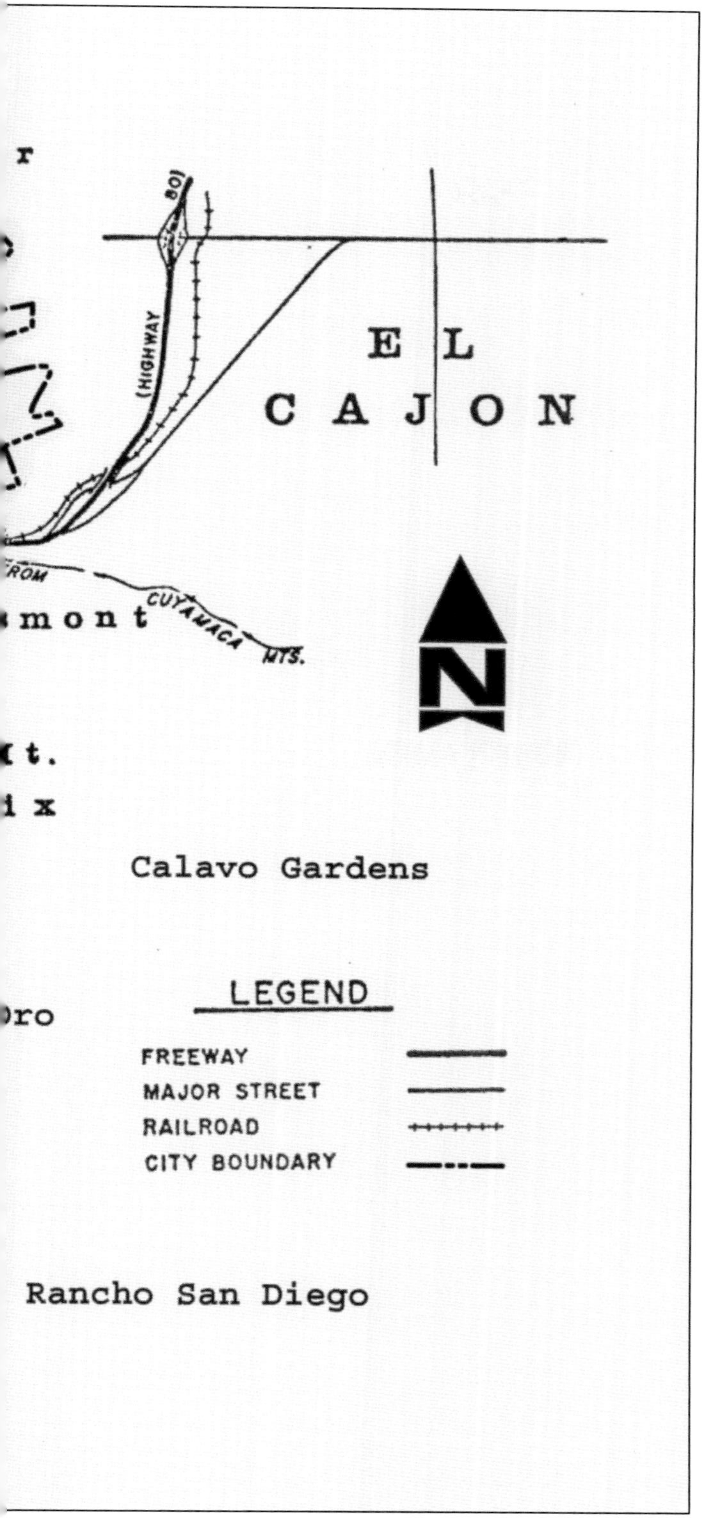

LA MESA AND VICINITY MAP, C. 1980. Modern La Mesa consists of numerous neighborhoods developed upon the tablelands between Cowles Mountain on the north, the El Cajon Valley and Mount Helix on the east, and Spring Valley and Lemon Grove on the south. This map, showing 1980s boundaries, includes the most recent western mesa-area annexations, such as Vista La Mesa, Rolando Knolls, and Rasonia, along with other formally associated neighborhoods lost to San Diego such as Rolando, Rolando Park, and the College Area. The postwar tract suburbs of Murray Manor, Lake Murray Village, and the Severin Manor area of Fletcher Hills stretch across the north, while unincorporated neighbors Grossmont, Mount Helix, and Spring Valley border to the east and south (base map from Bibb 1973:9).

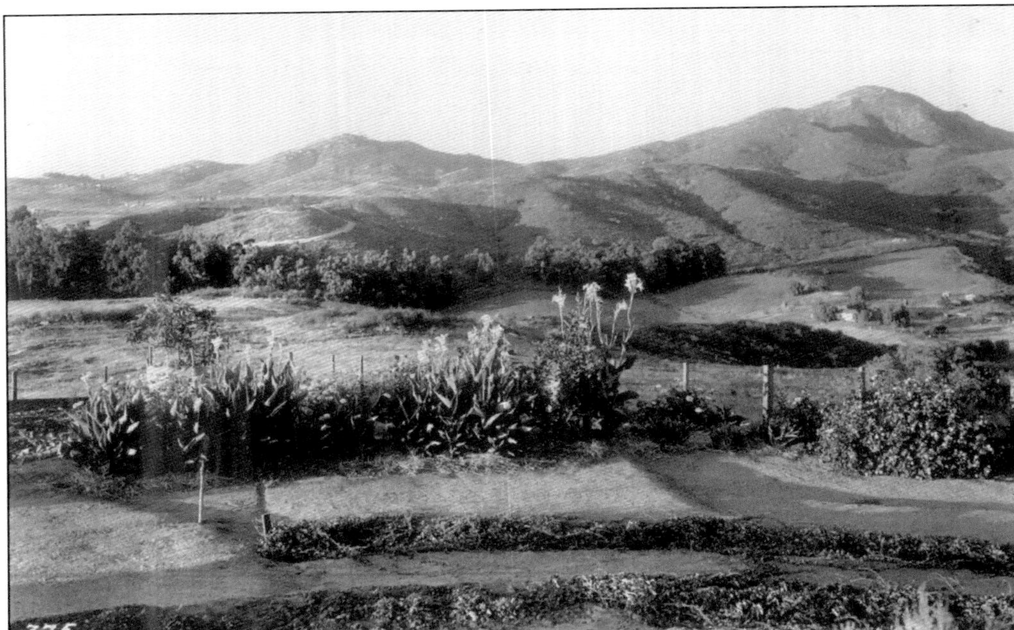

Grossmont Peak and Mount Helix, 1920s. La Mesa's eastern boundary includes these two distinctive landmarks. Progressive businessman, developer, and civic leader Ed Fletcher purchased the area in 1902, naming the peak and its residential development for his business partner and noted entertainer William Gross. Spring Valley pioneer Rufus Porter named Mount Helix after Swiss scientist Louis Agassiz discovered *Helix aspersa* snails there in 1872.

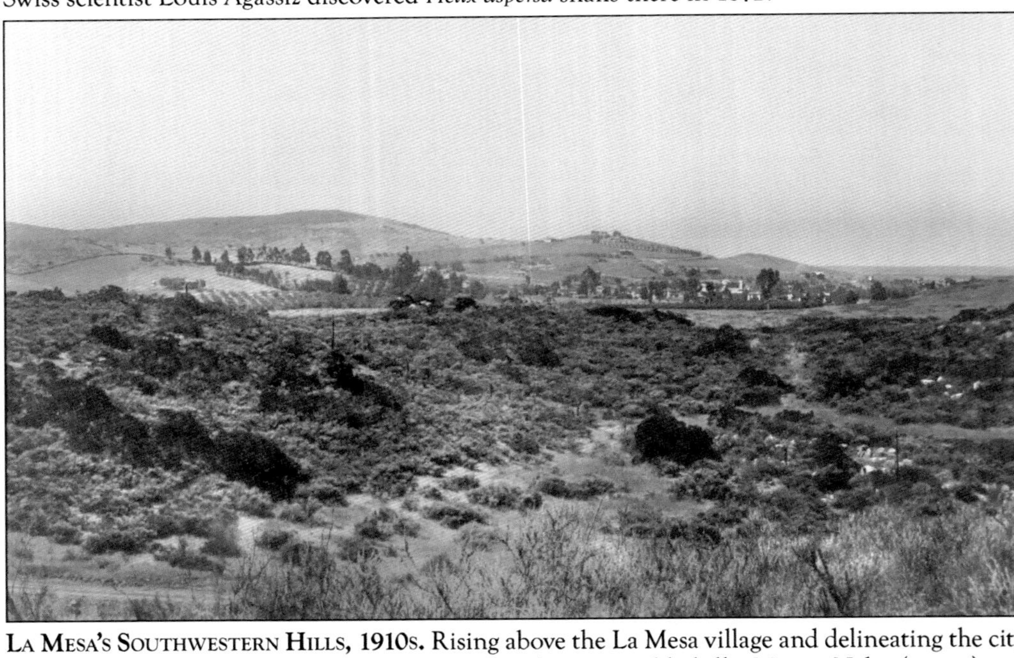

La Mesa's Southwestern Hills, 1910s. Rising above the La Mesa village and delineating the city from southern neighbor Lemon Grove are several recognizable hills. Mount Nebo (center) was the site of the city's first exclusive residential tracts. Eastridge, the left peak, became an exclusive home area in the 1950s. Murray Hill, to the right in the distance, rises above today's Helix High.

One

HISTORICAL ORIGINS
PREHISTORY TO 1886

La Mesa's cultural history is centuries old. Archaeological and ethnographic studies indicate that local native people, the Kumeyaay, lived in the area and used its resources for thousands of years. The Kumeyaay world changed significantly with the arrival of Spanish missionaries and soldiers. They introduced stock grazing and intensive agricultural practices, along with a new social system and epidemic-inducing diseases that rapidly weakened and displaced Kumeyaay society, altered the native environment, and forever changed the centuries-old cultural landscape. Mission San Diego de Alcala, established in 1769 on Old Town's Presidio Hill, was moved to its current site upriver near the village of Nipaguay in 1774. The mission's jurisdiction encompassed the lands throughout today's central and eastern county, including the tablelands south and east of Mission Valley that rose from today's East San Diego out to the El Cajon Valley, simply known as "The Mesa." After Mexican independence from Spain in 1822, new laws promoted private land holdings and foreign trade, reducing the mission's power and authority. Mexican Californios obtained private land grants, working to acquire the valuable mission lands. In 1846, the Mexican government sold the remaining lands of the then-destitute Mission San Diego to Santiago Arguello. U.S. occupation of California a year later introduced a new set of cultural values and brought more changes, including onerous laws and procedures for proving boundaries and title for Mexican claims. Arguello and his heirs and assignees would struggle for over three decades to clarify boundaries and clear their title, hampering purchases and development within the ex-mission grant. American settlers looking to introduce marketable crops and develop the physical infrastructure to connect with eastern markets eyed these former mission lands for their own. Starting in the 1850s, wagon roads east from San Diego passed through "The Mesa," requiring the establishment of Dan Manning and Christian Jepson's "road station" settlements and eventually attracting apiarist John Harbison and stockman and original community namesake Robert Allison to purchase several large tracts of former rancho land.

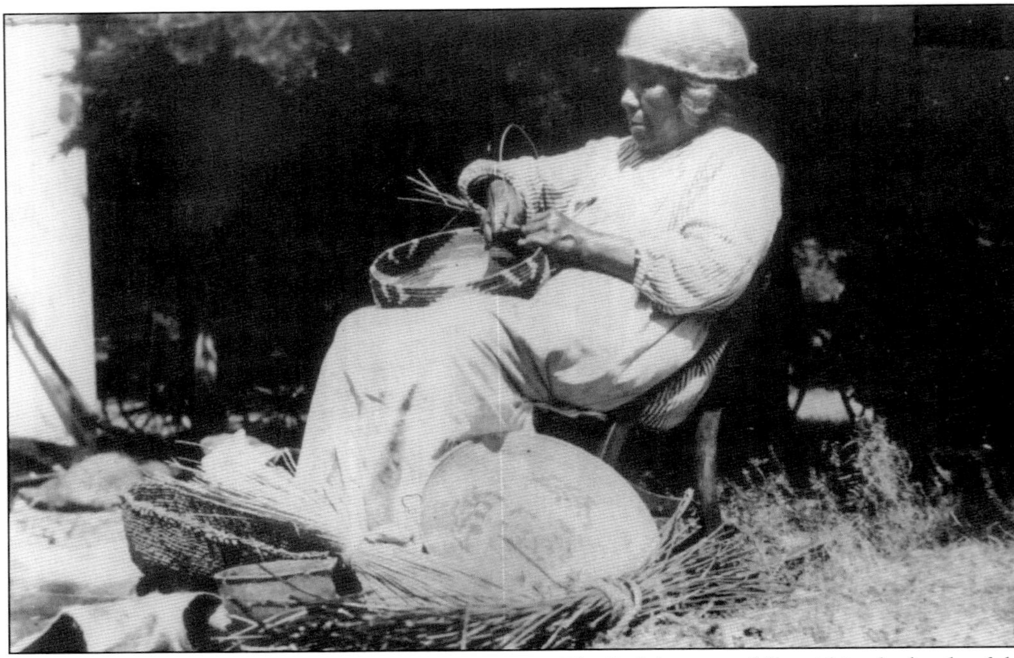

KUMEYAAY BASKETRY AND POTTERY MAKERS, C. 1900. The La Mesa area falls within the lands of the southern Kumeyaay (Tipai) cultural group, although the greater Kumeyaay territory extended from the coastal beaches and lagoons of San Diego County east across the Coastal mountain ranges to the Colorado Desert and south into northern Baja California. The Kumeyaay sustained themselves through hunting, gathering, and fishing but also practiced their own versions of land management, including brush burning, seed broadcasting, transplanting, and planting. They were expert basket and pottery makers and were skilled in fabricating stone tools and making ocean-worthy tule boats. They organized themselves into autonomous bands associated with villages, such as the local Meti, while establishing outlying and seasonal campsites at water sources.

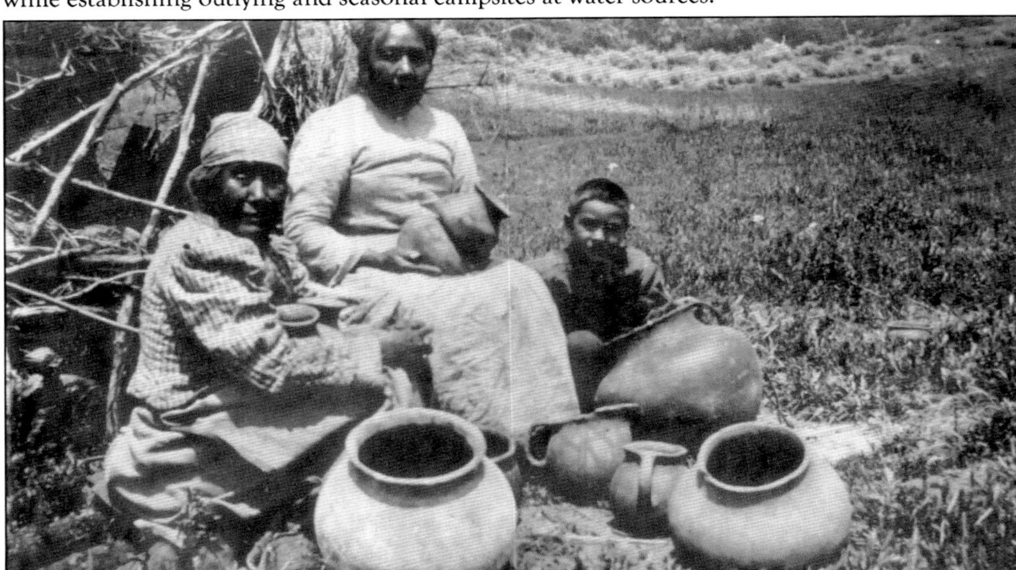

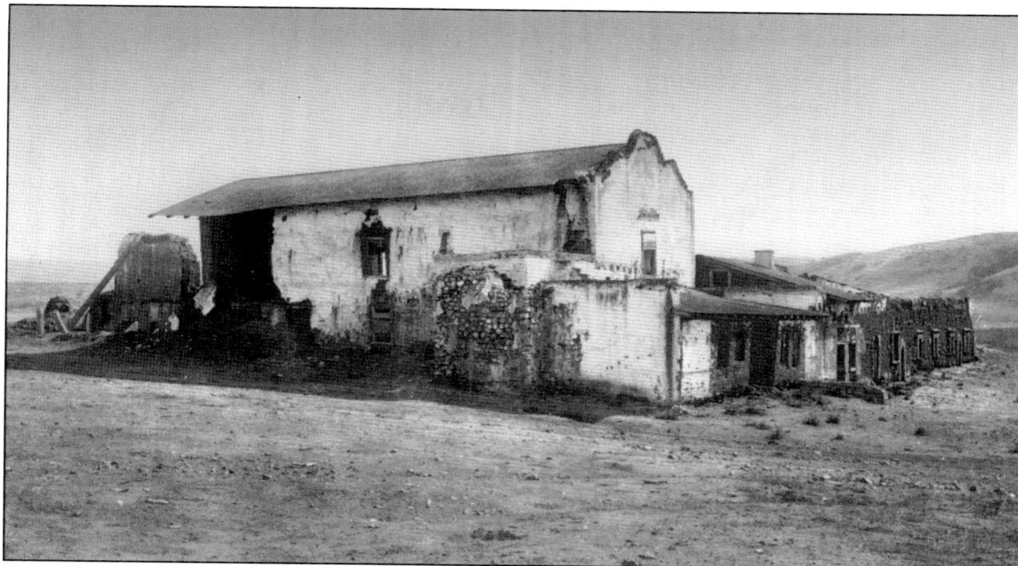

MISSION SAN DIEGO, C. 1886. Mission San Diego de Alcala was Alta California's first but struggled to achieve the success missionaries envisioned. Attempts to sow and harvest staple crops such as wheat, barley, corn, cotton, and beans were hampered by the arid climate and the local Kumeyaays' resolute and independent nature, many of who resisted conversion to mission life.

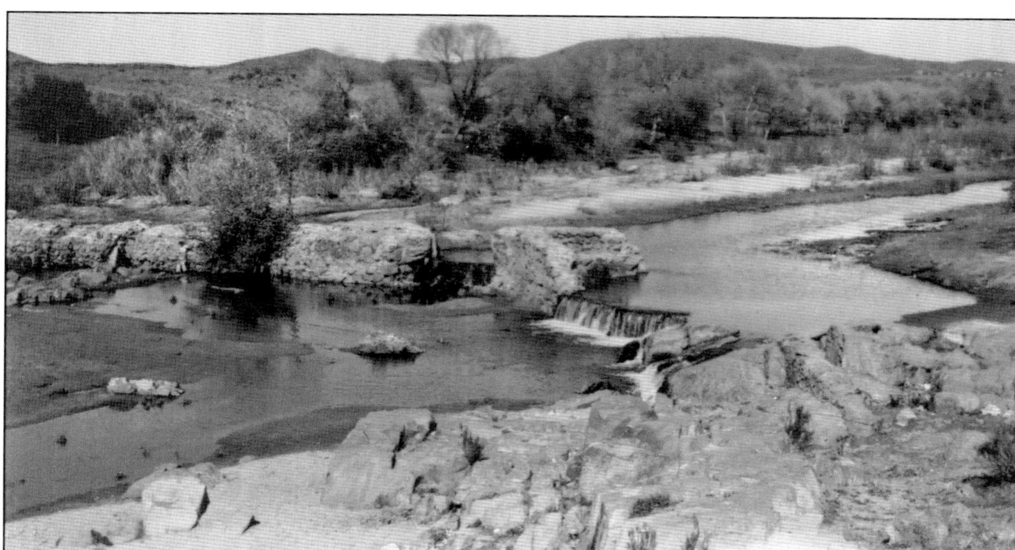

MISSION DAM, 1930S. At Mission Gorge's eastern entrance, this Kumeyaay-built dam helped secure a stable water supply for the mission's fields. Tapping the San Diego River would continue to be a key component to future development plans for the arid mesas that would become La Mesa. (USDA–Cleveland National Forest.)

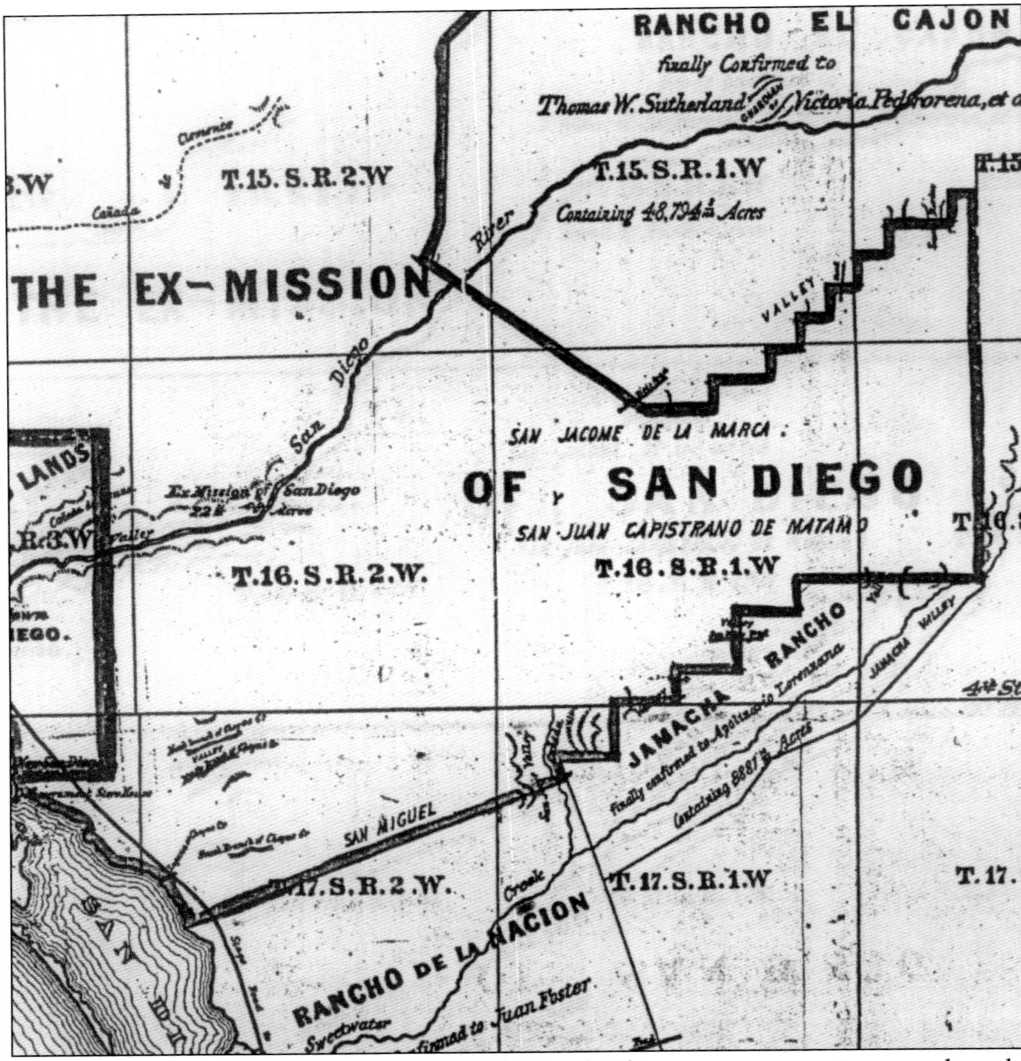

Ex-Mission Rancho Exception Map, 1869 (Portion). This court case map is cropped on the future La Mesa area and documents names established during the Mission San Diego days, some adapted from Kumeyaay names (*Jamacha, Matamo*). The missionaries and their neophyte workers accessed the mesa lands through Alvarado Canyon or by trails following Native American routes that went up Fairmount Canyon across today's College Neighborhoods toward Lemon Grove and out to the Valle de San Jorge (Spring Valley). An 1827 mission report noted that the well-watered area of San Jorge held mission sheep and was planted with cotton. Nearby San Jacome de la Marca (south El Cajon), San Juan Capistrano de Matamo (likely Helix/Calavo), and "la mesas" served as grazing lands for mission horses, sheep, and mules. Former mission ranch lands such as Jamacha and Santa Monica (or "El Cajon"), supported fields along the San Diego and Sweetwater Rivers as well as forage for grazing stock.

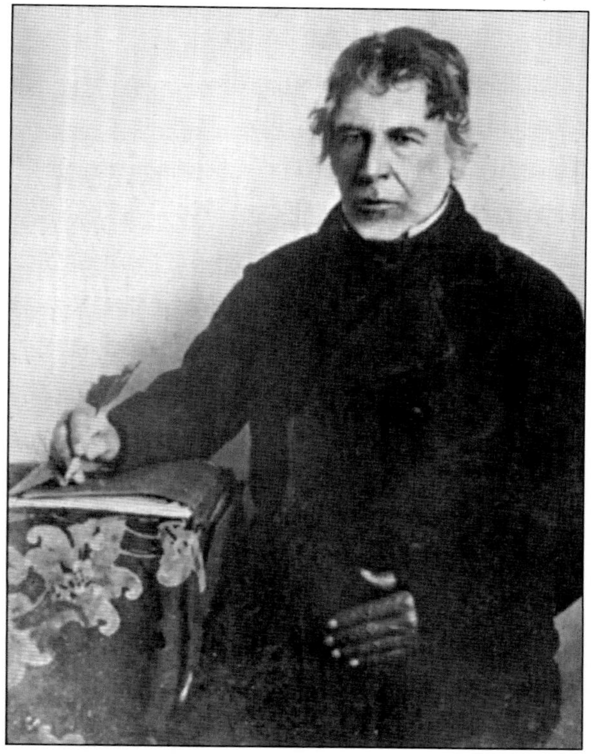

Santiago Arguello, c. 1856. The California missions declined rapidly during the Mexican Republic period. In June 1846, Gov. Pio Pico sold "all remaining lands and property of the Mission San Diego" to the former presidio commandant to help pay its debts. Although other mission lands, such as Jamul, Jamacha, and El Cajon, had already been granted away, these ex-mission lands would total 58,875 acres.

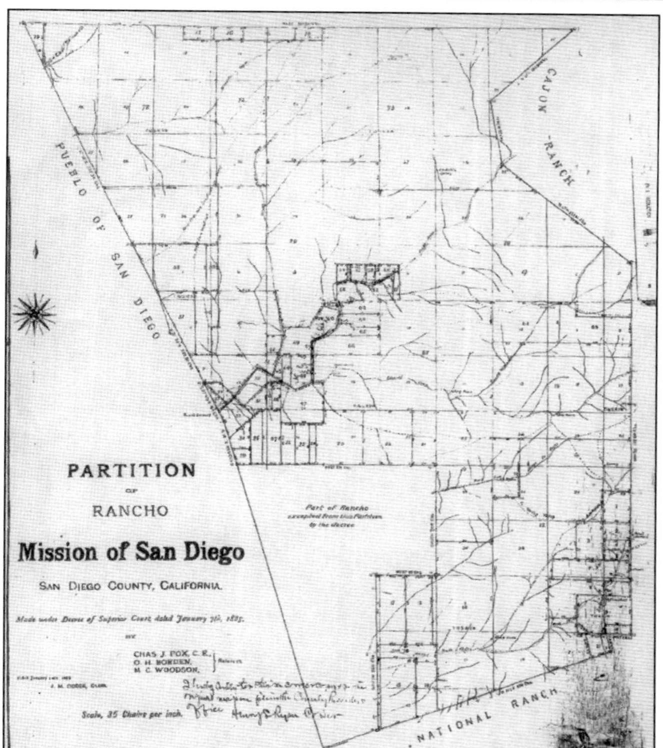

Partition Case Map, 1884. After U.S. occupation, California law created onerous and bureaucratic legal procedures for proving up previous Mexican land claims such as Arguello's. Although he initially filed in 1852, his title would not clear until 22 years after his death. The rancho's uncertain title hindered Arguello's heirs, land speculators, and settlers from developing the land.

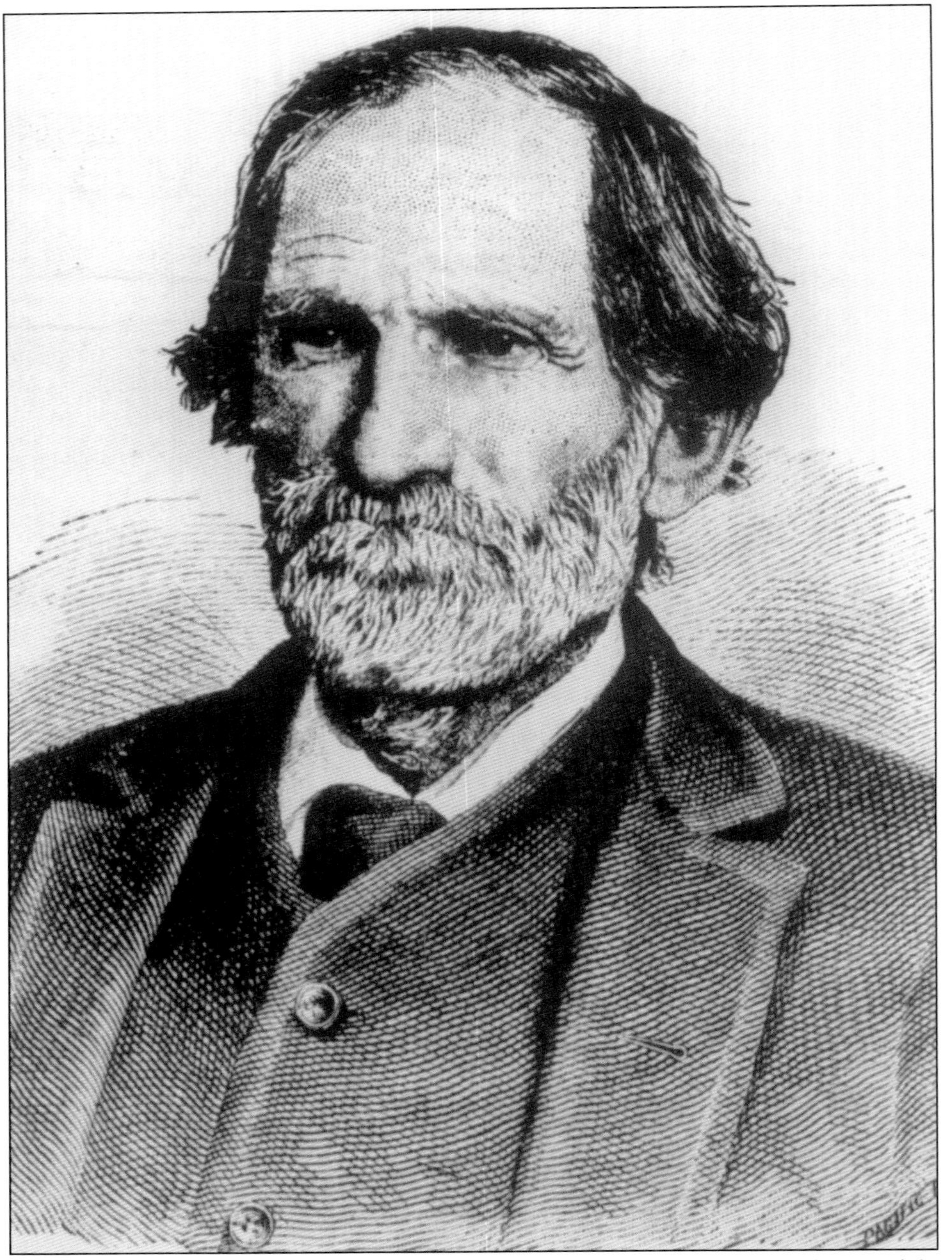

Robert Allison, 1880s. In 1851, Iowan Robert Allison moved his family to Northern California, where he prospered selling meat and supplies in the growing new state. In 1868, Allison moved his family to arid San Diego to improve his health. He began to purchase properties throughout the county to continue his stock business. In 1869, he purchased 4,282 acres of the ex-mission grant in Lot 12—the land now encompassing La Mesa south of today's University Avenue and west and south into Lemon Grove—on which he grazed sheep. Allison's San Diego investments would also include the Rancho Cuyamaca, extremely valuable after the 1870 discovery of gold in Julian and the Cuyamacas, and large grazing properties near Campo in today's east county. By the 1880s, Allison was one of the county's most prosperous businessmen and landowners.

John Harbison, 1880s. Another ex-mission lands purchaser in this period was pioneering apiarist John Harbison, who invented the sectional honey box that revolutionized honey production. In 1881, Harbison purchased the 4,185-acre Lot 19, which extended north and west from Allison's Lot 12 property.

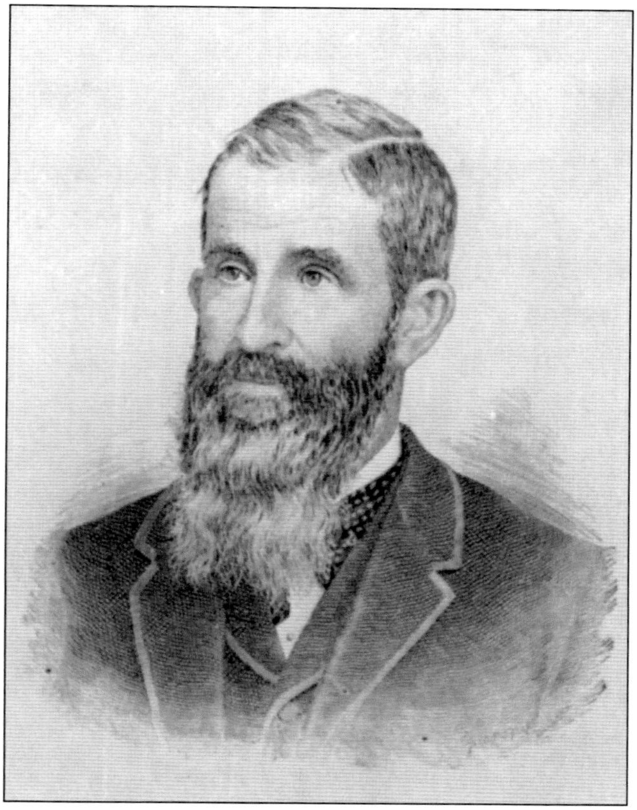

Spring Valley School c. 1897. In the 1860s, government surveyors confirmed that San Jorge was not within the ex-mission grant, opening it for settlement. Pioneers Augustus Ensworth, Rufus Porter, Robert Smith Campbell, and others claimed homesteads. In 1877, these pioneer families built Jamacha School, later renamed Spring Valley in the 1890s, predating similar community development on "the mesa."

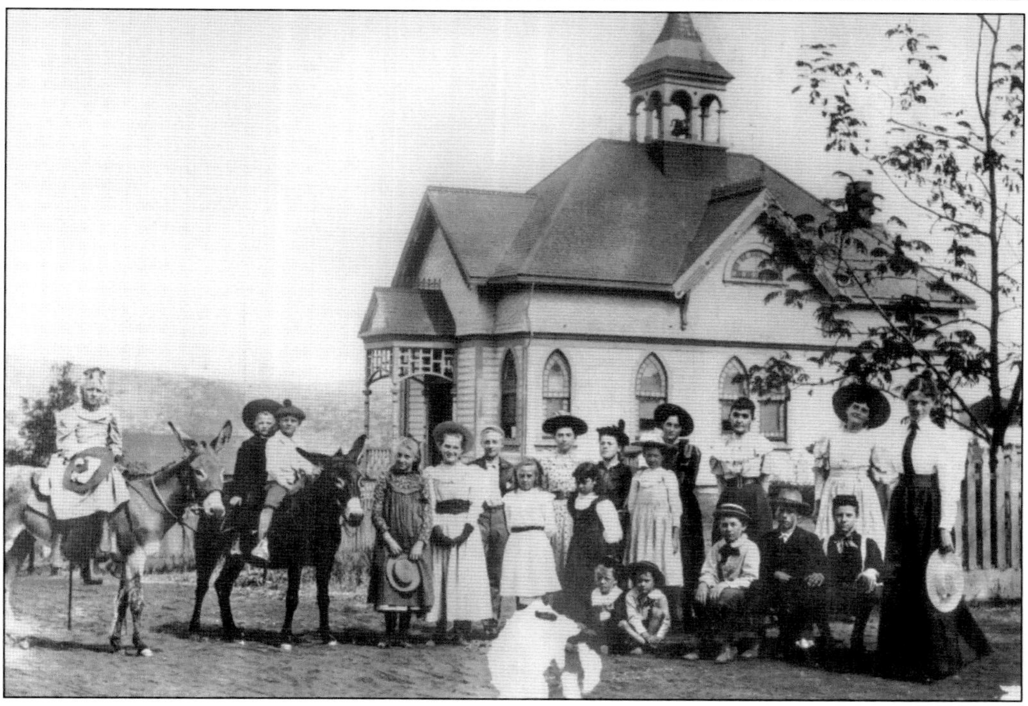

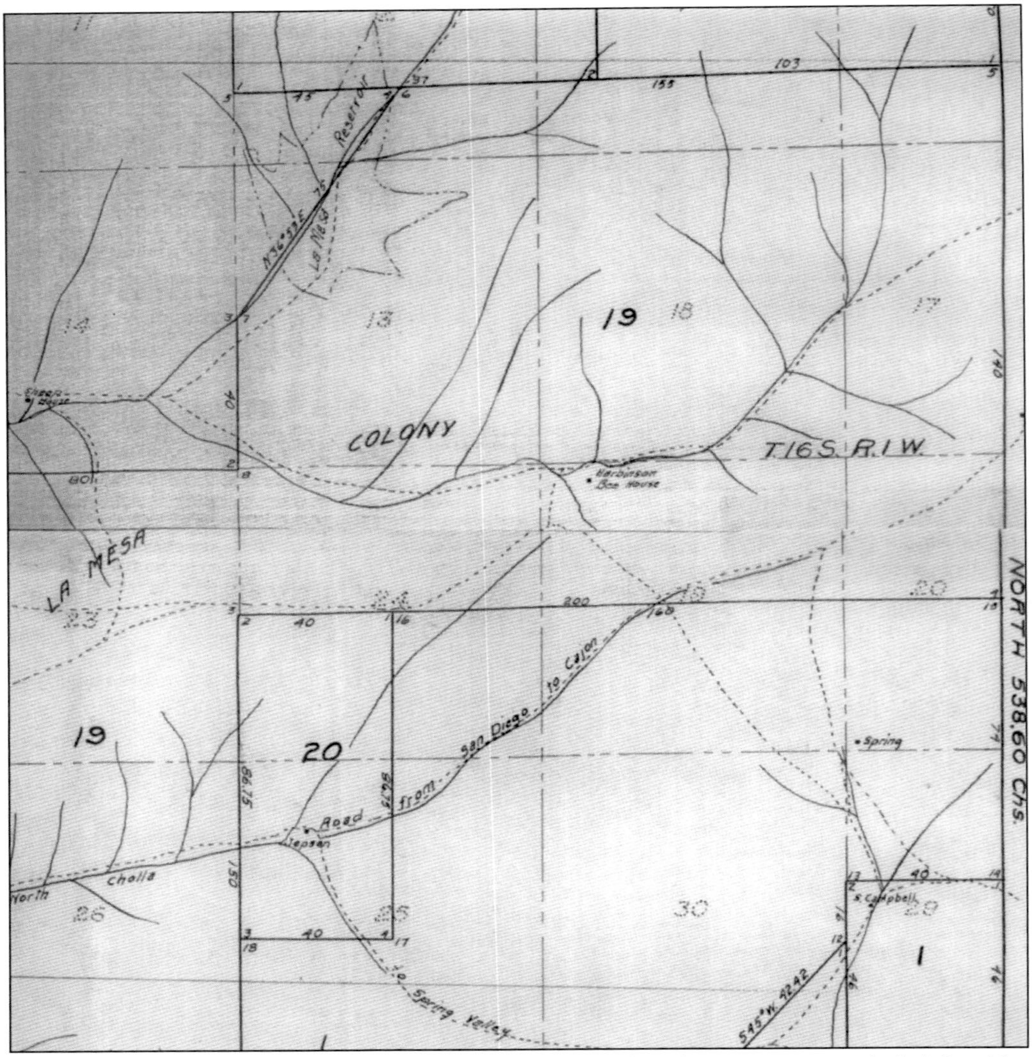

Partition Case Map, Mesa Area, 1884. The landscape before the community included the older Chollas Road, listed as "Road from San Diego to Cajon," and the future El Cajon Boulevard to the north. At the Chollas/"Road to Spring Valley" (Massachusetts Avenue) junction stood Christian Jepson's "Halfway House" (in Lot 20). Jepson kept a house, corral, stable, and well where he served travelers since 1875. Farther east was Dan Manning's Summit House (center edge of the map), where he and his wife also provided meals and accommodations (roughly where Interstate 8 meets State Road 125 today). One of Harbison's bee houses is shown along today's Fletcher Parkway. Allison's Springs is shown above Smith Campbell's Spring Valley ranch. He originally built a small reservoir and tank to capture the spring's water with corrals and a herder's cabin there. In 1883, Allison testified that he had occupied his mesa sheep ranch for 14 years, occasionally grazing on Harbison's lands to the north. Within two years of this testimony, Allison's Springs would begin changing from sheep ranch to community.

Two

Community Beginnings 1886–1912

The Ex-Mission grant's title cleared at the same time as the Great 1880s Southern California Land Boom. For San Diego, the Santa Fe Railroad's 1885 arrival triggered an influx of home-seekers that led speculators to purchase land and lay out new towns and rural communities to meet the demand. The San Diego Flume Company and San Diego, Cuyamaca, and Eastern Railroad (SDCE) were the keys to opening the mesa. The San Diego Flume Company's ambitious plans called for storing and transporting San Diego River water to the mesa through a wooden flume system ending at the La Mesa Reservoir, where it could be distributed to San Diego and the company's own development, the La Mesa Colony and Townsite (at today's Seventieth Street and El Cajon Boulevard). The company completed the flume in 1889, the same year that the SDCE was completed east from San Diego. The railroad traveled from San Diego through the Chollas Valley with a stop at Allison's Springs then over the summit to El Cajon Valley and beyond. Colony settlers opened La Mesa School at the colony town site in 1891, but with the railroad station at Allison's Springs, it eventually became the area's commercial, civic, and social center, especially after Allison's son Joseph and Lookout Ranch owner Andrew S. Crowder platted a small town called La Mesa Springs around the station and its new La Mesa Lemon Company packinghouse and store in 1894. A year later, Allison's Springs became known as La Mesa Springs, and a new school, Allison School, was built to serve the growing number of local citrus ranchers and home-seekers. Shortly after the beginning of the 20th century, a series of speculators arrived with plans for further residential and town development. Starting in 1907, La Mesa Springs rapidly attracted new settlers, ranchers, and businesses, including several hotels, a lumberyard, a sanitarium, stores, restaurants, and an opera house. Within five years, the community of La Mesa Springs had grown to over 700 residents who, concerned for local control of their economic and domestic livelihoods, were ready to join together as the growing county's newest city.

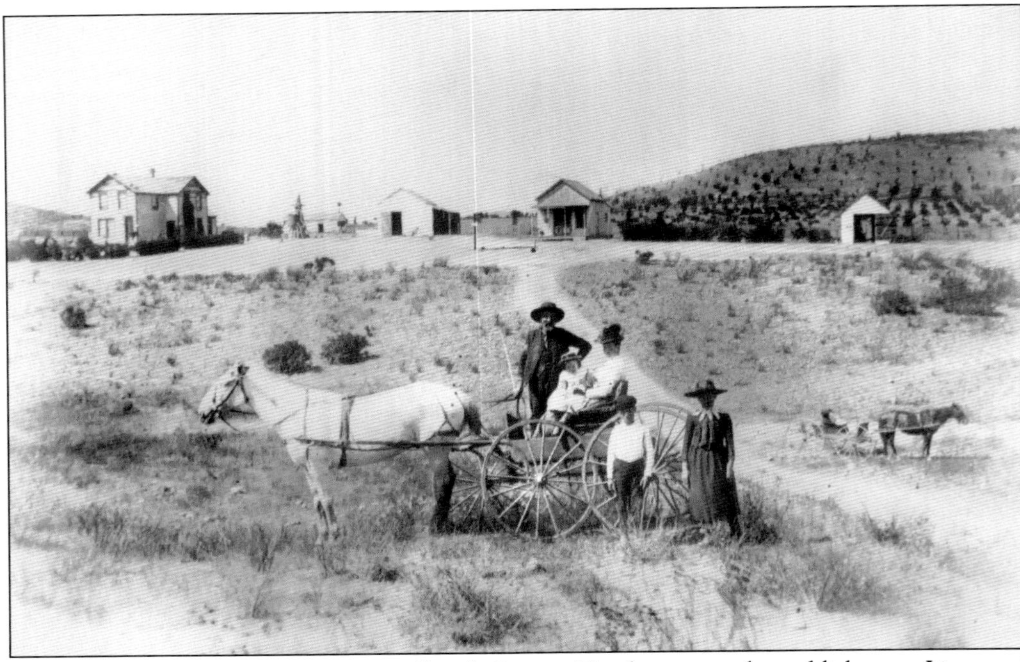

FELLOWS HOTEL AND FAMILY, C. 1887. Fellows's Cypress Hotel was an early establishment. Linus and Mary Fellows, who previously lived in the El Cajon Valley, purchased this property near today's University Avenue and La Mesa Boulevard in 1887. Mary was a noted hostess, and the Fellows housed many Flume and railroad construction workers as well as travelers of the old Chollas Road.

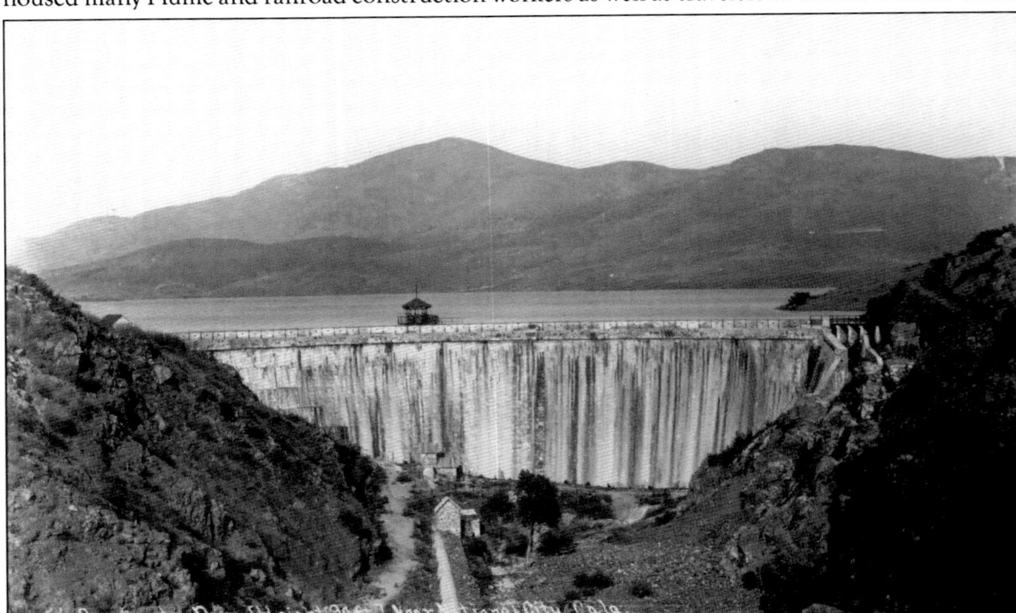

SWEETWATER DAM, C. 1890. This 1888 masonry dam was a landmark engineering feat. State engineer James Schuyler's structure was meant to supply National City and other boom-era developments at La Presa, San Miguel City, and Helix (Spring Valley/Casa de Oro area). Schuyler's purchase east of the Allisons' property in 1889 would result in the initial development of La Mesa's Lookout Ranch.

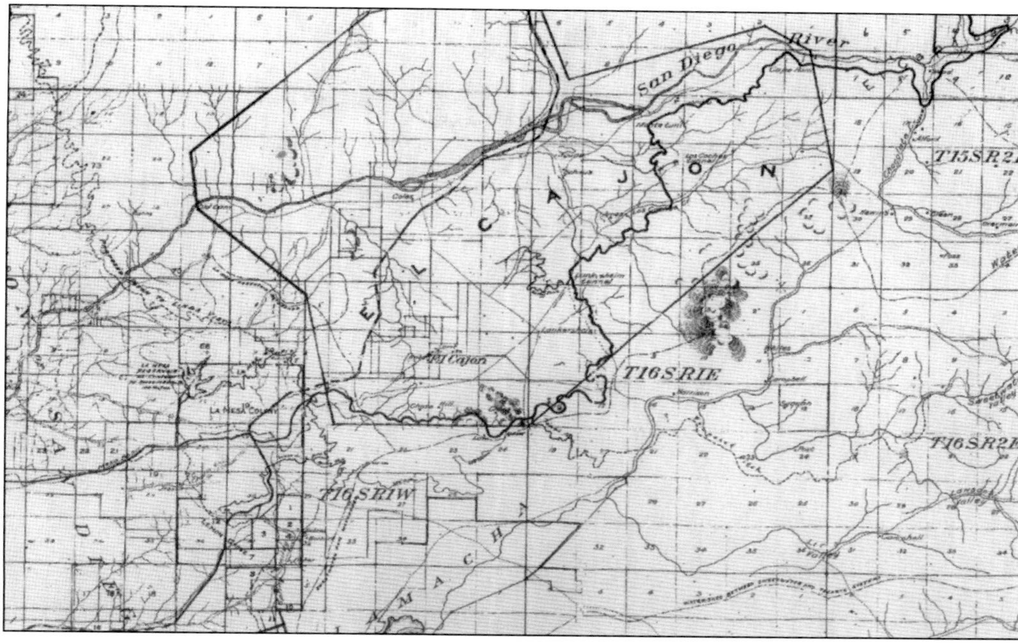

Flume System Plan Map, 1885, and Diversion Dam, 1887. Entrepreneur and author Theodore Van Dyke conceived of transporting San Diego River water to the mesa and beyond after seeing Northern California mining flumes. Working with San Diego investors, speculators, engineers, and landowners, including Robert Allison, Van Dyke looked to maximize the arid region's limited water sources. His plan called for a reservoir at Cuyamaca, headwaters of the Boulder Creek tributary. Below the creek's convergence, a diversion dam directed water into 36 miles of wooden flumes and eight tunnels to get it around the El Cajon Valley and up to storage reservoirs on the mesa for distribution to urban and agricultural properties in San Diego, City Heights, La Mesa Colony, El Cajon, and Lemon Grove.

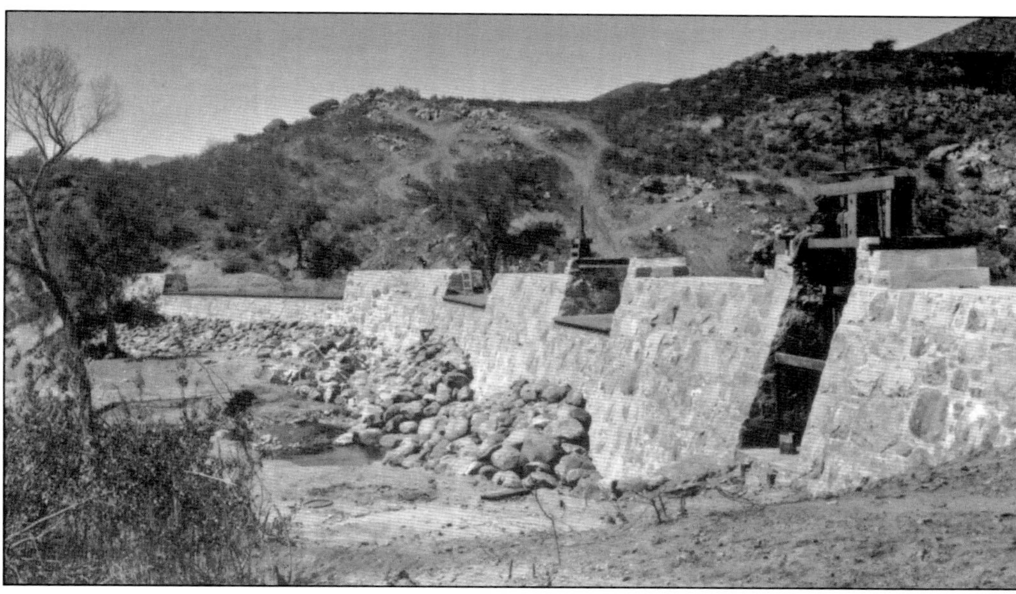

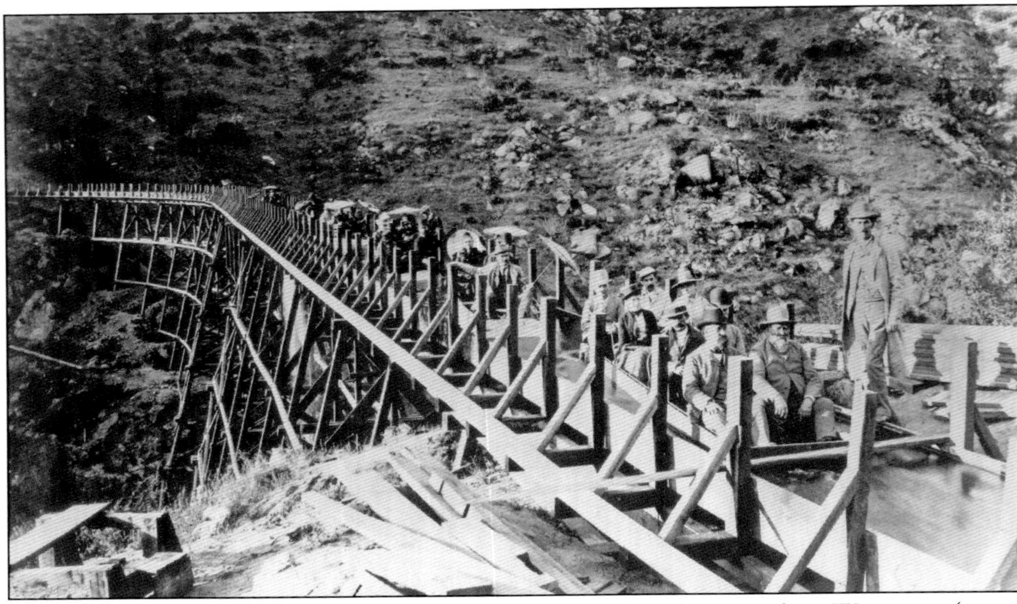

Flume Riders, 1889. Theodore Van Dyke (standing right) and Gov. Robert Waterman (sitting right), who owned Cuyamaca Rancho's Stonewall Mine and the SDCE, enjoy a flume ride with guests and dignitaries. Unfortunately for the San Diego Flume Company and its investors, the Great Boom ended the previous year, and the anticipated development would have to wait.

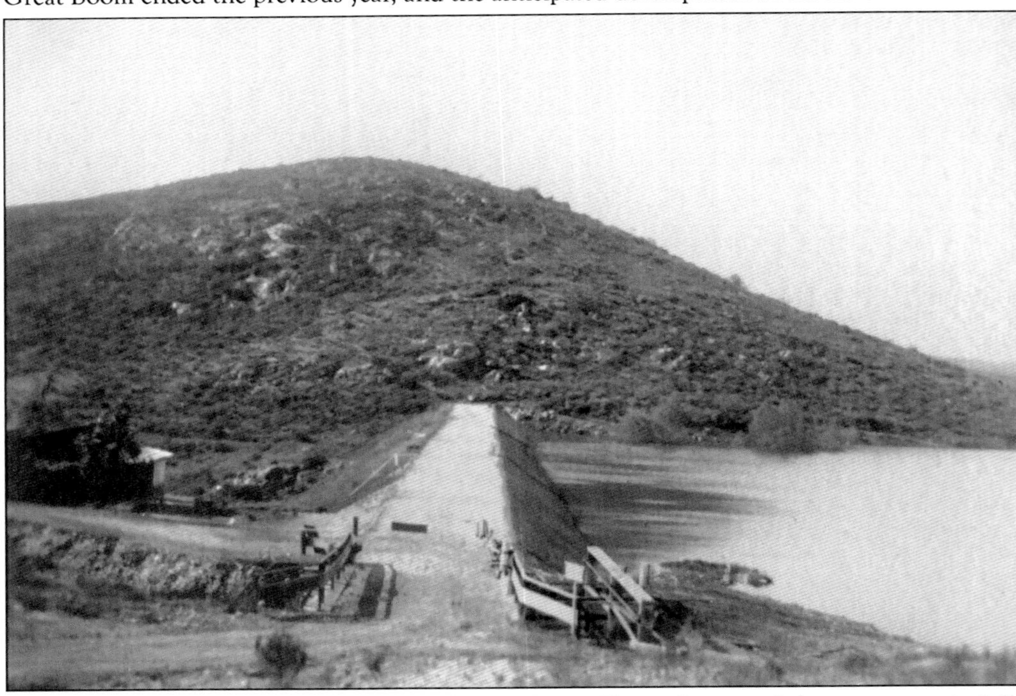

La Mesa Dam and Reservoir, c. 1900. The San Diego Flume Company's largest reservoir, fully completed in 1895, was built in Chappell Canyon, across Alvarado Canyon from the Colony Townsite. It was planned to serve the Colony and the lucrative urban markets of San Diego, including new boom-era suburban tracts such as University Heights and City Heights.

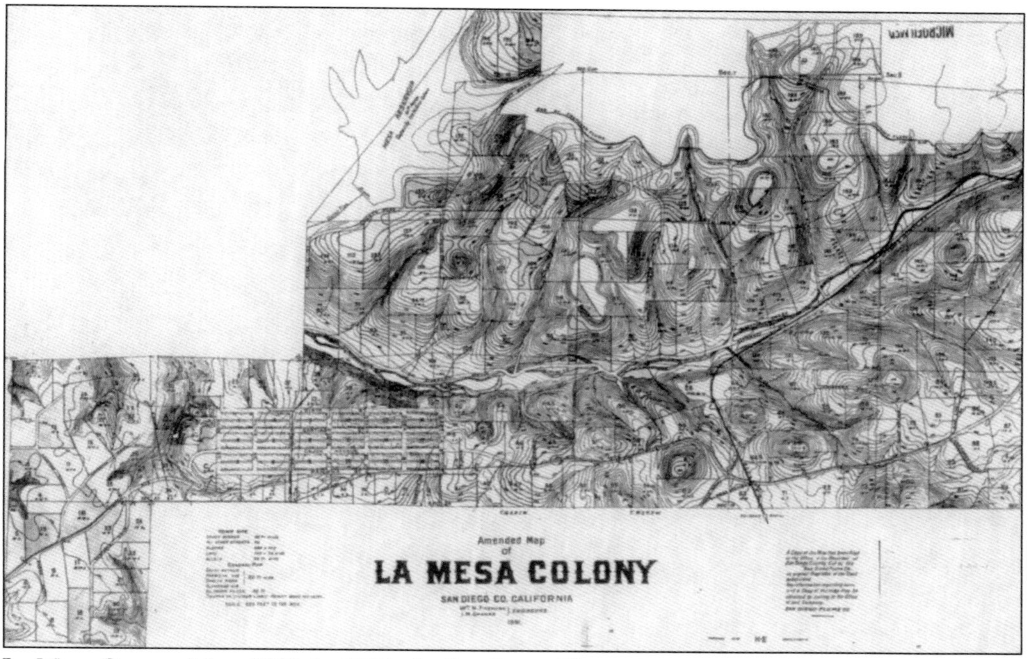

La Mesa Colony Map, 1891. In 1886, the San Diego Flume Company purchased Harbison's mesa land and subdivided it into flume water supplied 5- and 10-acre farm lots surrounding the Cajon Avenue–centered town site. The boom's bust stymied expected growth, but enough residents arrived to support opening the La Mesa School in 1891 and a community church by 1895.

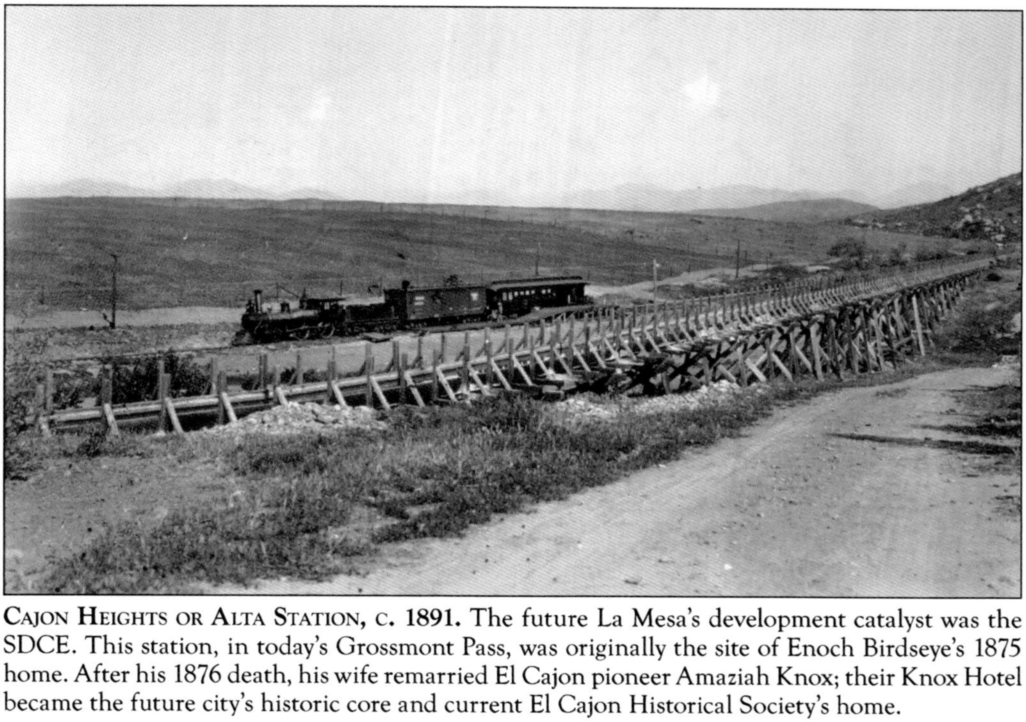

Cajon Heights or Alta Station, c. 1891. The future La Mesa's development catalyst was the SDCE. This station, in today's Grossmont Pass, was originally the site of Enoch Birdseye's 1875 home. After his 1876 death, his wife remarried El Cajon pioneer Amaziah Knox; their Knox Hotel became the future city's historic core and current El Cajon Historical Society's home.

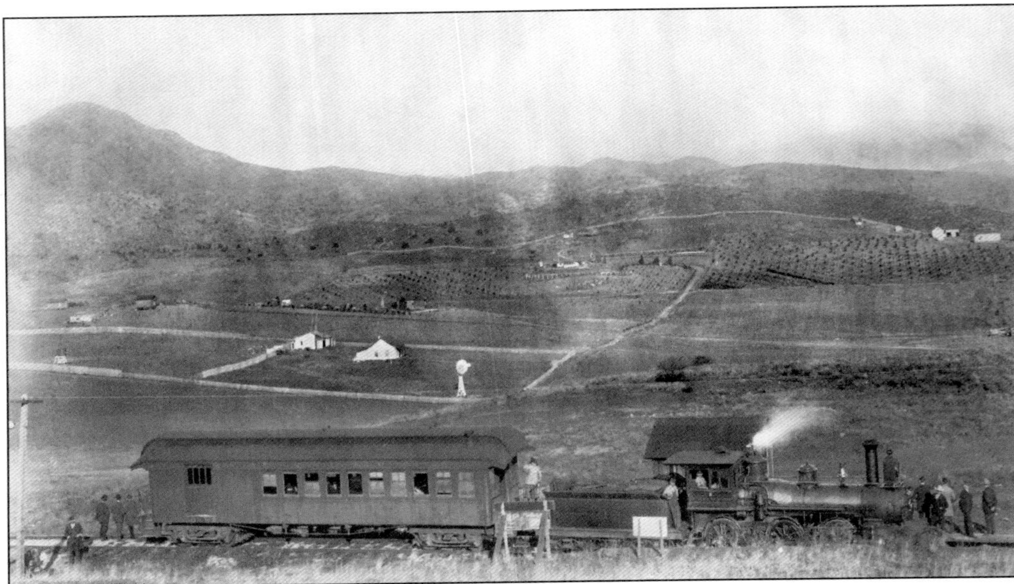

SPRING VALLEY STATION, 1890s. This station, site of today's Spring Street Trolley Station, served the already established rural community. The boom era had attracted new valley residents, including noted historian/publisher Hubert Howe Bancroft, who purchased the Porter and neighboring ranches. The Bancroft Ranch later became a community landmark and home to the Spring Valley Historical Society. (San Diego Historical Society.)

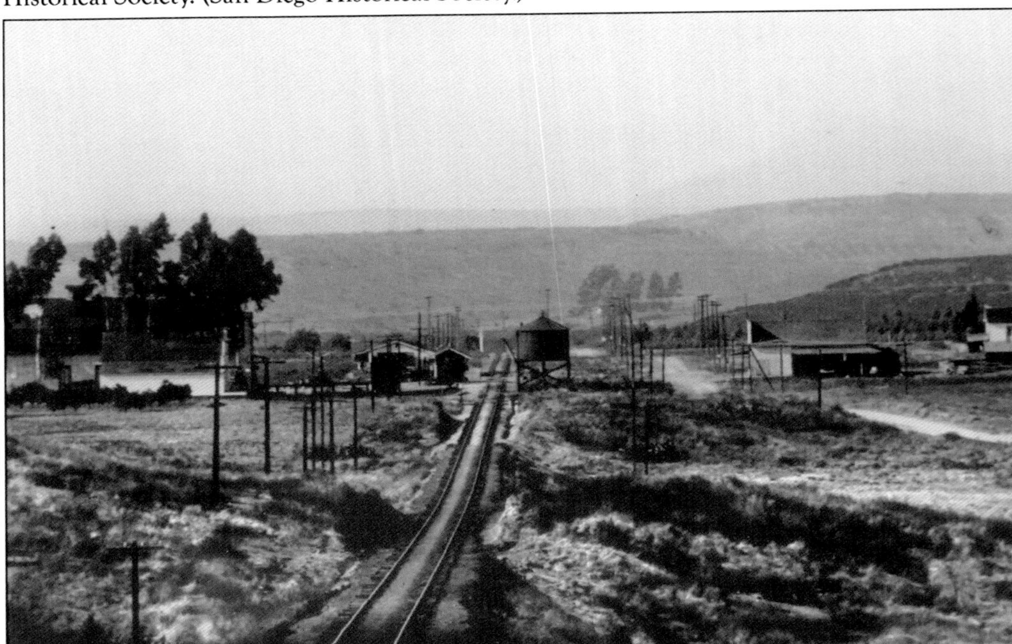

ALLISON STATION, c. 1900. Robert Allison was an initial investor in the SDCE, providing right-of-way and a station for the railroad. Although he died in 1891, his namesake station served both La Mesa Colony and Allison's Springs as the preferred location for area ranchers transporting produce to market and residents accessing San Diego.

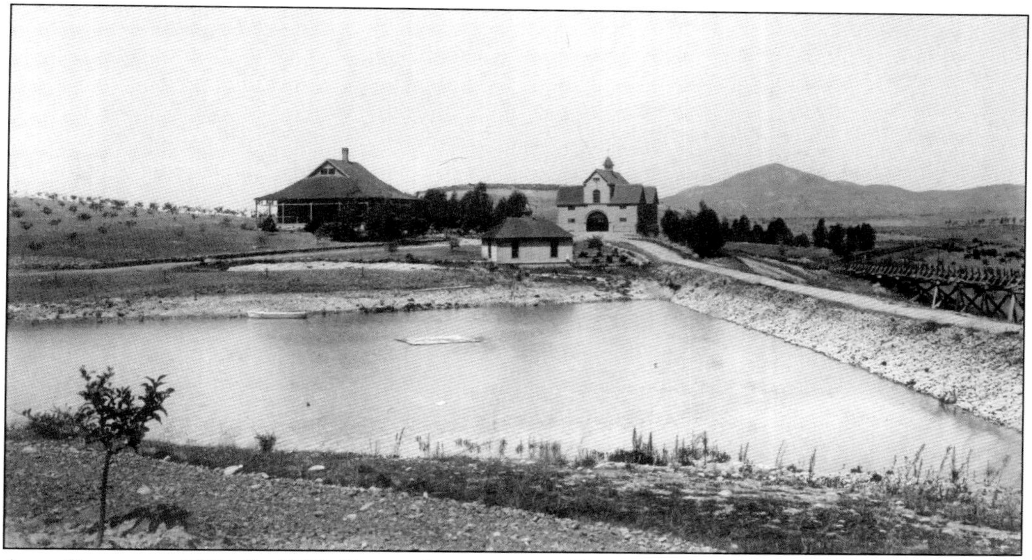

ALTA RANCH, c. 1895. In 1893, Detroit businessman Hervey Parke of the Parke-Davis Company purchased 600 acres from the El Cajon Vineyard Company. He developed the property with this house and elaborate barn around a small spring-fed lake (located at today's Anthony's Restaurant), planting lemons and other crops, and later added Sam Marshall's Villa Caro Ranch, which encompassed much of today's Grossmont and Fletcher Hills.

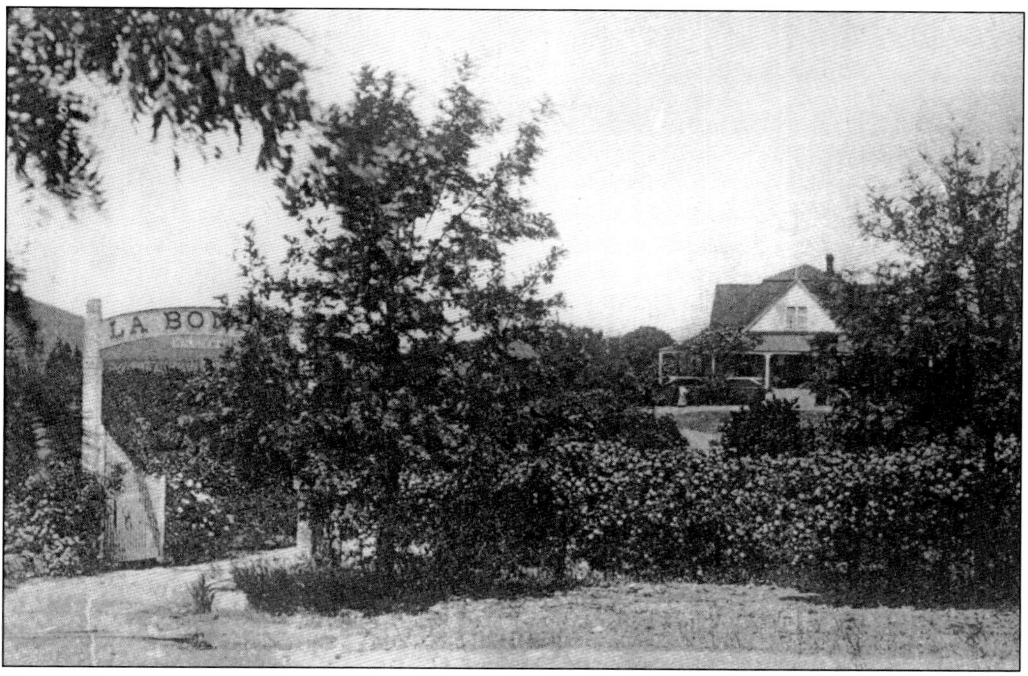

BONITA RANCH, c. 1900. Financial troubles resulted in English bondholders taking over the San Diego Flume Company, hampering improvement of the mesa area in the 1890s. Yet two examples of successful Colony developments were Dr. E. F. Wilson's guava ranch and DeWitt Williams's Bonita Ranch, both located along Cajon Avenue overlooking Alvarado Canyon west of Allison's Springs.

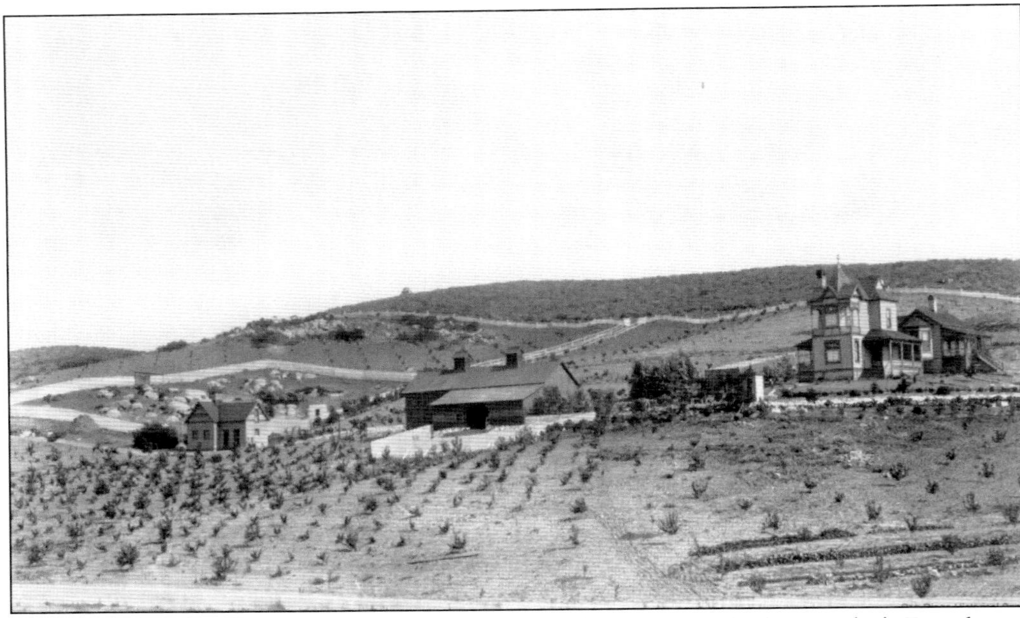

LOOKOUT RANCH, C. 1890. Engineer James Schuyler's hilltop ranch above today's Fourth and Lemon Avenues saw early improvement with this 1890 house and citrus orchard. In 1894, Schuyler sold the 65-acre ranch to investor and developer Andrew S. Crowder. Its showplace reputation led Crowder to name La Mesa Springs' main street Lookout Avenue. (San Diego Historical Society.)

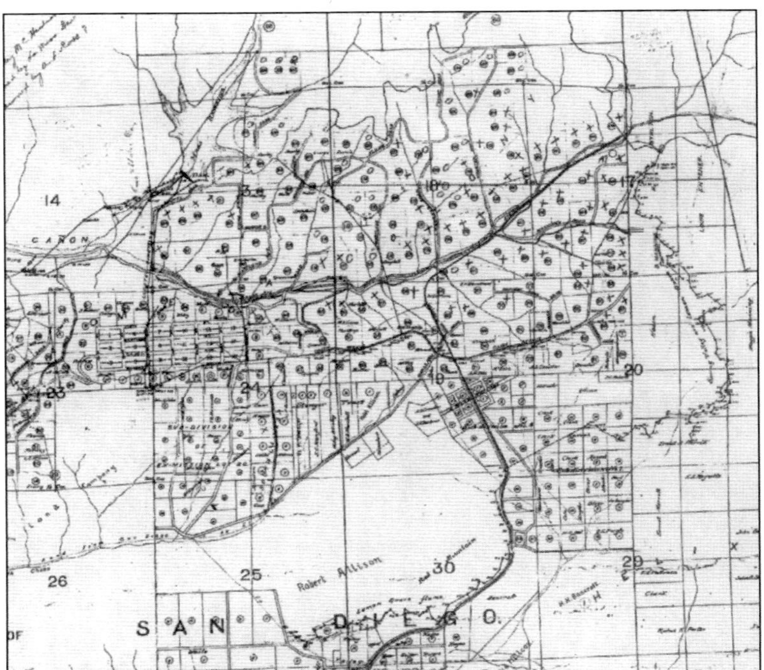

FLUME COMPANY SERVICE MAP, 1900. The San Diego Flume Company's receivership, compounded by the 1897–1904 drought, hampered its effectiveness. Joseph Allison, meanwhile, had remortgaged the family's La Mesa lands for his own flume company to serve Spring Valley and Lemon Grove. The failure of these efforts resulted in Allison's loss of these lands, effectively ending the family's development dreams. (Helix Water District.)

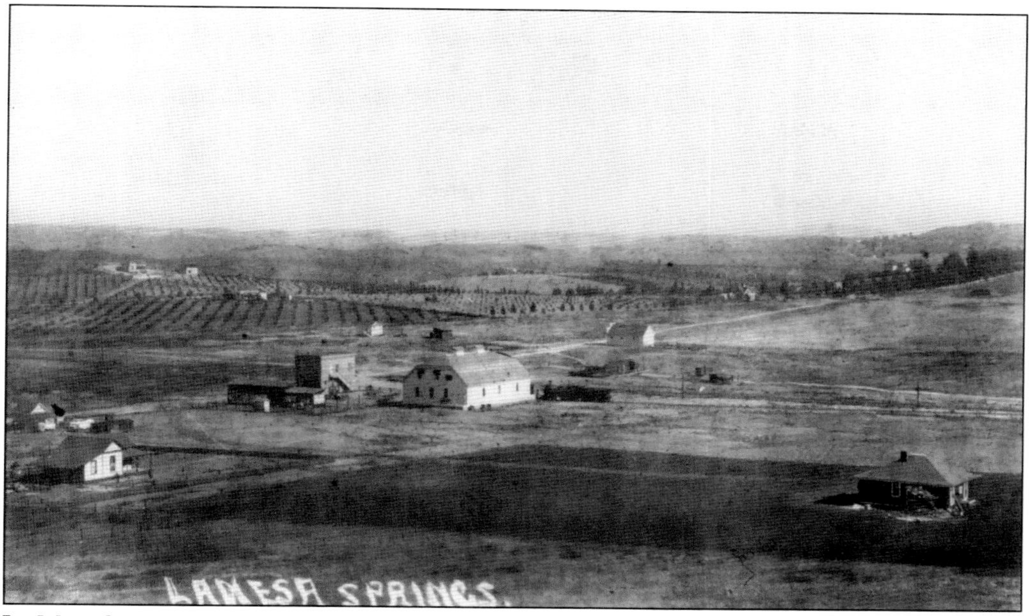

La Mesa Springs, 1895. In 1894, Joseph Allison and Andrew Crowder partnered in subdividing a tract centered on Allison Station. Its boundaries were today's Acacia and Allison Streets on the west and north, and Palm and Lemon Avenues on the east and south. Growing community spirit led to renaming the tract, station, and community from Allison to La Mesa Springs.

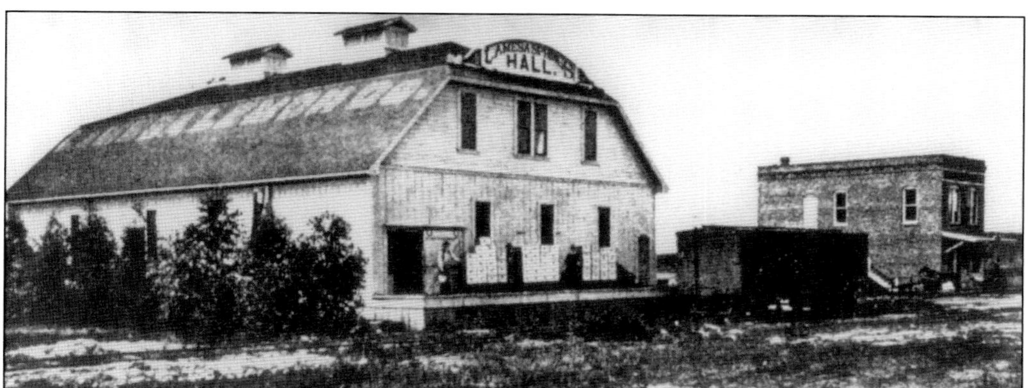

Packinghouse and Store, c. 1900. Crowder partnered with San Diego Flume Company investor and San Diego Commercial Bank founder Bryant Howard and his wife, Medora, to form the La Mesa Lemon Company in 1895, erecting these company facilities on Railroad Avenue (now Nebo Drive). The second floor's full-length hall provided space for community dances, performances, church services, and gatherings.

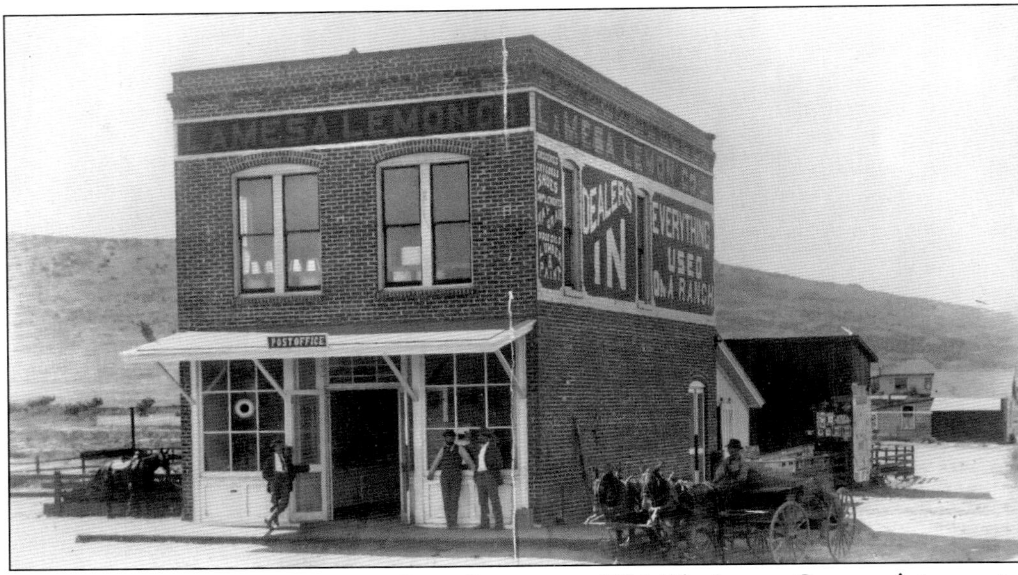

LEMON COMPANY STORE C. 1895 AND STORE INTERIOR C. 1900. The Lemon Company's impressive two-story brick store, at the southwest corner of Railroad Avenue and Lookout Avenue, was the first to supply settlers and ranchers of La Mesa Springs. The 1895 county directory listed 85 residents within "La Mesa (La Mesa Springs Station)," including the Colony lands. Bryant Howard had moved to La Mesa with his wife, Medora, after his San Diego Commercial Bank collapsed in the Panic of 1893. Also listed was postmistress Rocena Agnew. The interior photograph, which dates from around 1900, features her husband, then-postmaster Sam. Today this building is the oldest standing commercial structure in the city.

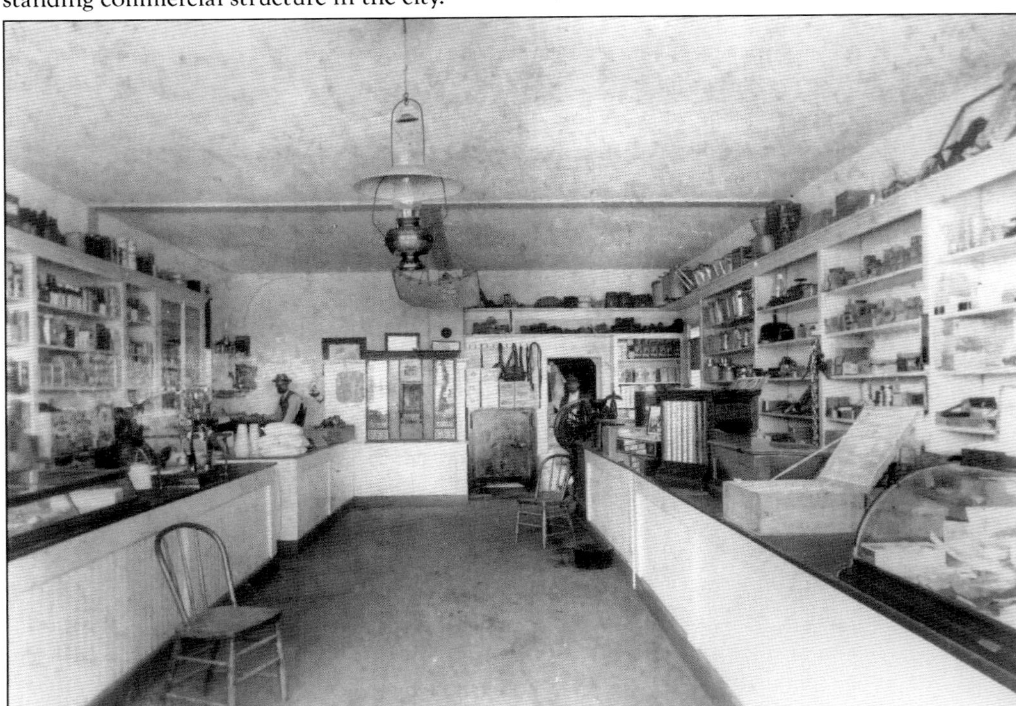

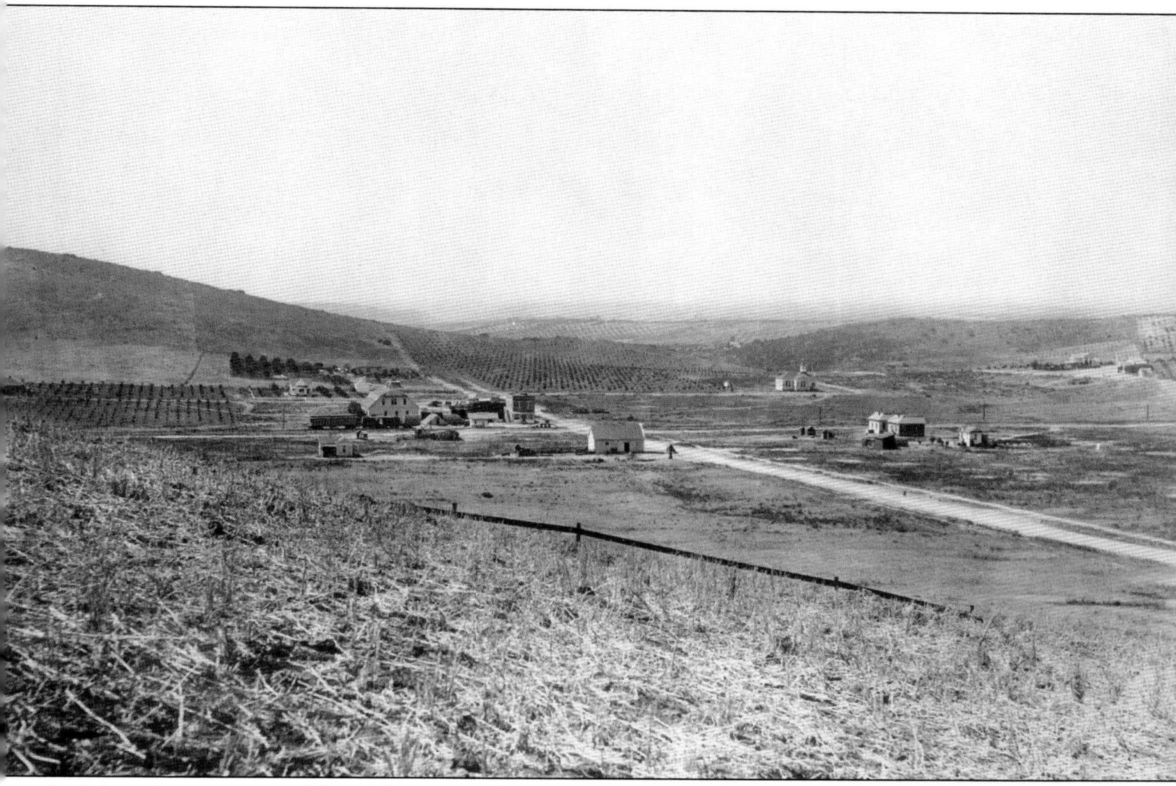

La Mesa Springs, 1897. The 1897 county directory entry for La Mesa (served by La Mesa Springs Station) indicated that both the Colony and the "Springs" were progressive sections of 5- and 10-acre lemon and orange ranches. Community assets for both locations included stores at each site, schools (La Mesa at the Colony and Allison at Springs), and churches (a Methodist church at the Springs and a Congregational church at the town site, both founded in 1895). The directory listed over 120 La Mesans between the two settlements. The Springs' rural nature is seen, with the packinghouse and blacksmith shop near the depot and the new Allison School dominating the landscape. At this time, the two settlements' relationship was still good-natured and of mutual benefit. As the drought took hold at the end of the 19th century and times grew difficult, the relationship would turn more competitive.

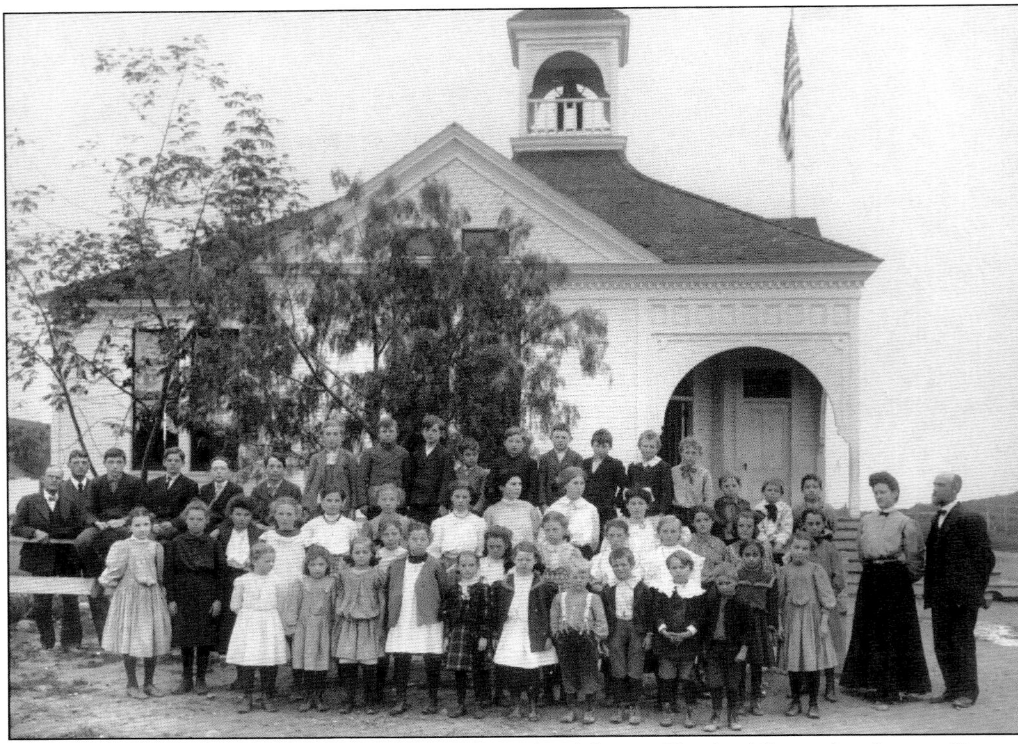

Allison School, c. 1907. Constructed in 1895 on land donated by the Allison family near Orange and Date Streets, Allison joined the already established area schools Jamacha/Spring Valley (1877), La Presa (1888), and the Colony's La Mesa (1891). As with all late-19th-century rural communities, the building also served as a community meeting and civic center.

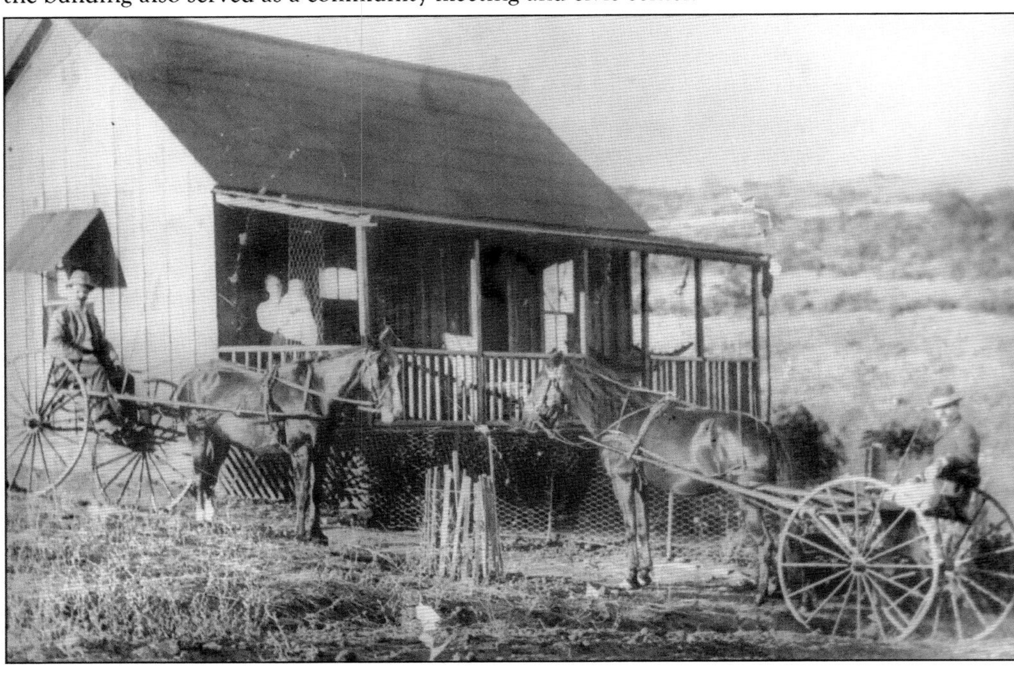

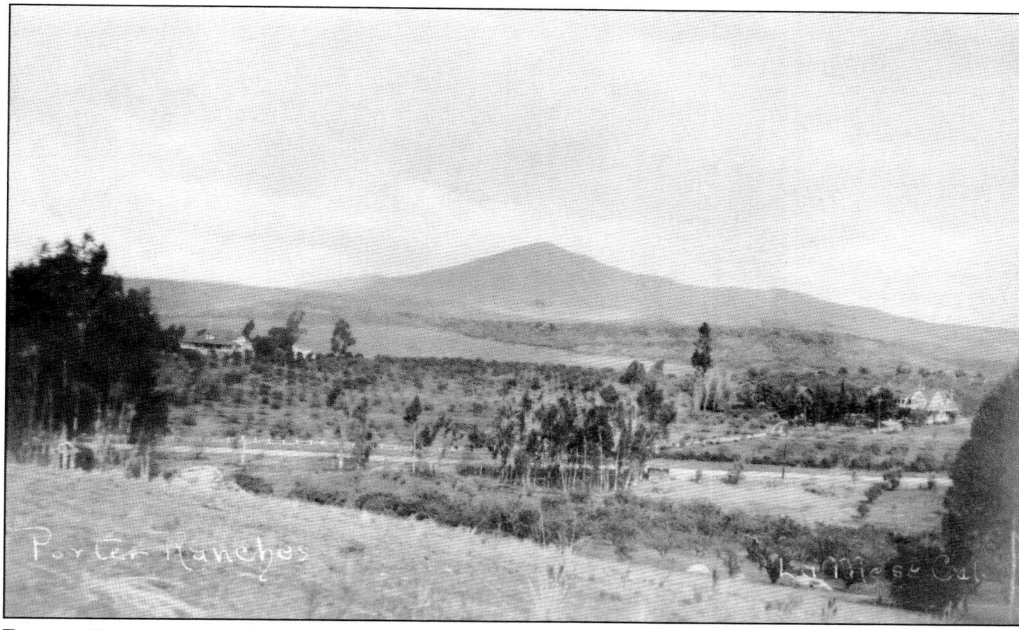

Porter Ranches and Orchard View, c. 1907. Former Civil War officers Col. James Randlett (arrived 1895) and Maj. Henry Roach (arrived 1892) were two notable La Mesa gentlemen ranchers, both building hilltop homes and orchards north of the Cajon Avenue. In 1905, Dr. Henry Porter, a noted emissary and missionary to China, purchased Roach's property for his family upon their U.S. return. They renamed Roach's ranch *Ping An Shan*, or the "Hill of Peace." The house is still located on Porter Hill Road. Randlett, who introduced Hervey Parke to the area, was often away from his ranch in high-level government appointments. After Randlett's death in 1916, Henry's brother James purchased Randlett's property, cementing a long-standing family commitment to support, service, and philanthropy in the community.

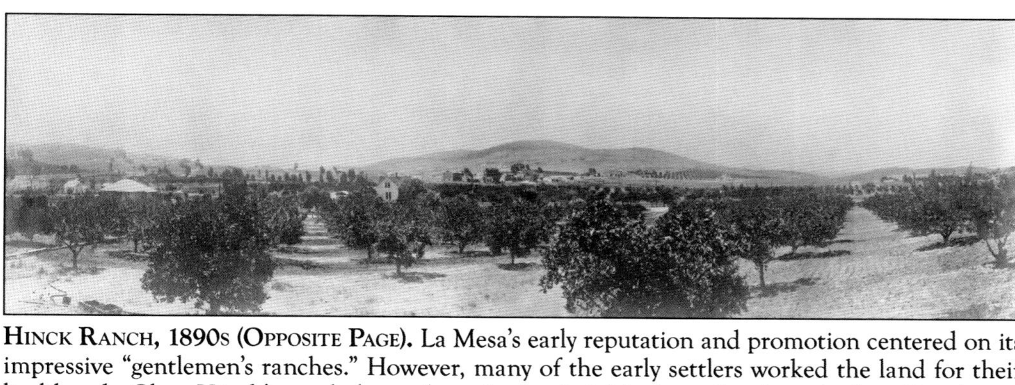

Hinck Ranch, 1890s (Opposite Page). La Mesa's early reputation and promotion centered on its impressive "gentlemen's ranches." However, many of the early settlers worked the land for their livelihoods. Claus Hinck's ranch, located north of today's Mariposa Road overlooking Eucalyptus Park and Spring Valley, reflects the simpler vernacular style of a typical hardscrabble homestead.

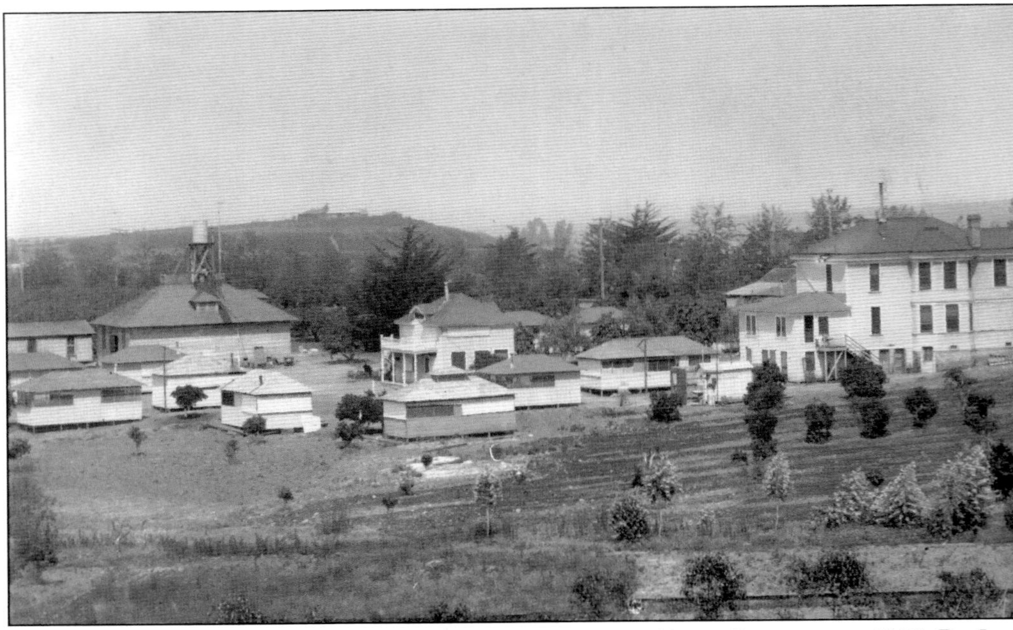

Parks Sanitorium, 1908. Dr. J. A. Parks, a respiratory disease expert, established this tubercular hospital in 1905 on Cajon Avenue west of Lookout Avenue. Parks closed the sanitarium in 1909, providing the children's Resthaven Preventatorium in today's El Cerrito neighborhood with some of these cottages. "Dr. Joe" continued to live in La Mesa, serving admirably in many civic and social organizations.

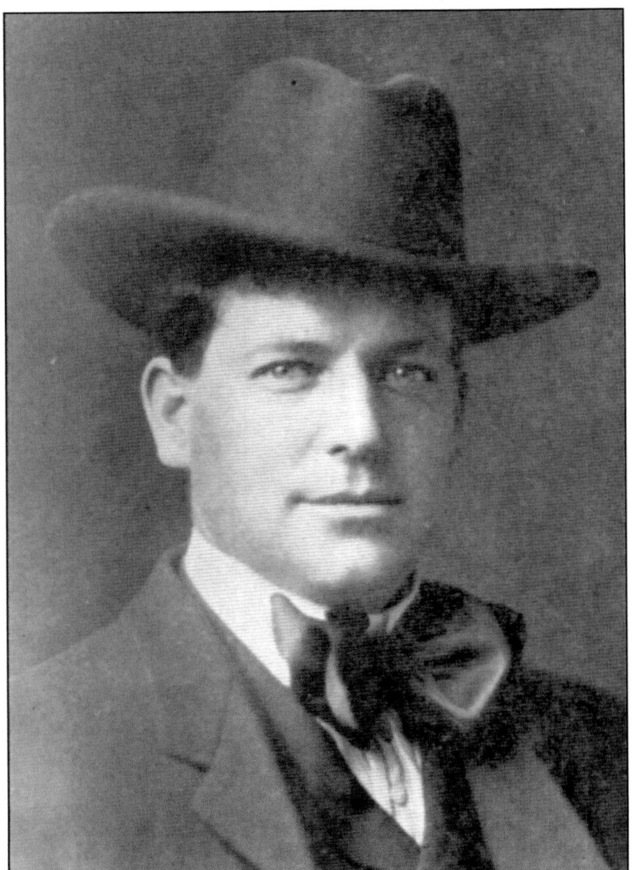

D. C. "Charlie" Collier. A proven land developer in Ocean Beach, University and Normal Heights, Collier triggered La Mesa Springs' suburban growth. He acquired the former Allison lands on the south of the Springs tract, adding Lookout Ranch by 1905. To promote La Mesa, Collier improved the old springs area, eventually donating the land for today's Collier Park.

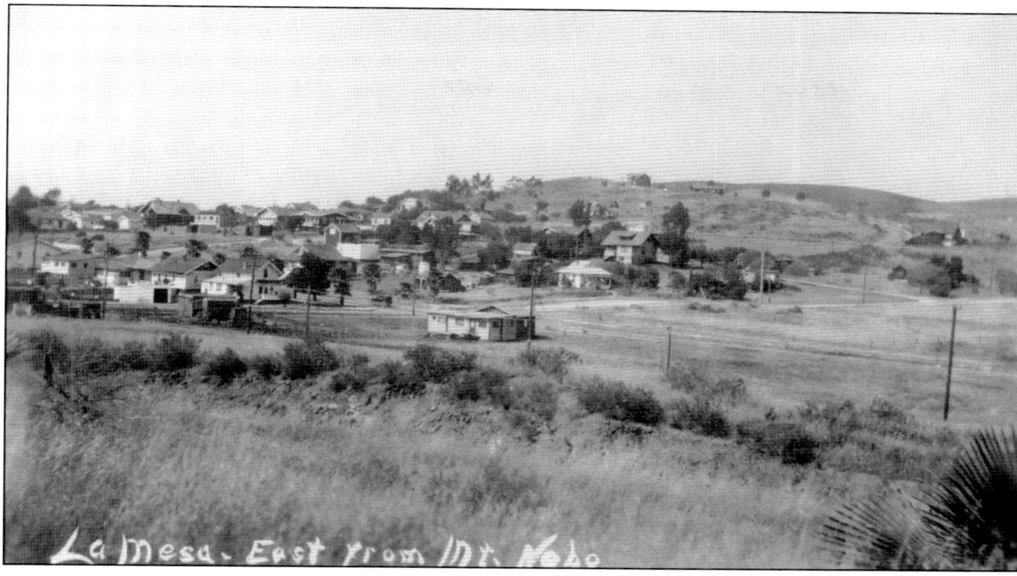

PARKS AND COLLIERS ADDITIONS AND PARK-GRABLE OFFICE, c. 1911. San Diego's 1907 real estate boom motivated Collier to subdivide the lands south of Fresno Avenue and surrounding Boulder Heights as Collier's Addition in 1908. He followed with Outlook Terrace, comprising much of the old Lookout Ranch, which was briefly owned by presidential son U.S. Grant Jr.—the inspiration for Grant Street. Collier's most notable effort was introducing Sherman Grable (at desk) to La Mesa in 1906. When Grable requested a house lot, Collier would not sell less than 100 acres. He agreed, developing Grable's Addition south and west of Lemon Avenue and the depot. Grable soon partnered with C. C. Park to subdivide another 200 acres, which became Park's Addition, east of Spring Street.

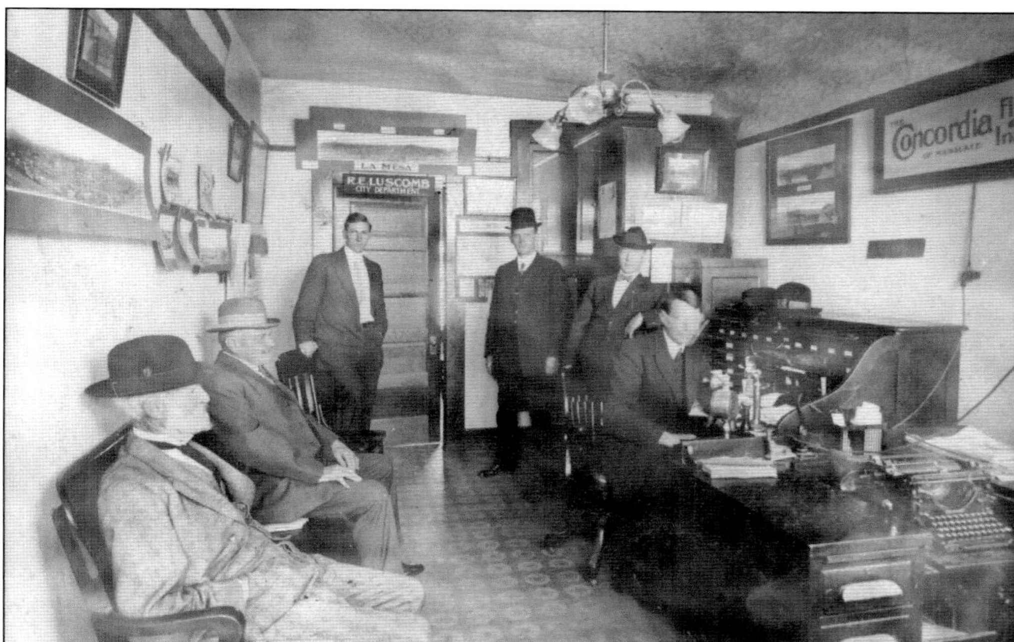

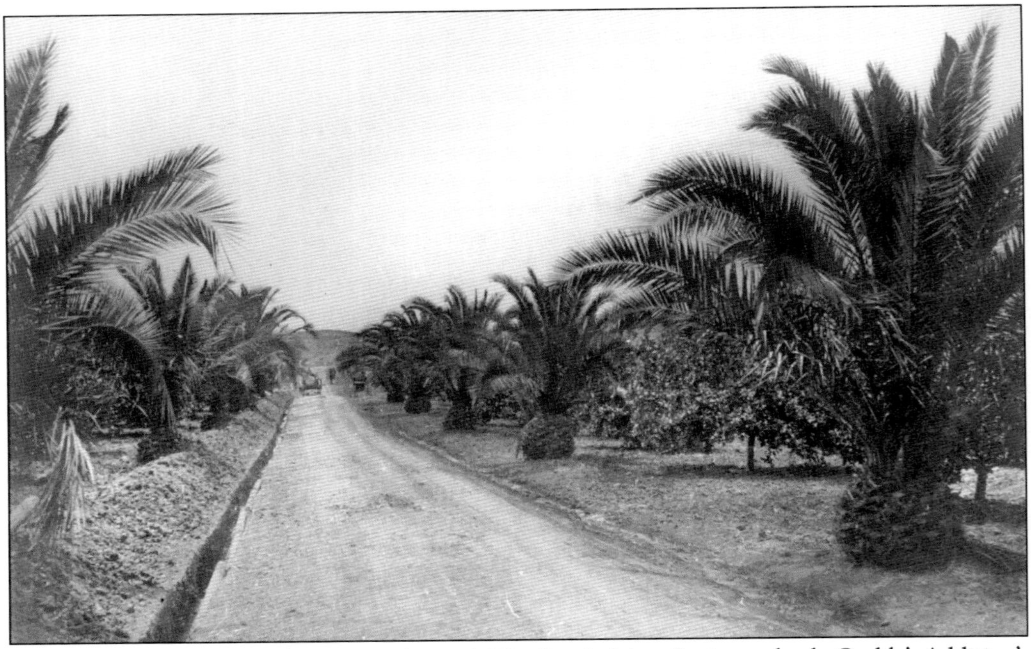

Date Avenue, 1908 (above) and 1910 (below). The first La Mesa Springs suburb, Grable's Addition's selling point was Date Avenue. The addition was laid out in an orchard, and Grable moved the namesake trees out another 15 feet to accommodate the home lots and the necessary utilities (being installed above). Within a few years, many of the tract's 1,000 lots were sold, concrete curbs and sidewalks in place, homes built, landscaping installed, and the addition had become the scene of suburban bliss seen below. The success of Park-Grable's real estate ventures would help both Park's Bank of La Mesa in 1909 and his investment in the La Mesa Lumber Company, the city's oldest active business, opened in 1907.

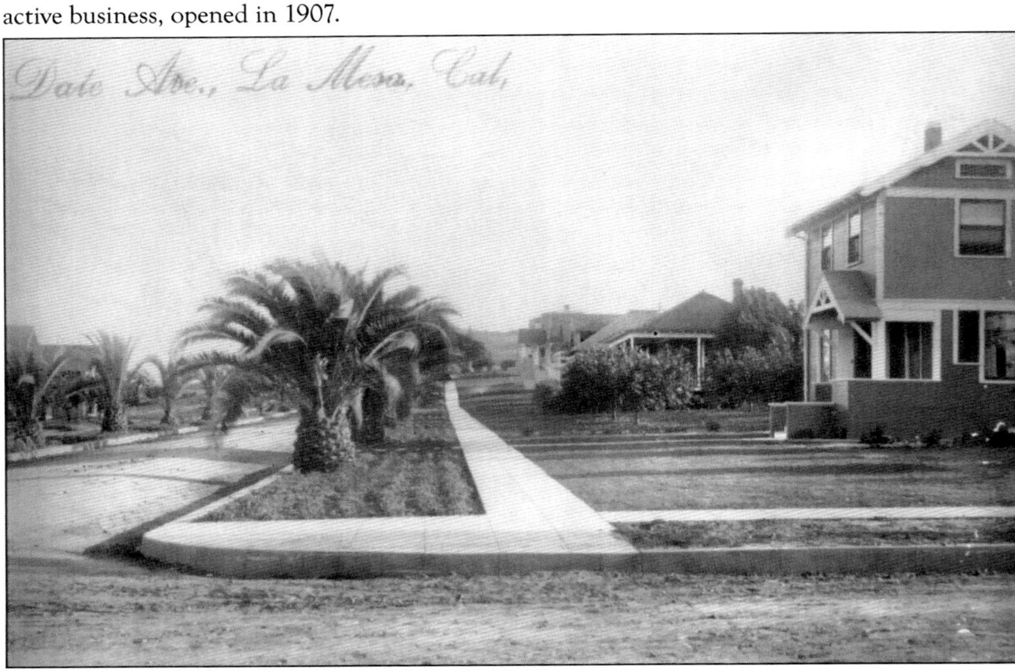

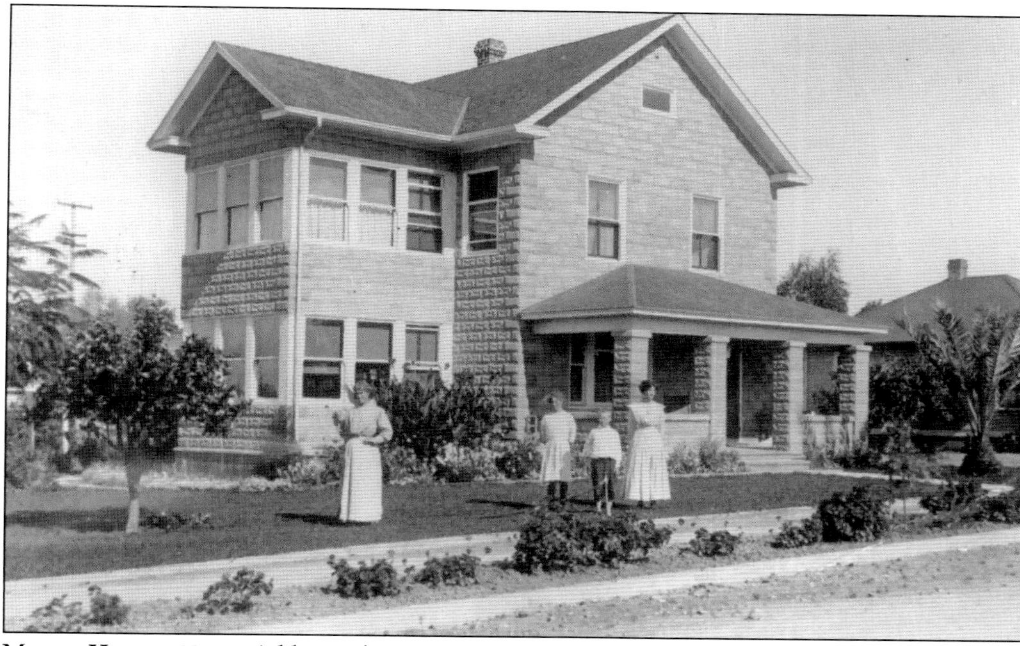

MOORE HOUSE, 1910S. Additional tracts were carved out of old orchards and filled with high-quality houses like this one. The Moore House features the latest in traditional foursquare design. Located on North Palm Avenue in the Wheeler Tract, this home, with its faux-brick siding, is still standing today.

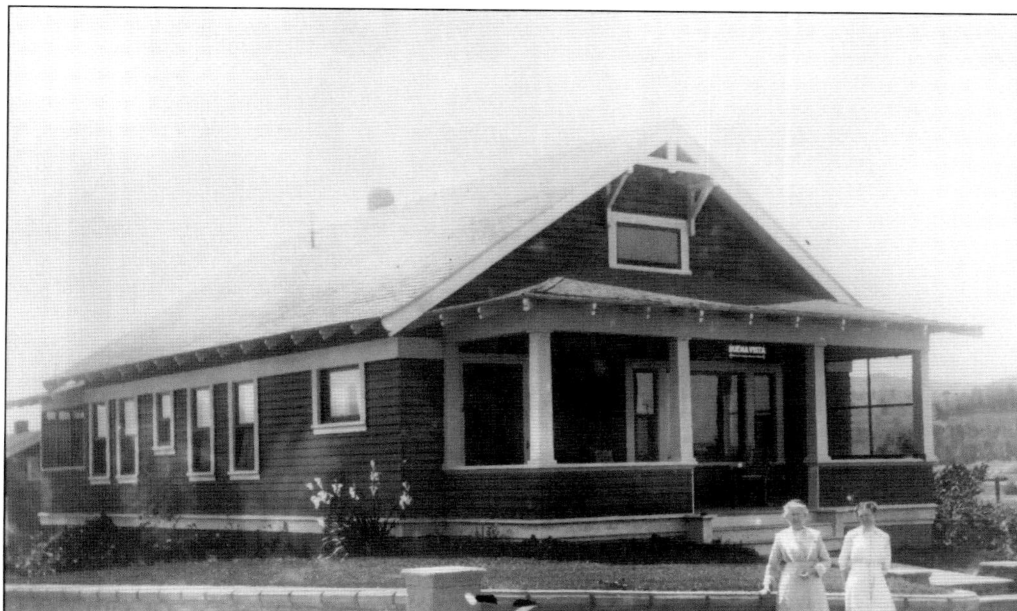

WINSLOW HOUSE, 1910. La Mesa contractor John Hurlburt built this popular California bungalow-style home in 1908 for his mother-in-law, Julia Winslow. Such affordable homes were often built for retirees and health-seeking homebuilders. This simple but well-built home is located at the corner of Third Street and Finley Avenue in Park's Addition.

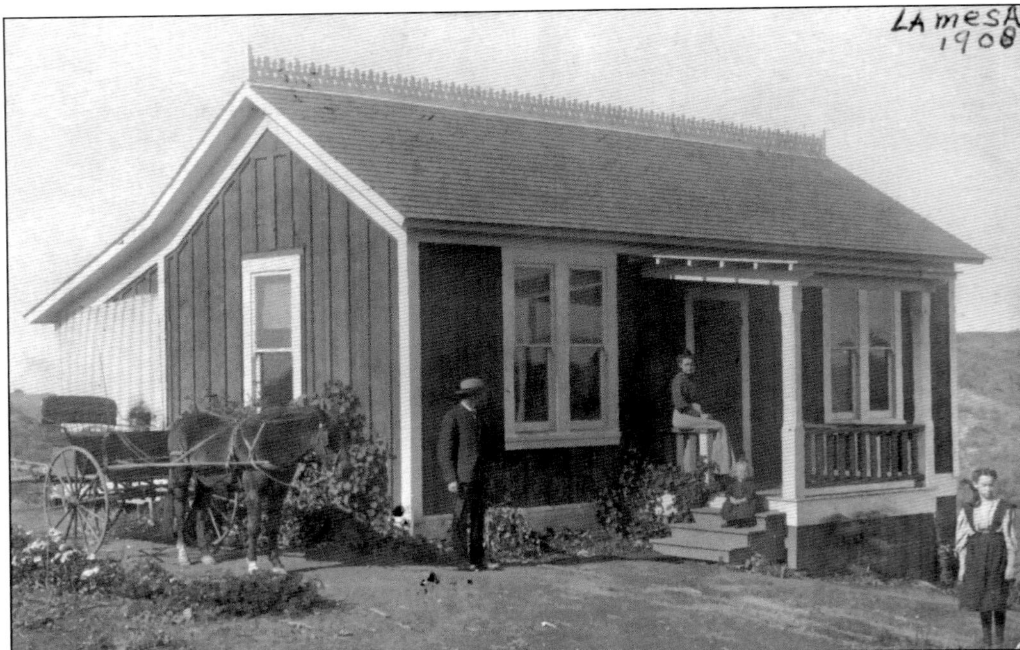

BEN LYSTER HOUSE, LEMON CIRCLE, 1908. This small hall-and-parlor-style house, built for Park-Grable employee Ben Lyster, was located on Lemon Circle in the Lookout Park tract. Confusingly, Grable subdivided this tract on Mount Nebo—the opposite side of town from the historic Lookout Ranch on Boulder Heights—where the Lysters also constructed a hilltop Sunrise Avenue home for his father in 1910.

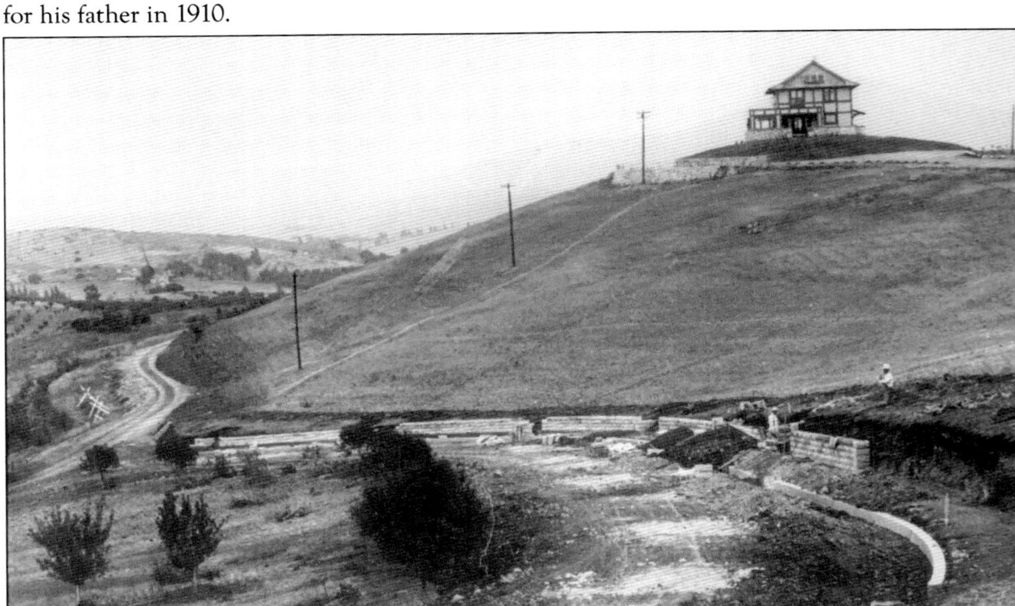

GRABLE'S "HILLCREST," C. 1912. Grable's standing as a developer, banker, and promoter was represented by his hilltop home on Date Avenue. This modern showplace home took in views south to Mount Miguel as well as to La Mesa Springs and his Mount Nebo tracts, such as here on Summit Drive, featuring the distinctive La Mesa cut-stone-block retaining walls.

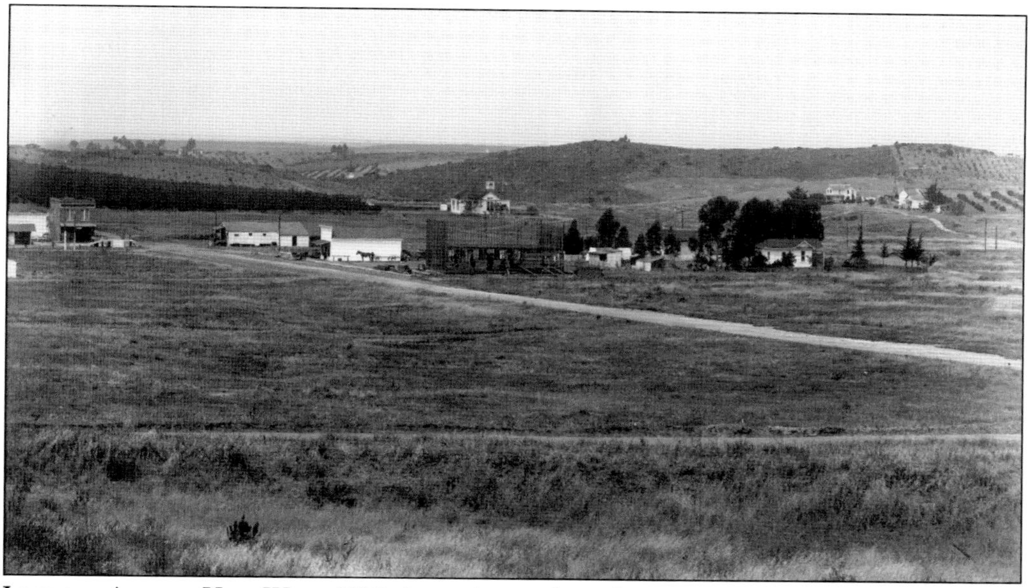

Lookout Avenue, View West, 1907. A growing residential community required the development of a thriving commercial district. This 1907 image shows the still-rural landscape. The two-story building under construction at the corner of Lookout and Palm Avenues is the Dorothy Hotel. The graded but empty Third and Fourth Streets are evident south of Lookout Avenue.

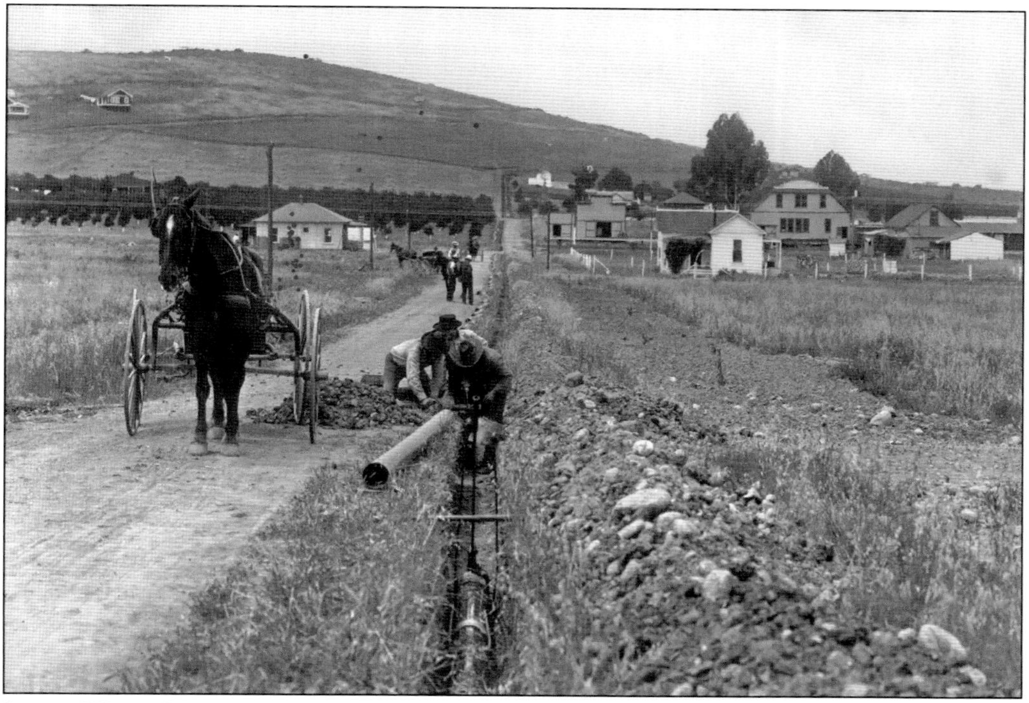

Laying Water Pipes, Lemon Avenue, 1907. Modern infrastructure was also necessary. Here water pipes are installed along Lemon Avenue between Palm Avenue and Third Street, requiring both civil engineering and horsepower. This infrastructure was essential for La Mesa Springs' residential and commercial development.

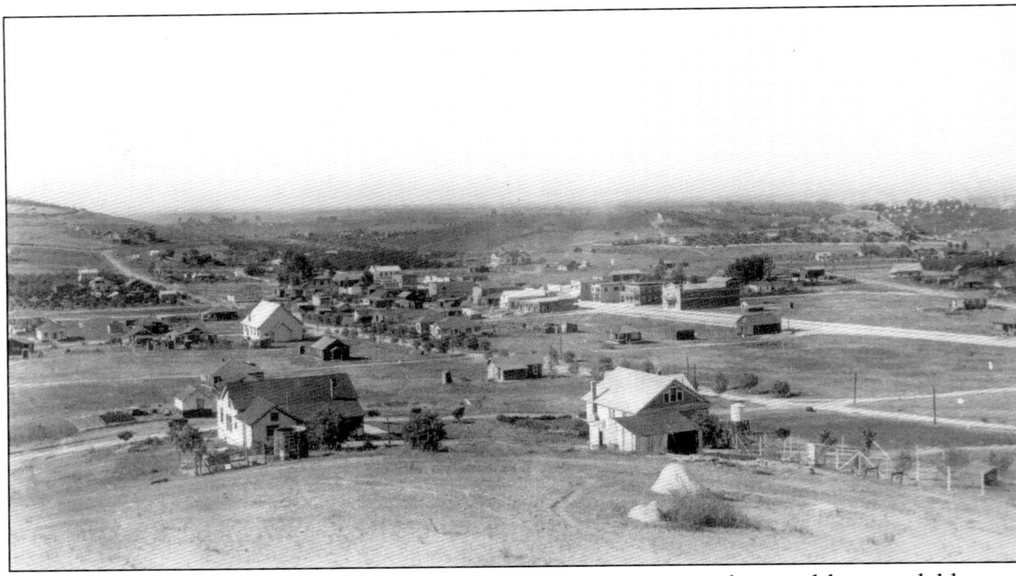

Lookout Avenue, View West, c. 1909. With infrastructure in place and lots available, new businesses and homes quickly sprang up. New businesses adjoined the Dorothy Hotel on both sides of Lookout Avenue. The new Methodist church is seen at the southeast corner of Lemon and Palm Avenues, and houses appear on previously empty streets and within old groves.

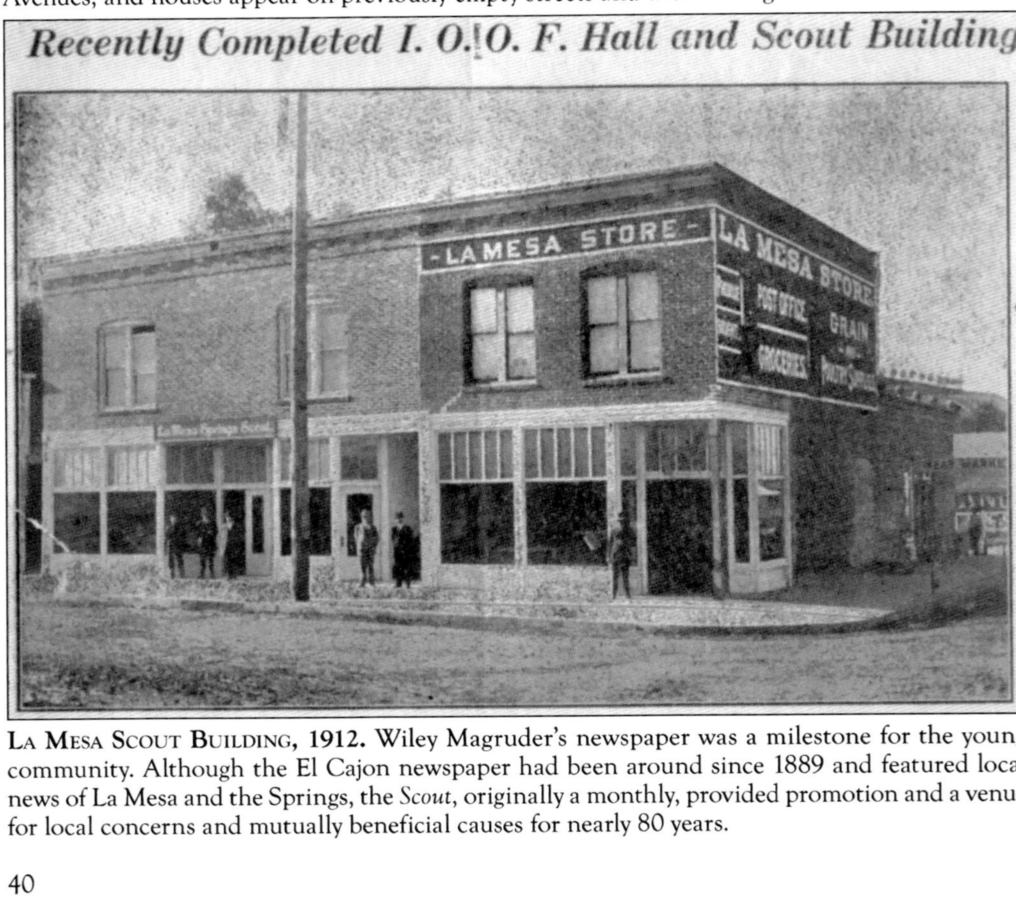

La Mesa Scout Building, 1912. Wiley Magruder's newspaper was a milestone for the young community. Although the El Cajon newspaper had been around since 1889 and featured local news of La Mesa and the Springs, the *Scout*, originally a monthly, provided promotion and a venue for local concerns and mutually beneficial causes for nearly 80 years.

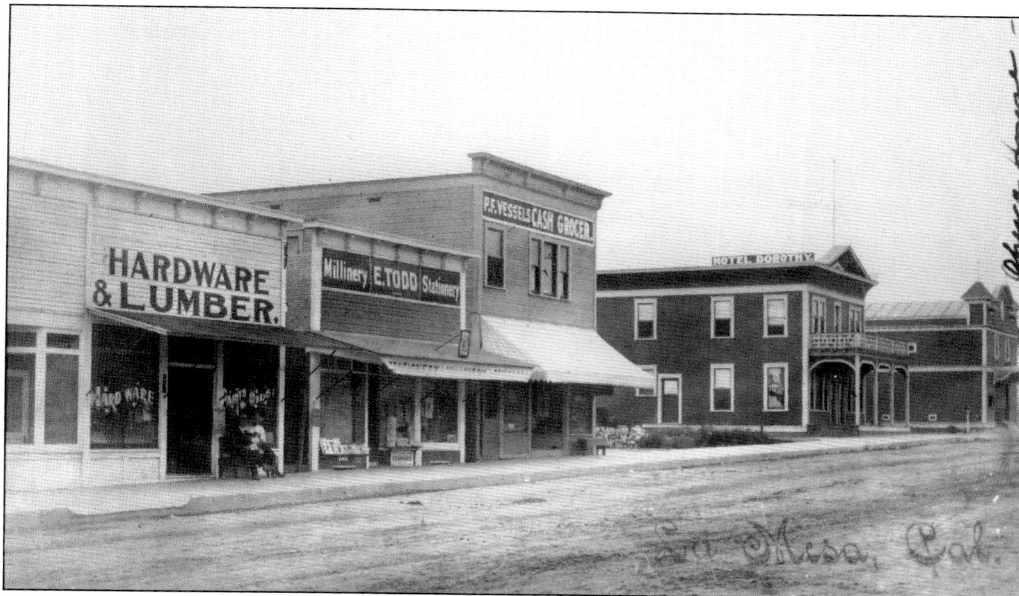

PIONEERING BUSINESS ON LOOKOUT AVENUE, C. 1908. New merchants established businesses to serve the growing population, such as these on the north side of Lookout Avenue east of Spring Street. The La Mesa Springs Lumber Shop, Todd's Millinery, and Vessel's Grocery join the Dorothy Hotel, with the new opera house situated on the northeast corner of Palm and Lookout Avenues.

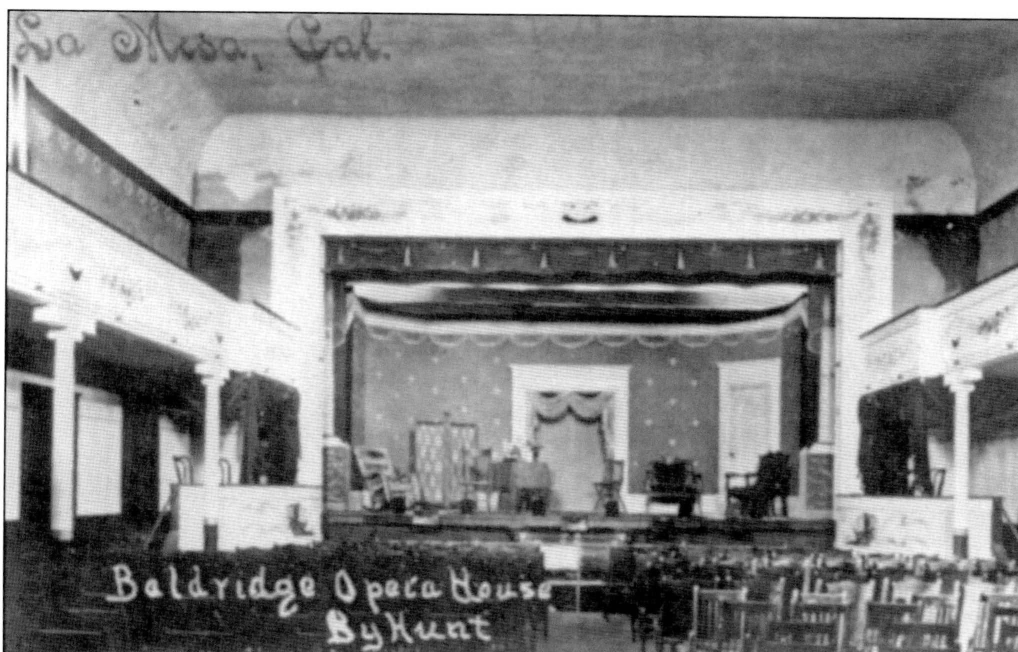

OPERA HOUSE INTERIOR, C. 1908. The Baldridge Opera House began a long-standing appreciation and support of performing arts for La Mesa. This rare photograph shows the grand interior decor and elaborate stage settings that rivaled any outside of San Diego. The opera house would provide locals with theater, vocal, and musical performances for nearly two decades.

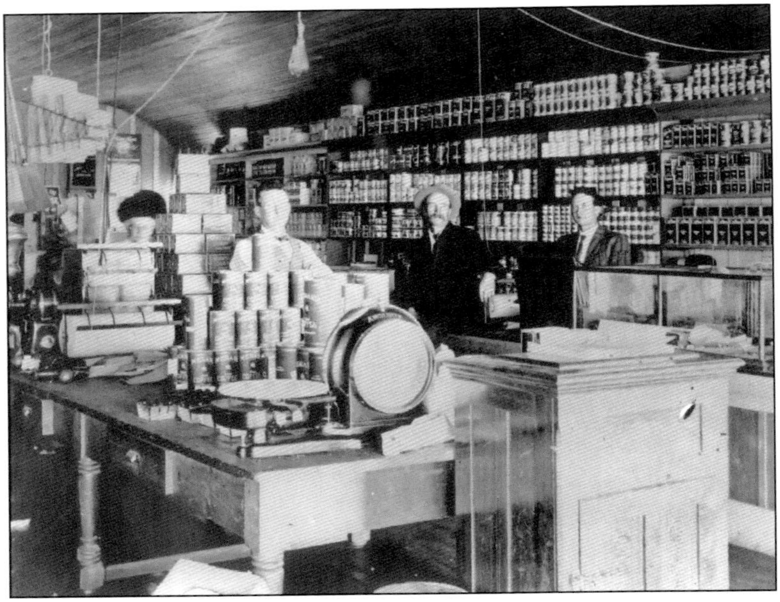

Interior of a La Mesa Store, c. 1910. Soon a series of new stores, such as this dry goods store, were opened to serve the growing community. Merchants Thomas McCarthy, Arthur Stone, and Charles McCarthy stand ready, with the latest variety of commercial and household items.

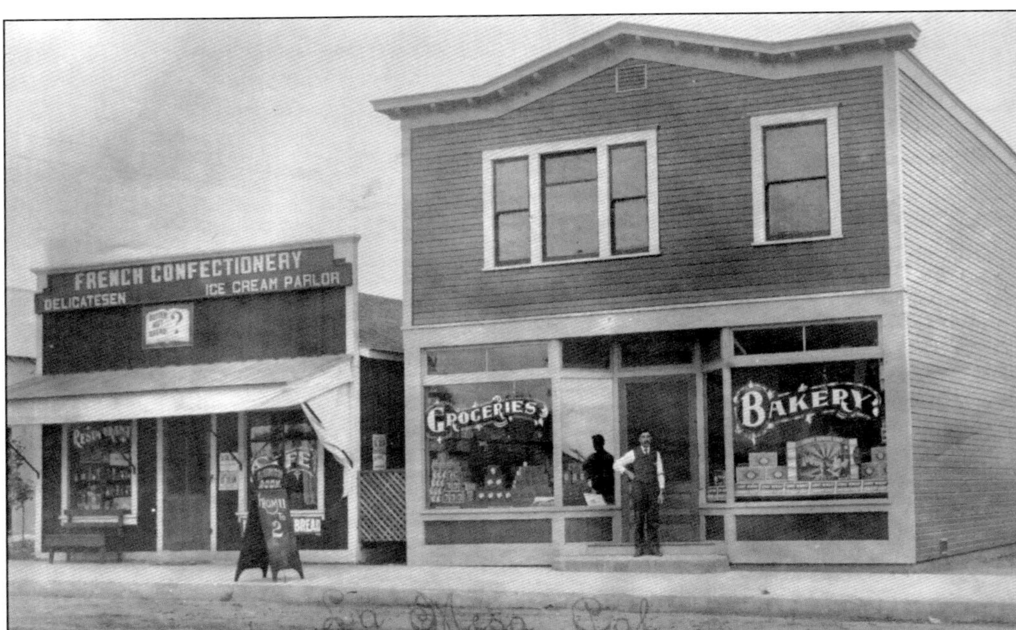

Deli, Ice Cream Parlor, and Bakery, c. 1910. Additional service-related businesses were added, including this restaurant-delicatessen, ice cream parlor, and grocery-bakery on the south side of Lookout Avenue between Spring Street and Palm Avenue. The key to supporting such business enterprises was the growing number of new suburban residents and automobile travelers.

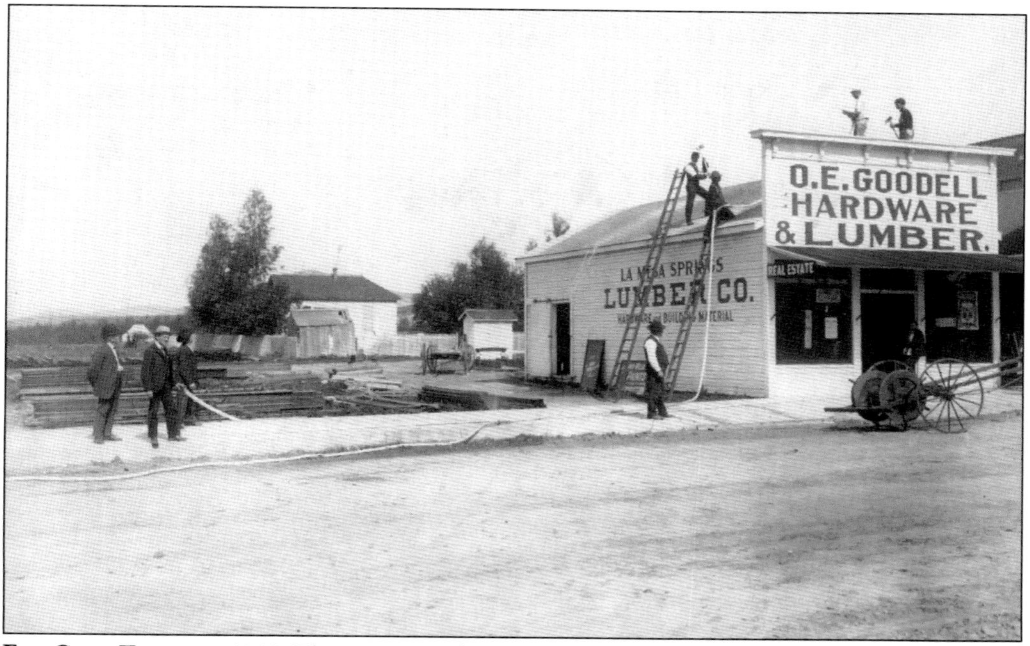

Fire Crew Training, 1908. The community's sense of civic responsibility is demonstrated with this testing of the new hose-reel cart—the oldest documentation of a formal "volunteer" fire company. Although local men had assisted with fires, such as when the Lookout Ranch house burned in 1903, this fire equipment purchase is the origin of the current La Mesa Fire Department.

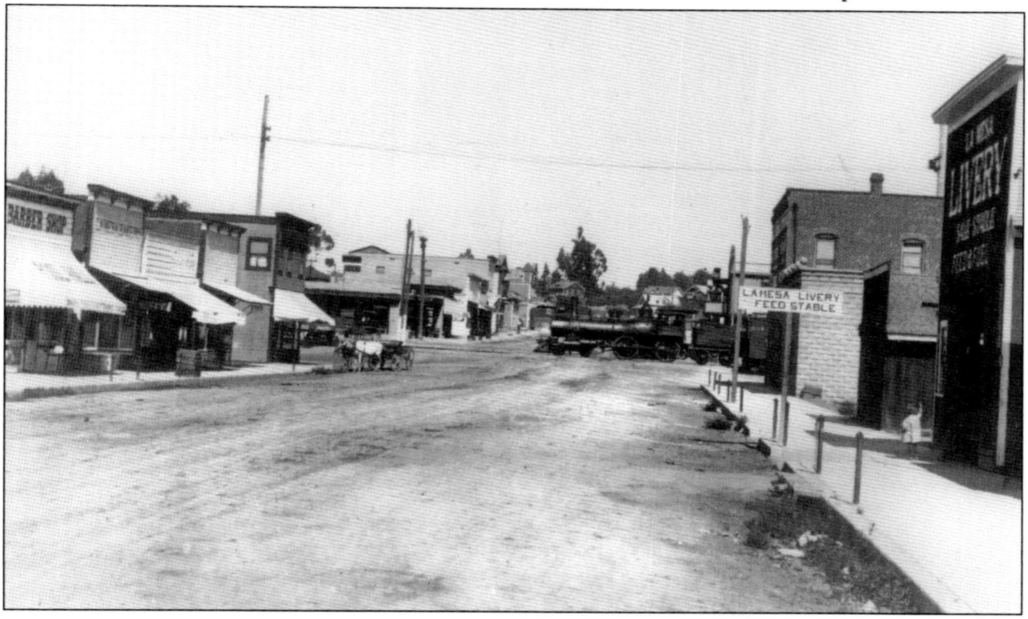

Lookout Avenue, View East, c. 1910. This view from near Date and Lookout Avenues shows the growing business district. A SDCE engine travels north parallel to Railroad Street (now Nebo Drive). The railroad had recently been purchased by San Diego business leader John Spreckels. The hitching posts embedded in concrete sidewalks and curbs indicate the urban transition in process.

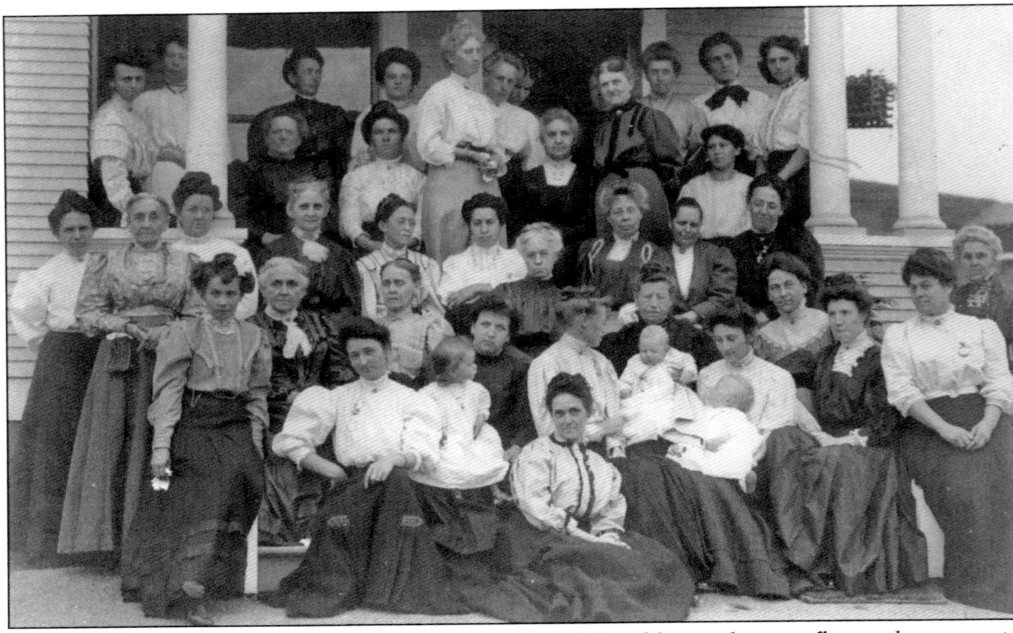

La Mesa Women's Club, 1908. Mary Ferguson formed this oldest and very influential community civic organization in 1902 along with a dozen other pioneering ladies. The club's efforts included charity and community events, mutual aid services for those in need, and regular community entertainment events, the first in July 1903 at the Peek-A-Boo Ranch in Maryland Heights near La Mesa Reservoir.

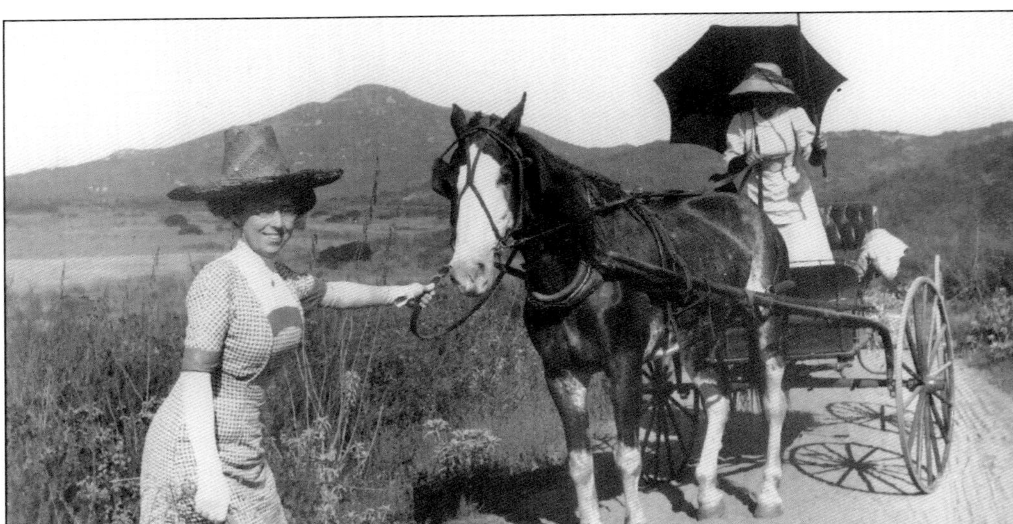

Lost in the Wilds of La Mesa, c. 1910. This promotional photograph poses two lovely La Mesa lasses near undeveloped Mount Helix. Although much documentation exists for the entrepreneurial spirit of La Mesa's predominately male developers, business and civic leaders, this is a reminder of the hearty pioneer women who also worked diligently in "civilizing" the La Mesa frontier.

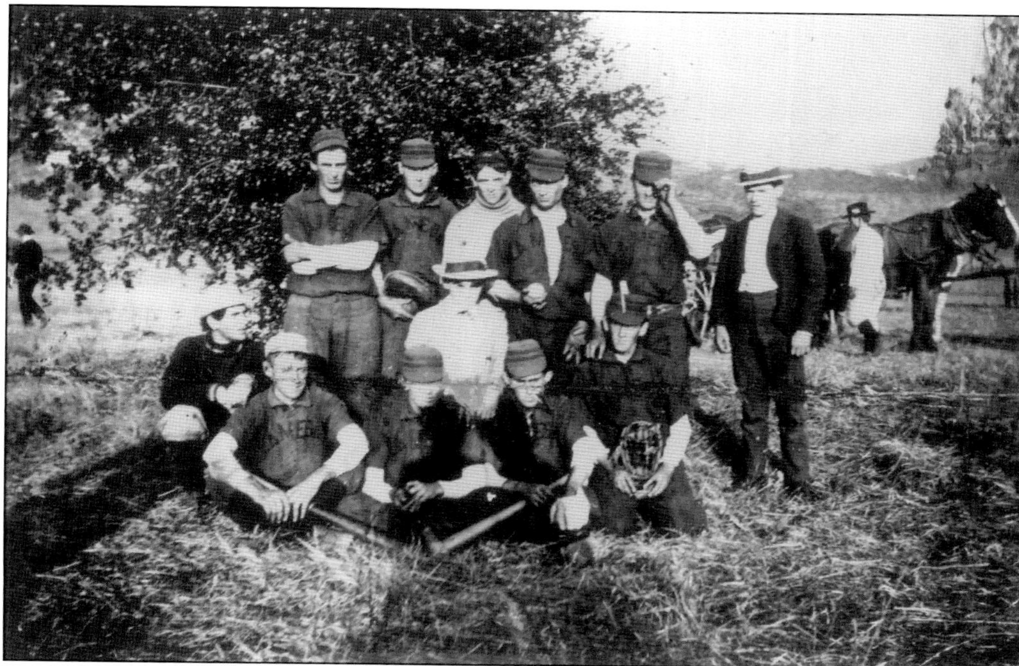

La Mesa Baseball Teams, c. 1896 and 1910. No other community activity has rallied La Mesans like baseball. Local amateur baseball in San Diego County dates to the 1870s. In the mid-1890s, La Mesa fielded its first team of young men to take on other local teams from communities such as El Cajon, Lemon Grove, Lakeside, La Mesa Heights, East San Diego, and San Diego. Initially played at special events, such games and rivalries would lead to regular leagues pitting community teams against each other with civic pride at stake. Business sponsors would help defray costs of uniforms, equipment, and travel expenses. In the early 20th century, school teams would introduce youth baseball to La Mesa, setting the stage for future success.

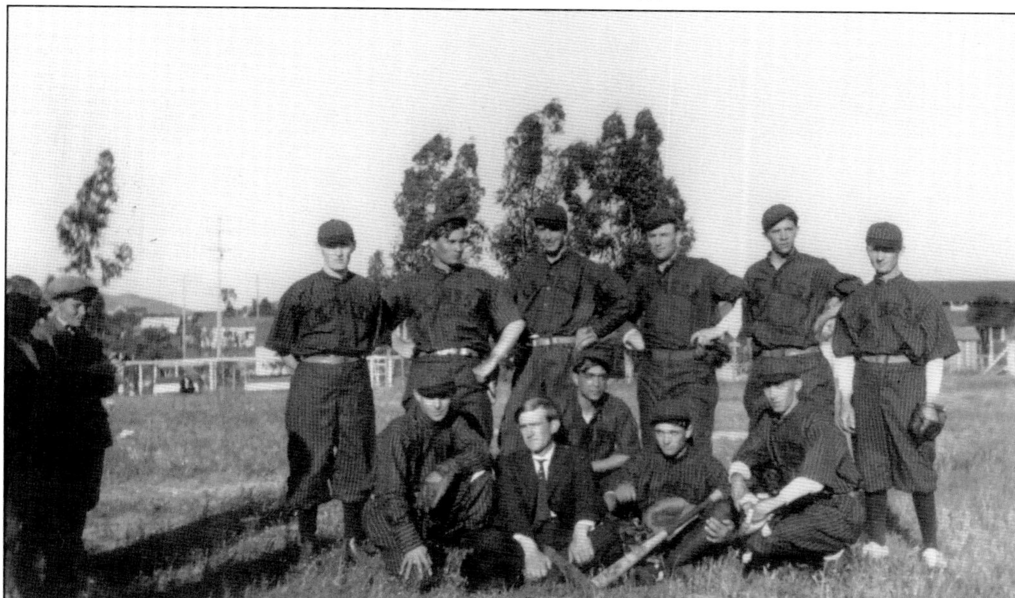

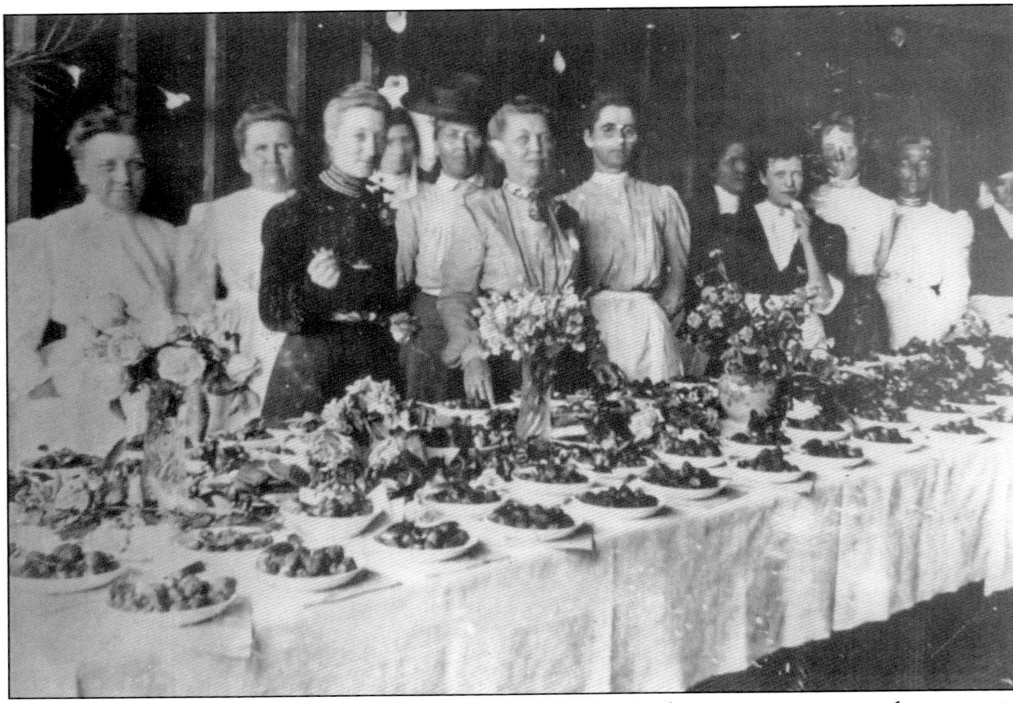

STRAWBERRY PROMOTIONS AND WATERMELON FEED, C. 1909. Real estate promotion and community events often intertwined. Developers Park-Grable would hold bimonthly "excursions" for prospective buyers and visitors. After a tour of available lots, guests would receive a complimentary plate of strawberries—these were from the Hawley Ranch, former site of Manning's road station and today the home of the Drew Ford dealership. Pictured inside Park's La Mesa Springs lumber store, such promotions cemented La Mesa Springs' reputation as a hospitable community that enjoyed opening the town gates for regular community events.

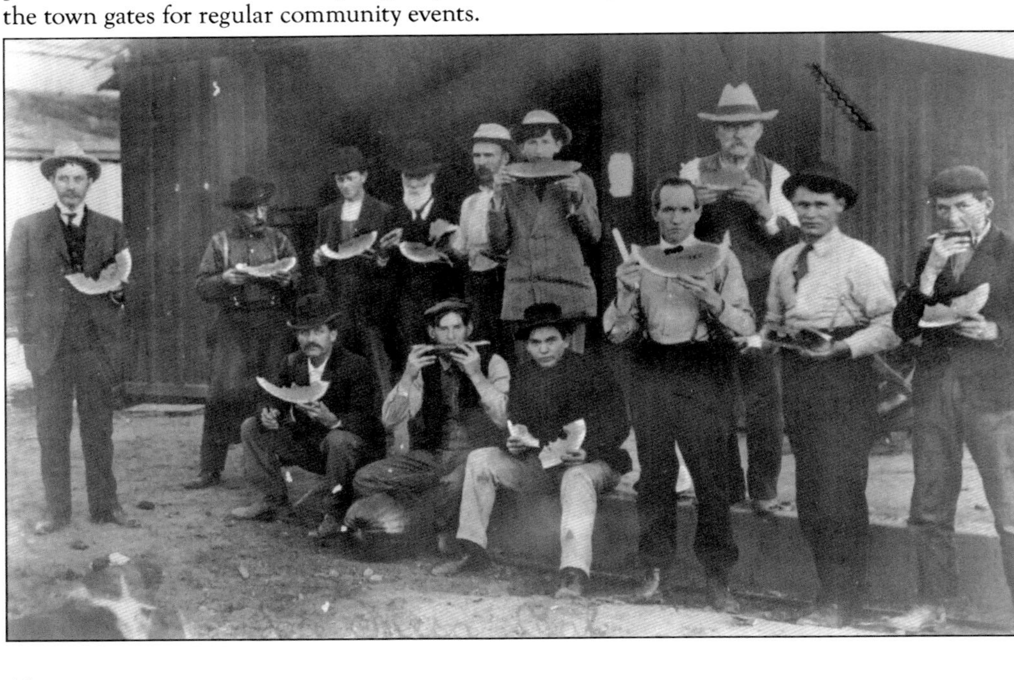

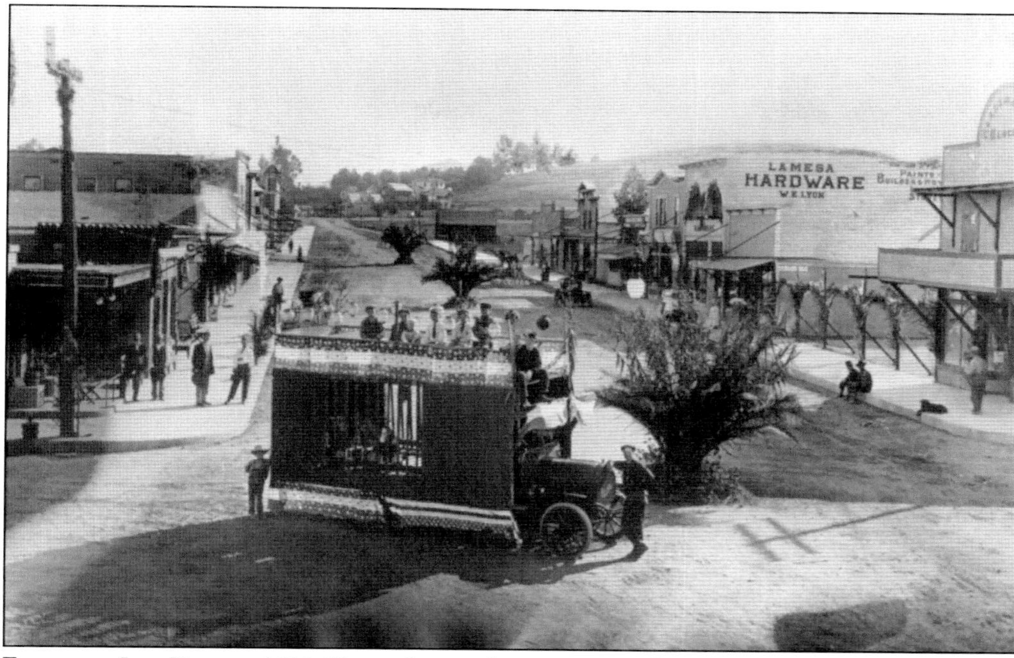

FOURTH OF JULY PARADE, 1910. The tradition of community-wide events dates to the annual Fourth of July parades started in 1908. All community groups, businesses, and voluntary organizations would participate, marching, performing, or, as shown here with one of the local auto stages, building or decorating parade floats. This popular annual event included a community picnic with games and barbecue.

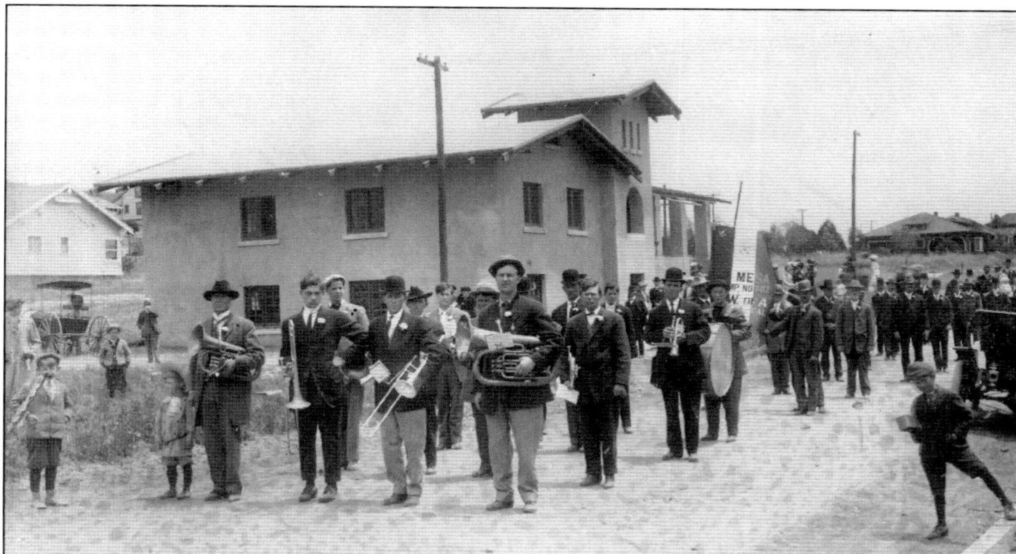

COMMUNITY BAND, C. 1911. THE La Mesa Springs Community Band lines up on Third Avenue to participate in the 1911 Fourth of July Parade. One of the community's fraternal organizations waits behind the band, ready to march onto the Lookout Avenue parade route. The bran-new Emmor Brooke Weaver–designed Congregational church building is an early example of La Mesa's interest in cutting-edge architectural design.

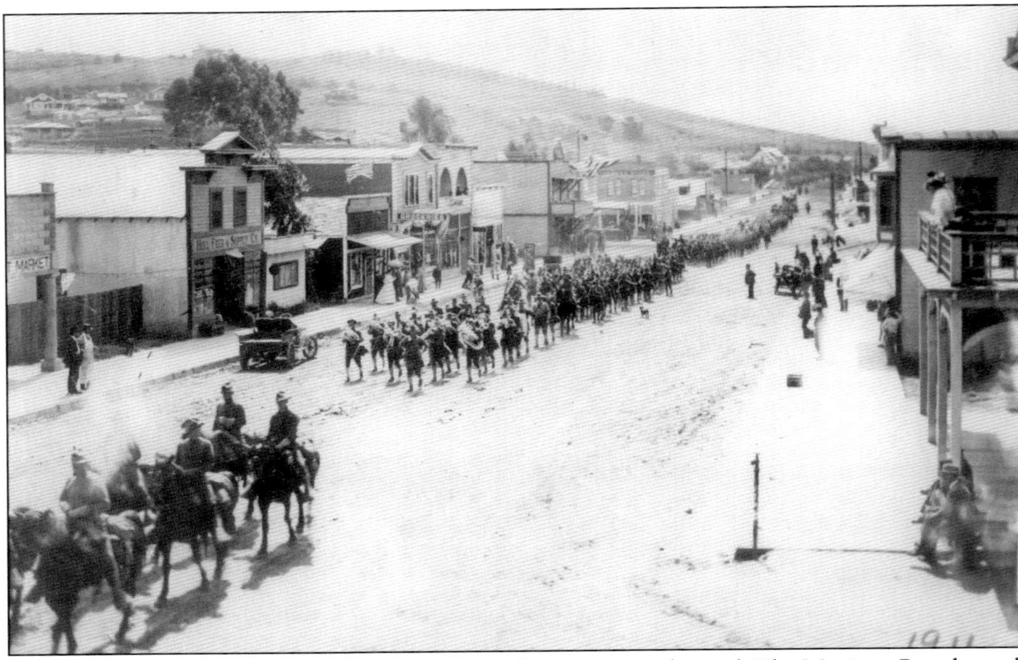

U.S. ARMY TROOPS, 1911. Not all community gatherings were planned. The Mexican Revolution's spread into upper Baja California in the spring of 1911 forced the army to establish border camps protecting locals against the fighting crossing into the United States. Here U.S. Army soldiers march through town, before camping at Fletcher Hills on their way to their border stations.

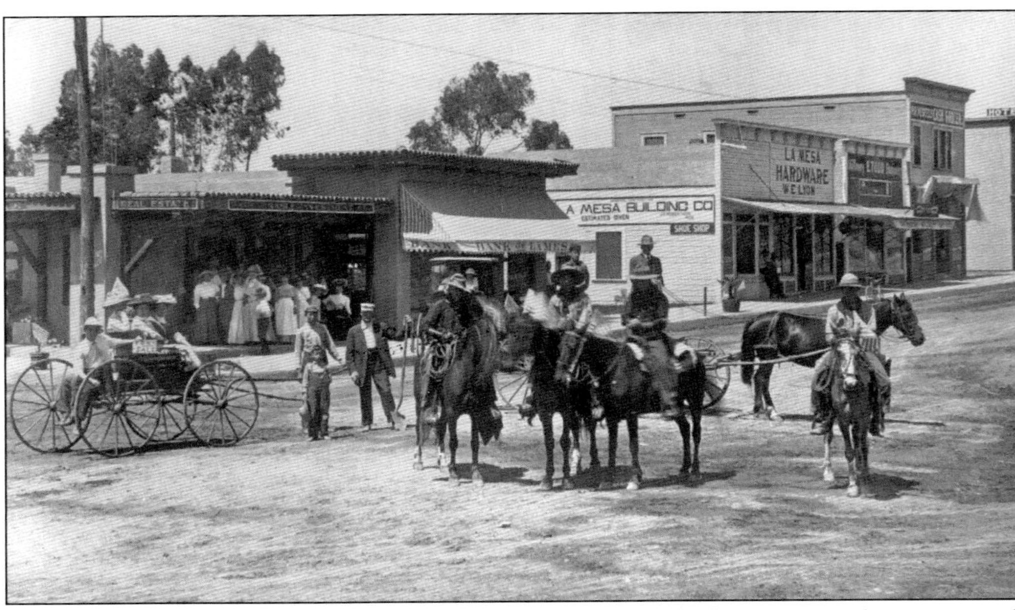

COMMUNITY CLEAN UP DAY, 1912. Community events sometimes had more practical purposes, such as Community Clean Up Day, planned to remove unwanted refuse and promote community spirit. Centered on the Park-Grable office and Bank of La Mesa at Spring Street and Lookout Avenue, the locals are joined by some "cowboys"—not real ones but well dressed for the part.

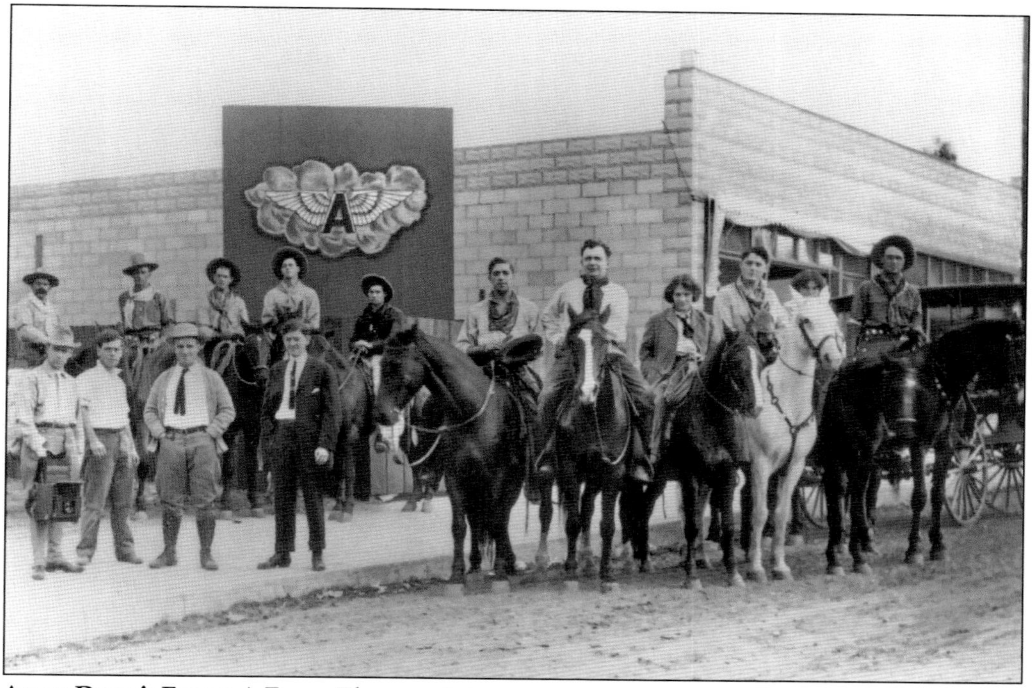

ALLEN DWAN'S FLYING A FILMS. Those cowboys were actors for the American Film Manufacturing Company. Pioneering motion picture director Allan Dwan moved his company to La Mesa Springs in August 1911. Dwan had already worn out scenery and settings in San Juan Capistrano and Lakeside before establishing his Lookout Avenue studio between Third and Fourth Streets, including an open-air stage set for interior shots. Dwan used the local settings for his popular Flying A western one-reelers, completing over 100 films in less than one year. Dwan (front row, third from left) would also tire of La Mesa, moving his company to Santa Barbara in July 1912 on his way to a 50-plus-year filmmaking career.

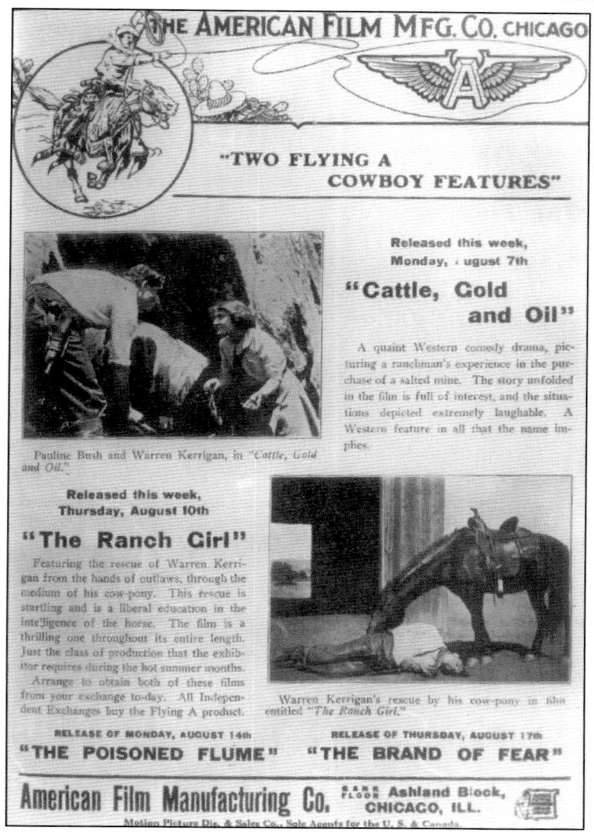

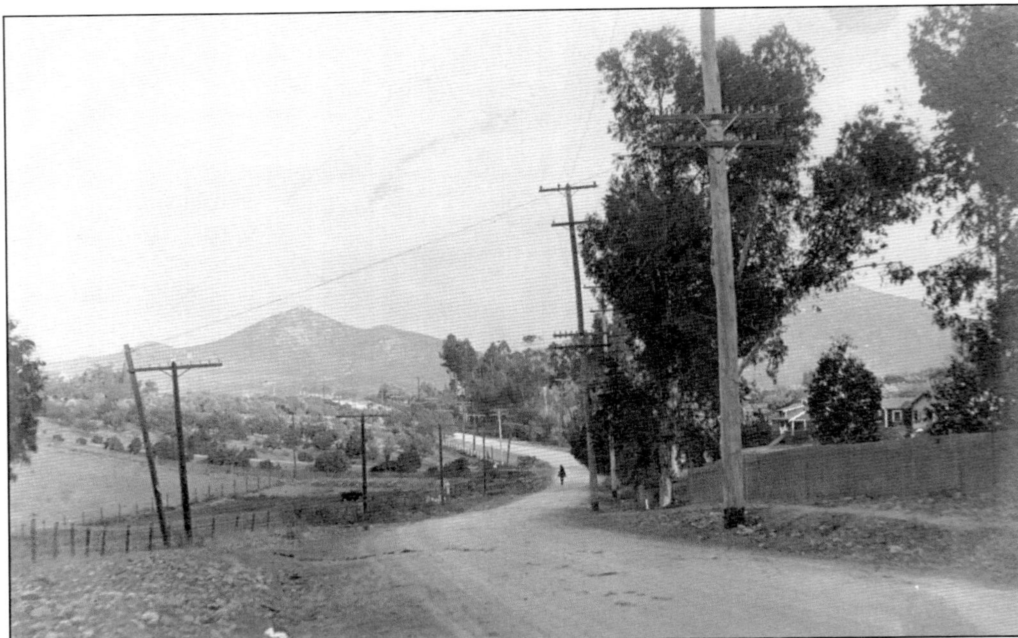

State Route 12, c. 1910. The automobile assisted suburban development and commerce. County residents in 1909, then state residents in 1911, passed highway bonds to pay for development of an all-weather highway system. State surveyors chose El Cajon Avenue as the official east-west state route from East San Diego to El Cajon, passing through both the Colony town site and Springs.

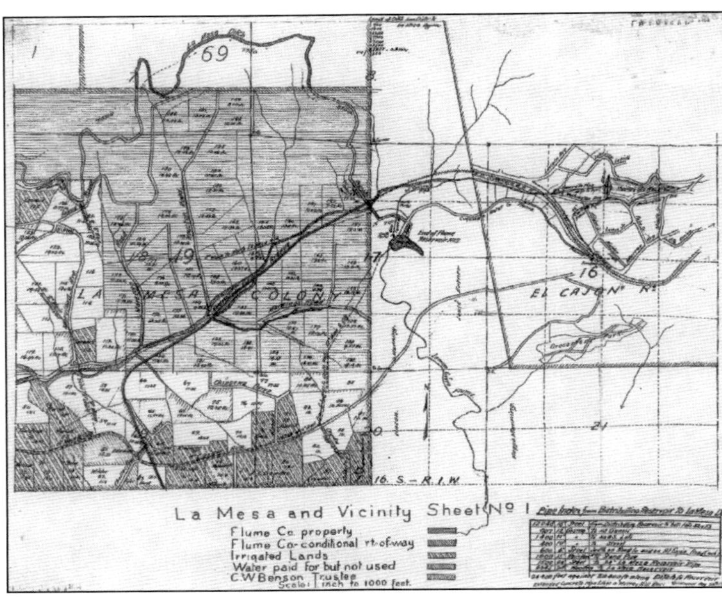

Cuyamaca Water Company Map, 1912. In 1910, Ed Fletcher, a merchant and the new owner of the Alta and Villa Caro Ranches, partnered with Montana capitalist James Murray to purchase and rename the insolvent San Diego Flume Company. Fletcher and Murray would spend significant funds to improve the dilapidated infrastructure, looking to provide necessary water for developing their lands and the region. (Helix Water District.)

Three

The Young City 1912–1925

The new Cuyamaca Water Company provided locals hope for fulfilling the area's growing urban aspirations. The San Diego Flume Company's earlier failures fueled increasing interest in local control to ensure community priorities and prosperity. By mid-1911, the 700-plus residents of La Mesa Springs, concerned not only with water and infrastructure issues but also with the county's ability to meet their public safety, commercial, and civic needs, turned to California's revised Municipality Act. Local leaders, including Sherman Grable, Drs. Charles Samson and J. A. Parks, attorney Lester Welch, developer E. A. D. Reynolds, and banker Edward Upp, among others, gathered support for municipal incorporation. Their petition was initially sent to county supervisors in December 1911, and on February 7, 1912, an election was held, with electors voting 249–60 to incorporate La Mesa Springs as the City of La Mesa—distinguished from the Colony (renamed La Mesa Heights). On February 16, 1912, the City of La Mesa filed its formal incorporation papers. The concurrently elected board of trustees including Reynolds, Samson, Parks, S. R. Canon, and John McRea. The board selected Dr. Samson as chairman (the first "mayor"). In response to this civic infrastructure, local merchants quickly formed a chamber of commerce, and local property owners formed a new irrigation district that would be key to their future civic independence. The next decade provided steady growth, both in city services and local institutions, including a new school, new churches, and new civic institutions and groups. New suburban tracts were platted, including the notable La Mesa Boulevard Addition with its presidential street names and Fletcher's Grossmont Colony tracts among others. With the newly designated state highway passing through town, the Lookout Avenue business district also grew and prospered, serving the increasing commercial and auto traffic along with the rising city population. Challenges with water service would continue to rally locals as the young city rode out the trials of World War I and prepared to participate as a civic player in the region's 1920s boom times.

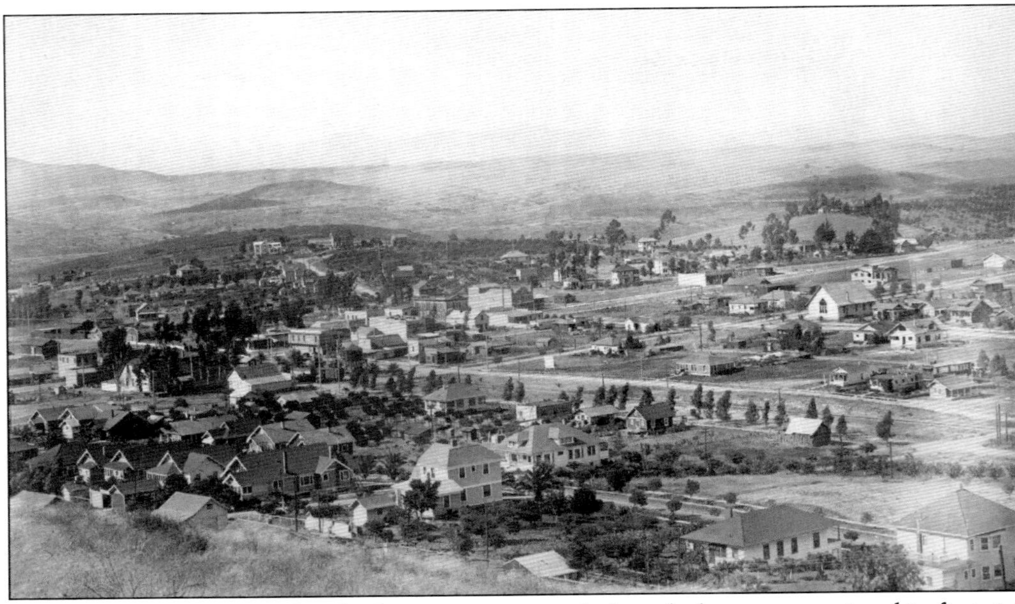

CITY OF LA MESA C. 1912. Shortly after incorporation, the board of trustees appointed its first civil servants, including a part-time engineer, recorder, and attorney, balancing its $2,360 annual budget. Other early elected officials included City Clerk Edward Upp, Treasurer Kellogg B. Finley, and City Marshal Frank Oliver. Oliver's multiple duties included law enforcement, license collection, and building inspection.

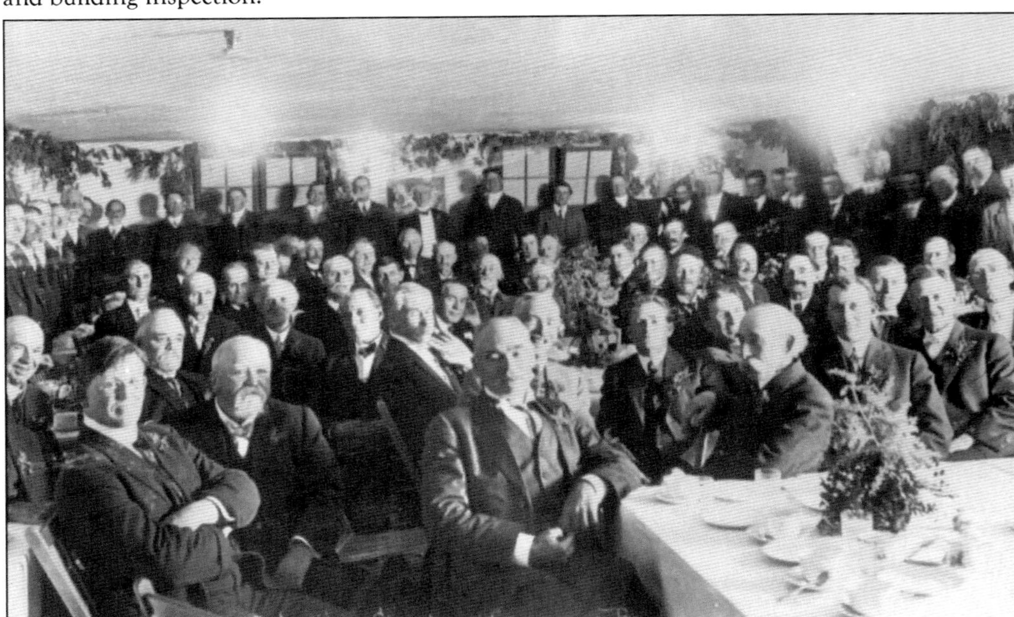

CHAMBER OF COMMERCE BANQUET, 1915. The chamber, formed in 1912, tirelessly promoted La Mesa and was a cornerstone of the town's long-recognized reputation for business opportunity and secure residential investment. Seen here is the chamber's membership of pioneer businessmen, civic officials, and leading residents of the early City. Dr. Charles Samson, the first mayor, is at bottom left with arms folded.

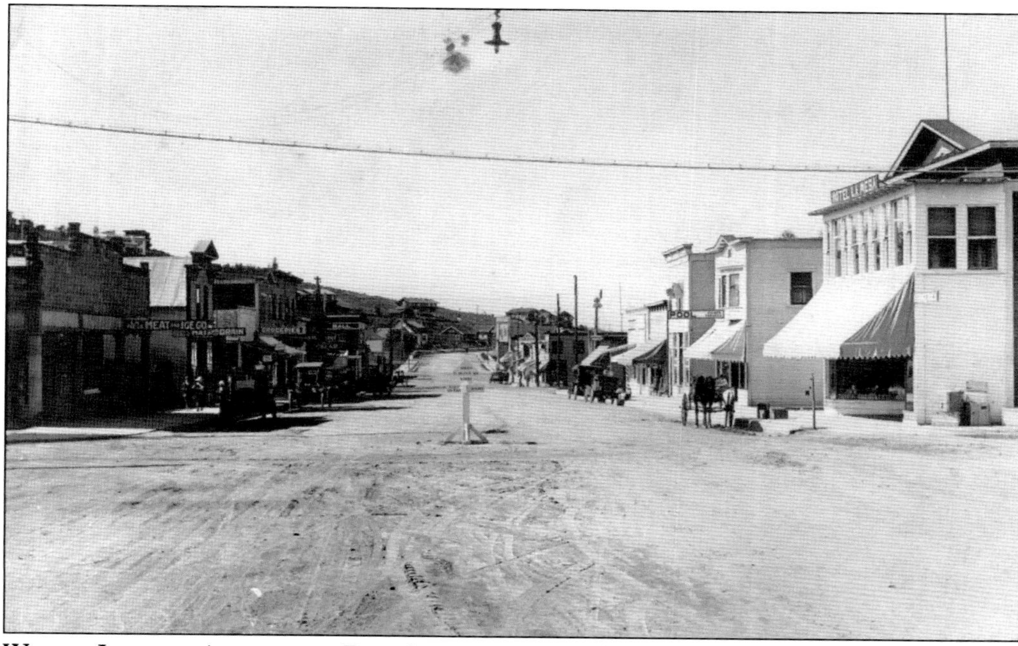

West on Lookout Avenue from Palm Avenue, c. 1916. The business district is seen in its transition to automobile traffic and commerce. Autos share the road with horse-drawn buggies, and auto garages are replacing livery stables. Electric streetlights and telephone lines crisscross the streetscape, while older buildings, such as the 1907 Dorothy Hotel (Hotel La Mesa), sport new storefronts.

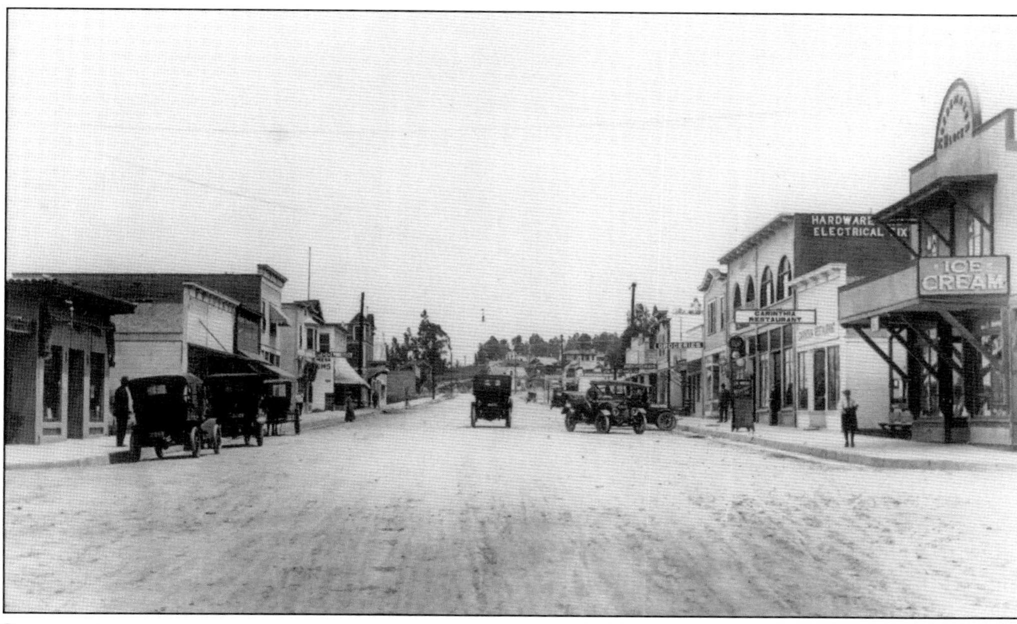

East on Lookout Avenue from Spring Street, c. 1919. This shot was taken after the California Highway Commission provided all-weather paving for this section of the highway, putting in the infrastructure for the increasing auto commerce that would come after World War I. The Bank of La Mesa is seen at left center.

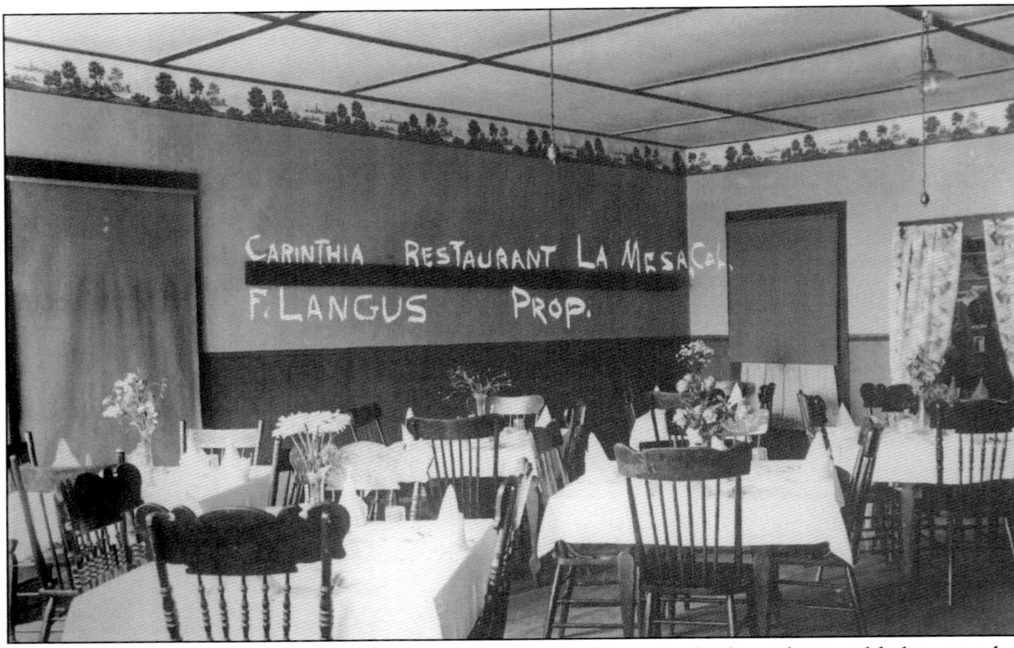

CARINTHIA RESTAURANT, C. 1919. This rare interior shot shows the high-quality establishments that served both local and traveling customers. Former Park-Grable land agent William Maxwell sold La Mesa Restaurant to Mr. Langus, allowing Maxwell to move into his furniture business, which served the community for decades.

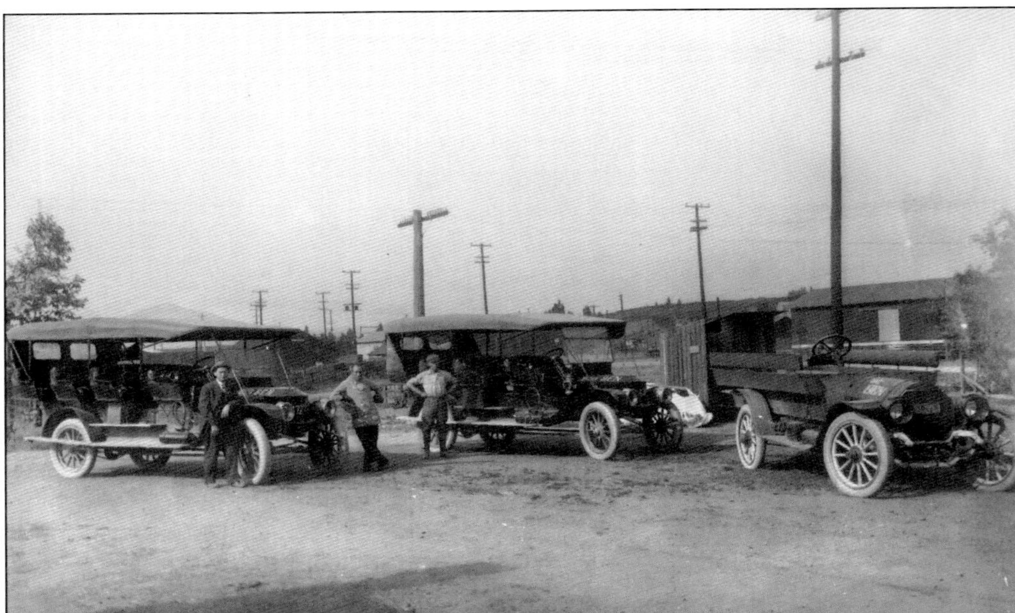

"BIG BEN" MOTOR STAGES, 1912. In the 1910s, personal automobiles were rare, and most relied on the services of various auto stages to travel to and from La Mesa. The Big Ben Company was locally owned. Owner Ben Atkins (center) is flanked by *La Mesa Scout* editor T. M. Hancock (left) and driver Ross Orsborn (right).

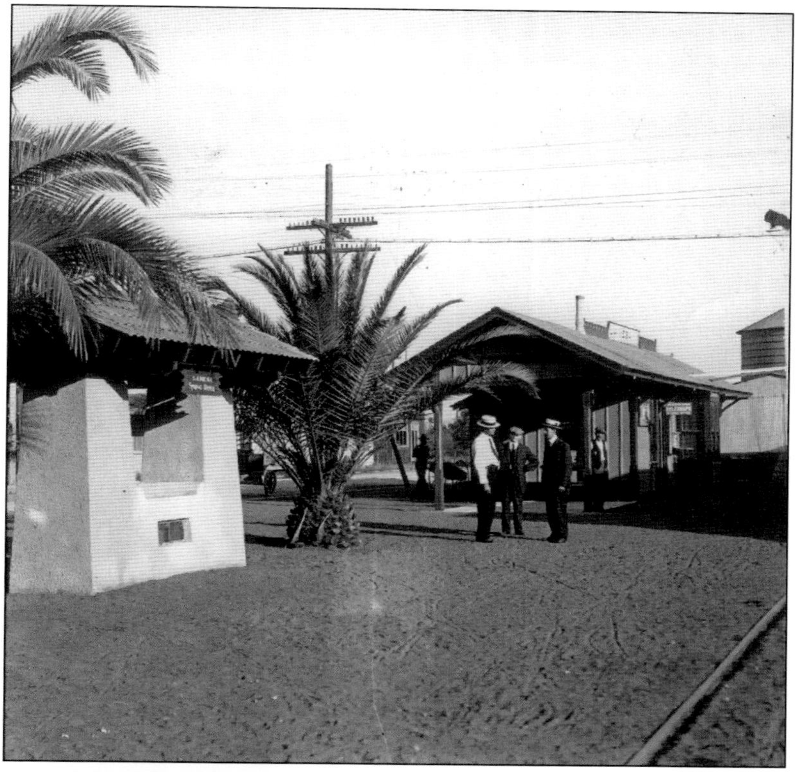

DEPOT AND SPRING FOUNTAIN, 1914. The SDCE continued to be the key commuter route to San Diego. The depot and telegraph station are shown along with the new spring fountain. Promoting the abundance and purity of La Mesa's local resources, the water was pumped from Collier Park's Spring House to this public fountain until its 1960s relocation to the park.

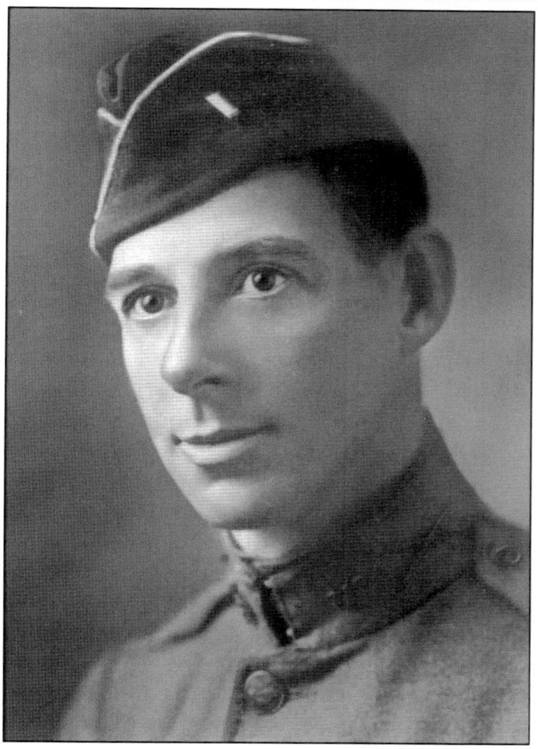

LT. RUEBEN LEVY, 1918. La Mesans participated in America's World War I efforts, buying war bonds and sending young men to serve. Notables included Rueben Levy, who was awarded the Distinguished Service Cross and was later a long-standing merchant and Helix Water District director. The president of La Mesa Women's Club, Mrs. Howard Worth, earned home-front praise for organizing programs for visiting servicemen and war industry workers.

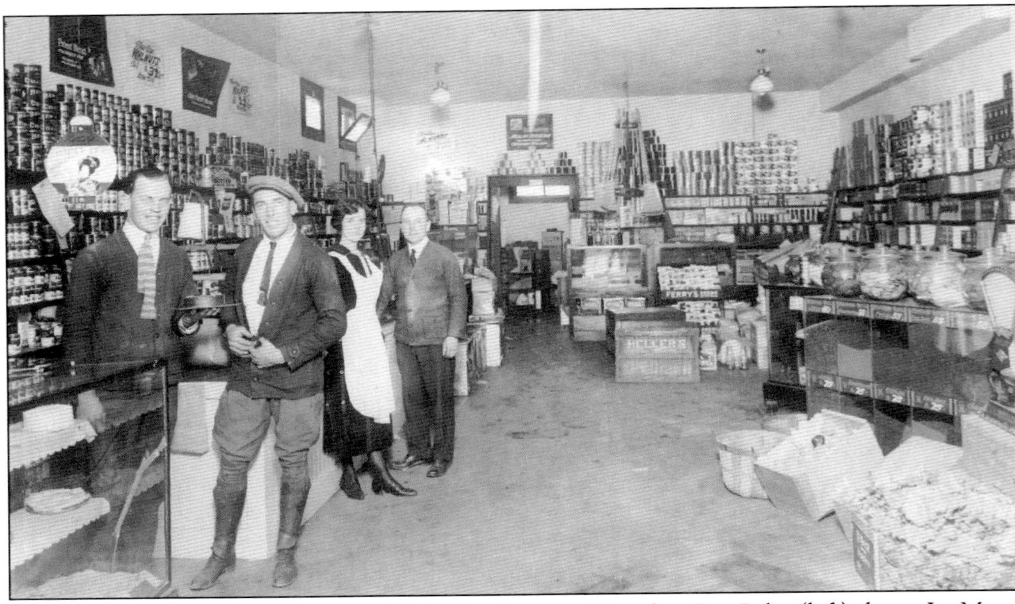

LYLES STORE, HELLER BUILDING, C. 1924. Merchant and butcher Ray Lyles (left) shows La Mesa's 1920s prosperity with baked goods from his well-stocked grocery store. Luther Gordon, owner of one of the first radio shops in town, is to his right. Both were later city fire chiefs. Ray's father, Alvin, is at far right next to clerk Violet Coleman.

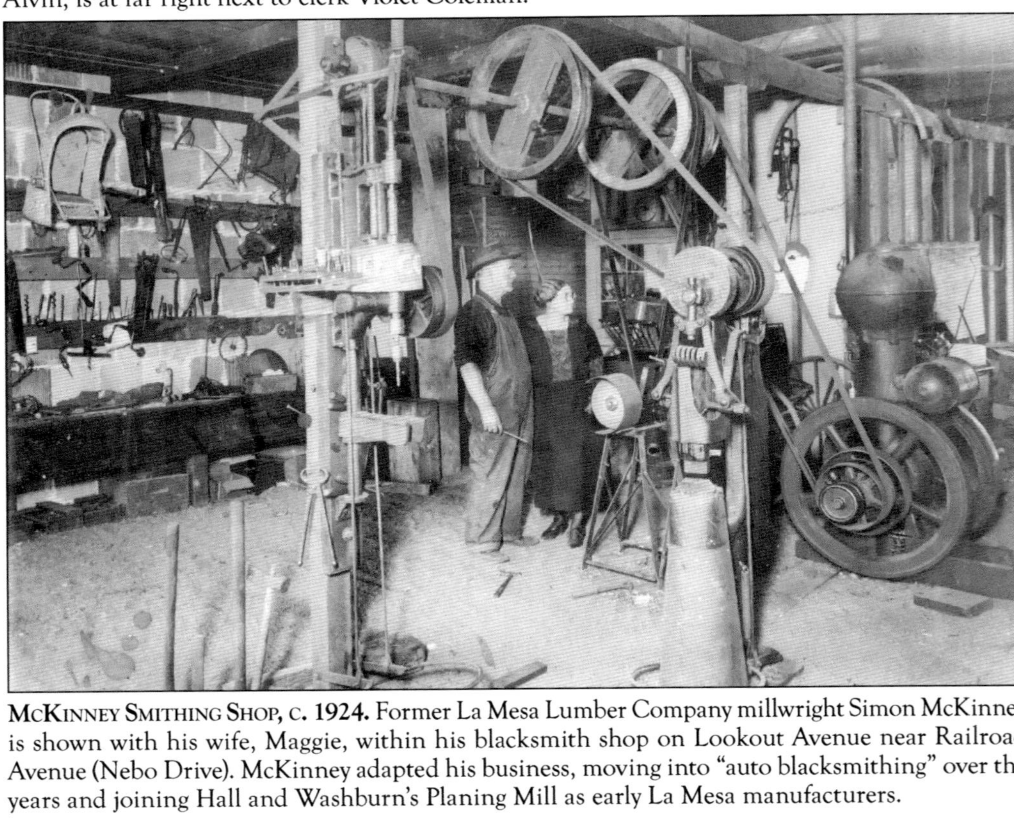

MCKINNEY SMITHING SHOP, C. 1924. Former La Mesa Lumber Company millwright Simon McKinney is shown with his wife, Maggie, within his blacksmith shop on Lookout Avenue near Railroad Avenue (Nebo Drive). McKinney adapted his business, moving into "auto blacksmithing" over the years and joining Hall and Washburn's Planing Mill as early La Mesa manufacturers.

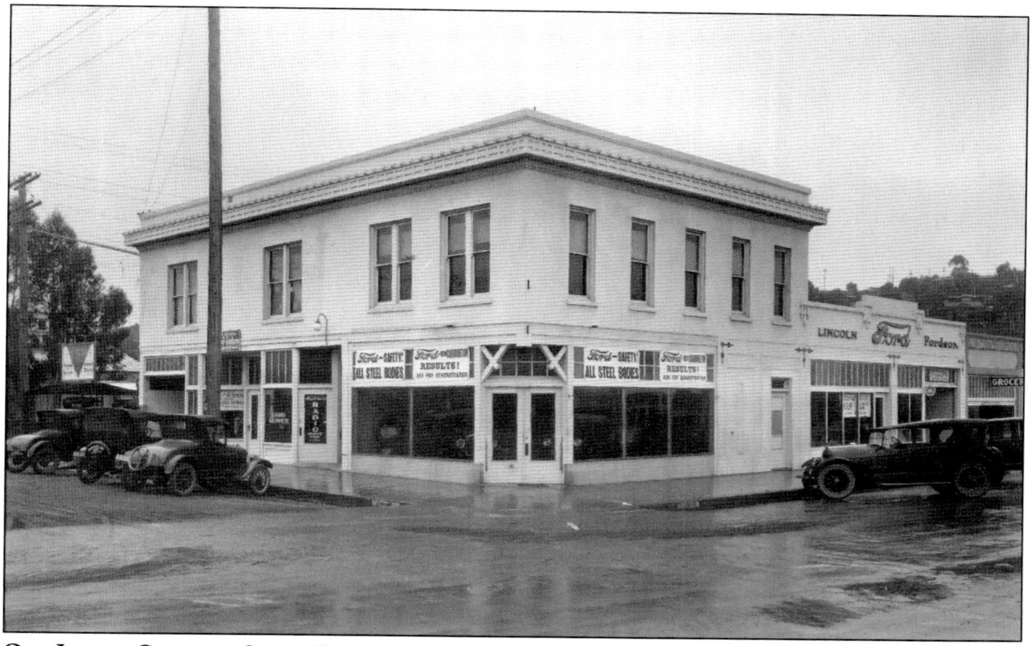

OLD LEMON COMPANY STORE BUILDING, C. 1925. As the community moved from agricultural to urban, the old mainstays changed with the times. This landmark 1894 building gets a face-lift to serve as the new Ford Motor Company dealership. Elmer Drew would later take over the local Ford dealership, moving it to his repair shop at Lookout Avenue and Allison Street in 1934.

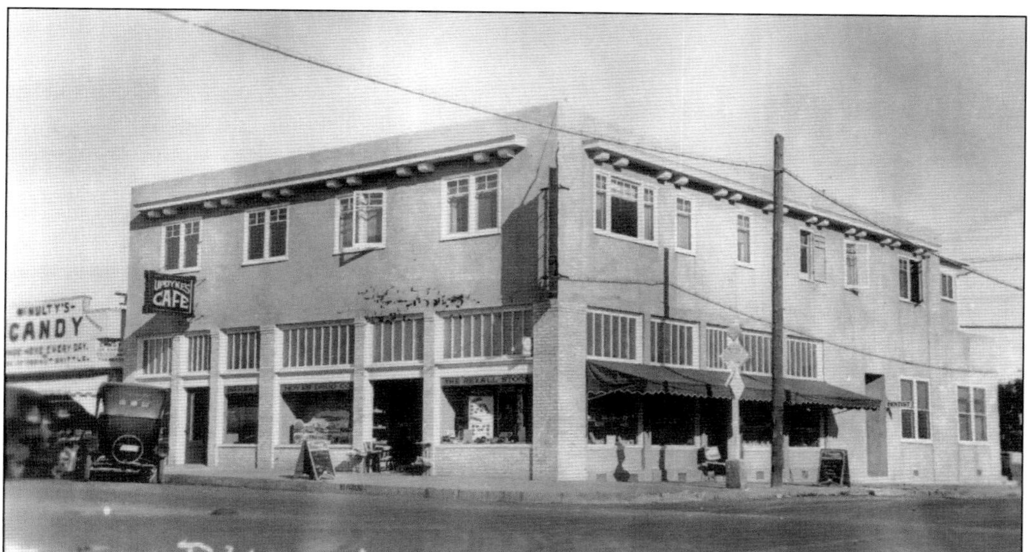

LA MESA DRUG STORE, C. 1923. Charles Noyes purchased the original town drugstore at Spring Street and Lookout Avenue in 1911. In 1922, he had local contractors Marker and Russell construct this impressive building at Palm and Lookout Avenues. Noyes sold it in 1923, but the building's long-standing soda fountain and community-minded owners such as Murray Kellock have kept the building a time-honored community landmark.

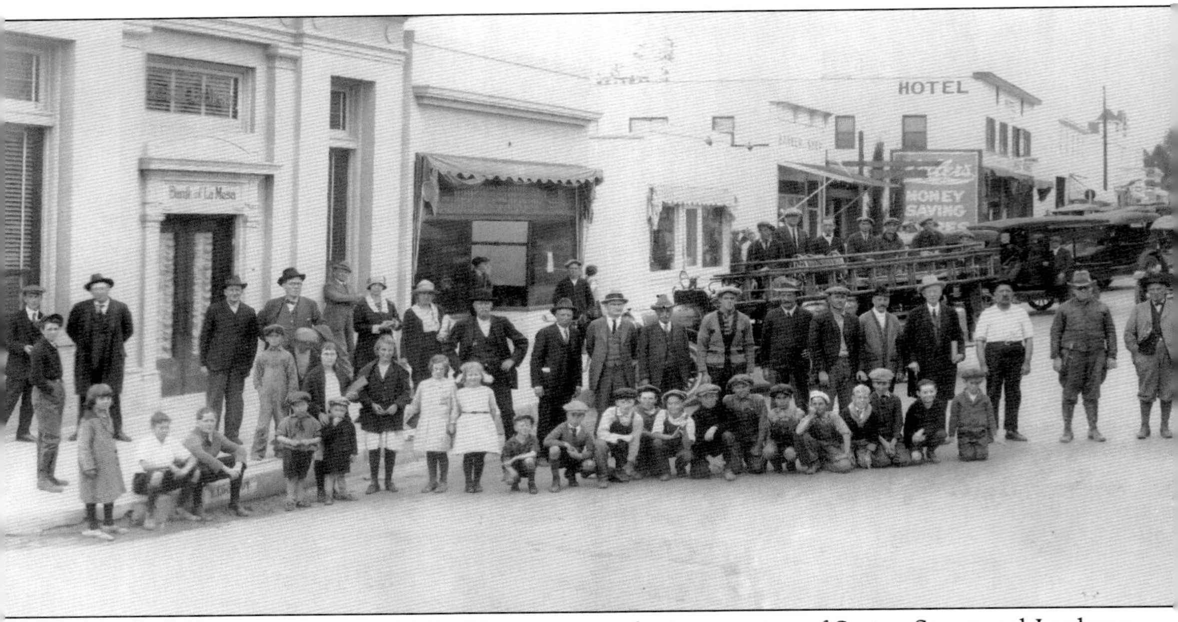

COMMUNITY PORTRAIT, 1924. La Mesa poses at the intersection of Spring Street and Lookout Avenue. The new Bank of La Mesa building has replaced the original Park-Grable office and bank building at far left. The fire department is represented with Chief Luther Gordon and its Moreland ladder truck. Jack Mercer's police force of five is found at right with its two patrol motorcycles. Civic and business leaders are spread out with a cadre of "junior businessmen," including the

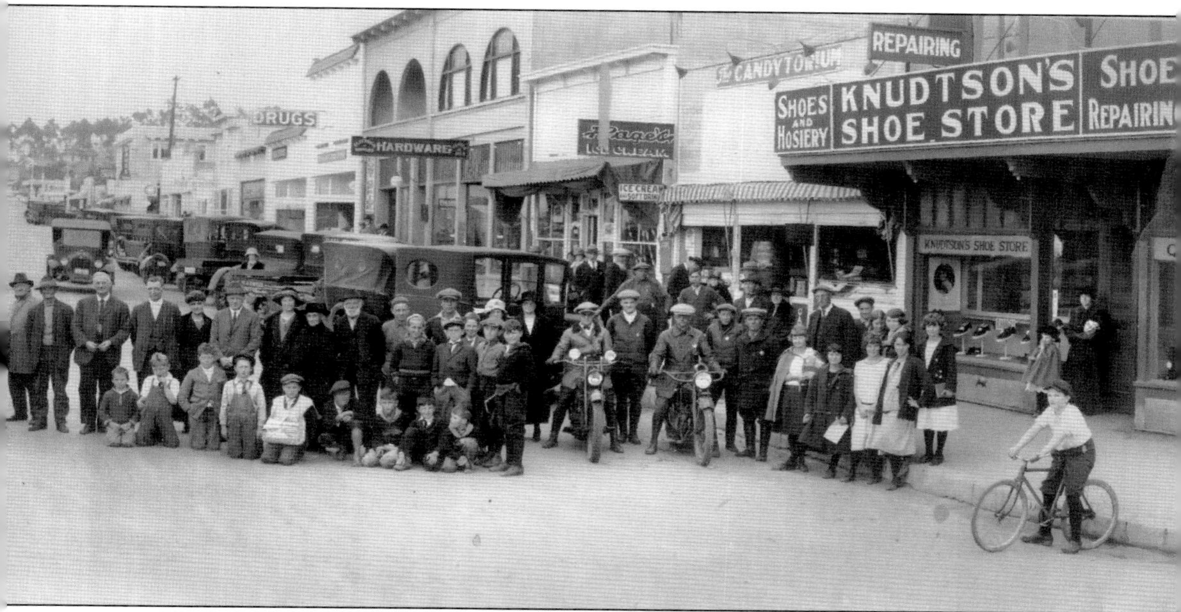

newsboys at front center-right. This photograph illustrates the young city ready to take advantage of the Roaring Twenties. "Mayor" David Jones (center with hands up) served from 1924 to 1926 and followed early chairmen Dr. Samson (1912–1914), Henry Hall (1914–1918), Dr. John Mallory (1918–1920), John Scott (1918–1920), and Edwards Porter (1920–1924) of the noted Porter family.

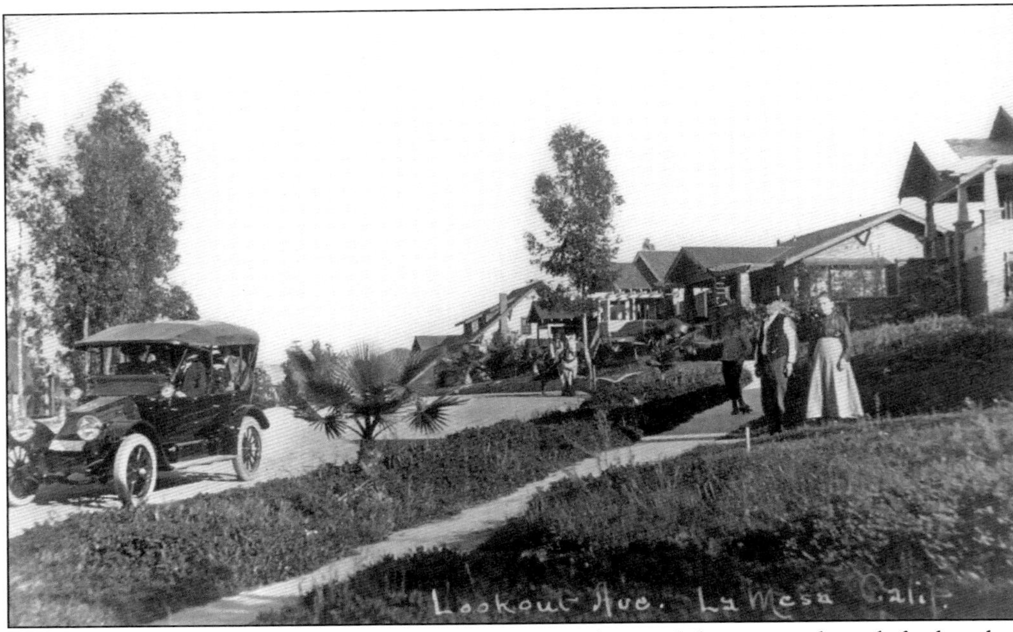

LOOKOUT AVENUE HOUSES, C. 1912. The early business district did not extend much farther than Palm Avenue on the east and Date Avenue on the west. These California bungalows, popular during this period in La Mesa, were located on the curve between Acacia and Normal Avenues, at this time the outskirts of town.

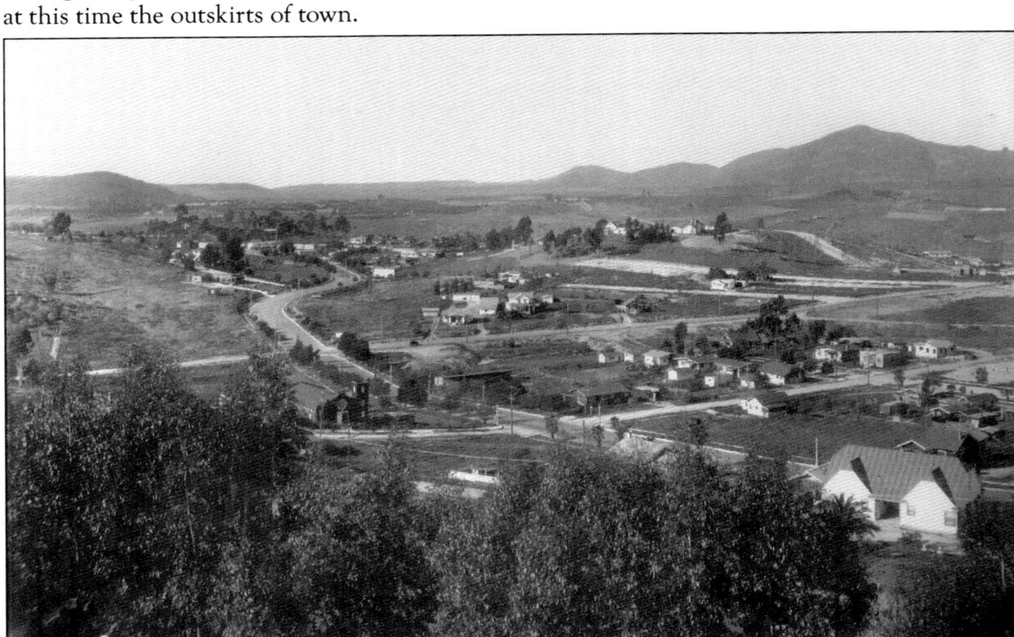

NORTHWEST ON LOOKOUT AVENUE FROM UNIVERSITY AVENUE, C. 1922. Seen From Mount Nebo overlooking the Sunnyside Tract below Lookout Park, the old Fellows Hotel is just right of the intersection, and the original St. Martin's Catholic Church is on Normal Avenue a half-block from Lookout. Lookout Avenue then twists north between Roseland Heights (left) and El Capitan hill (right).

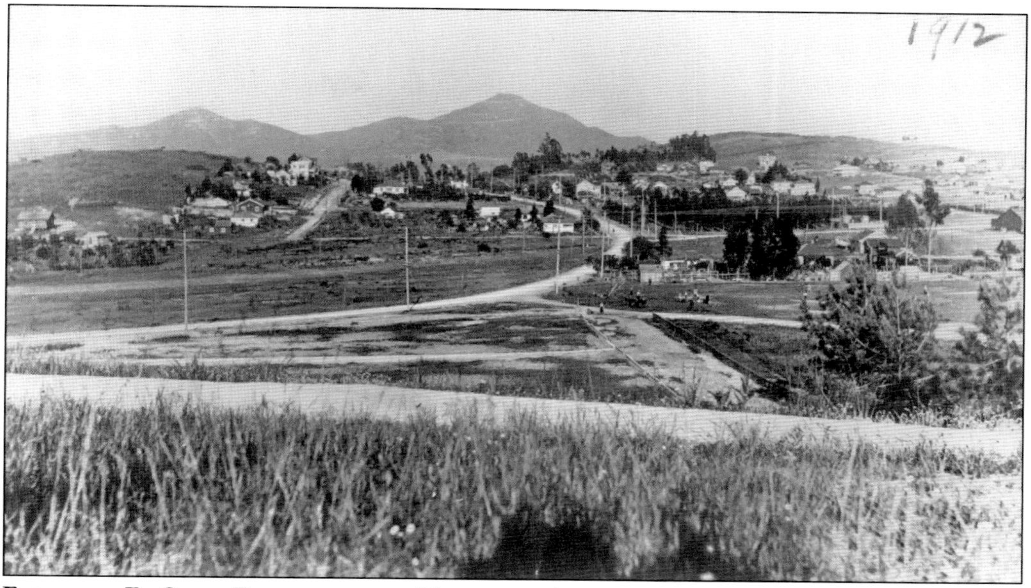

EAST FROM EL CAJON BOULEVARD AND UNIVERSITY AVENUE, C. 1912. The young city's northern area is seen from El Capitan hill in the Morningside Tract. The state highway (now University Avenue) passes between Porter Hill (left) and the urbanizing Petaluma, Wheeler, and Magruder tracts north of Allison (right). The community baseball field, with a game in play, is at the Chollas Road intersection.

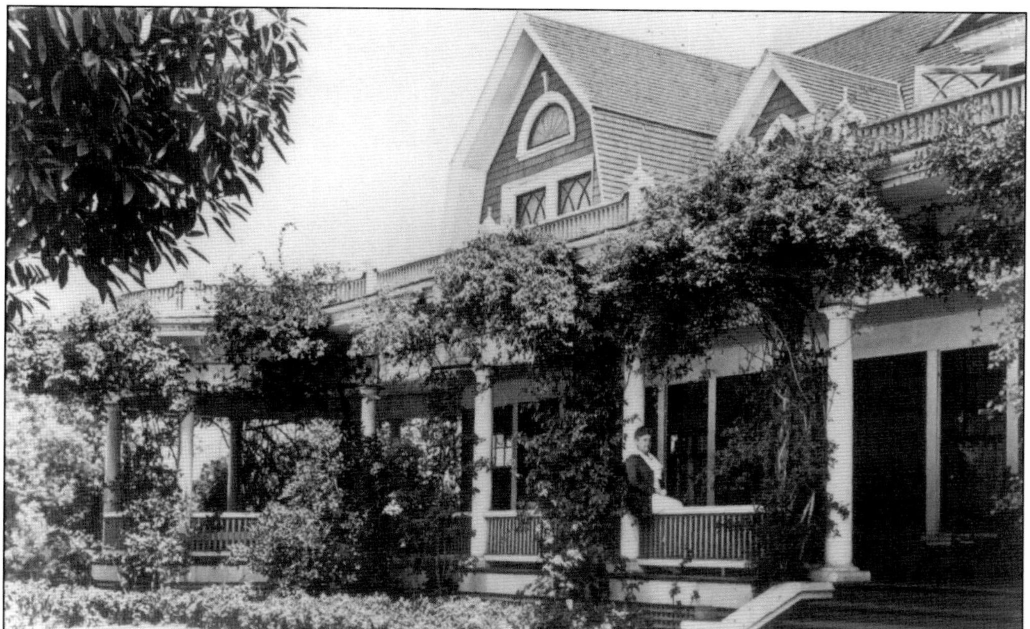

ROSEHEDGE MANOR, C. 1916. James Wallcott Porter and his sister Mary developed this lavish residence they named for the surrounding rose hedges on the former Randlett property. Brother Edwards Porter, a mayor and civic leader, also lived here. James's civic leadership included donation of parkland at Lookout Avenue and El Cajon Boulevard and the landmark Porter Hall in memory of his family's accomplishments.

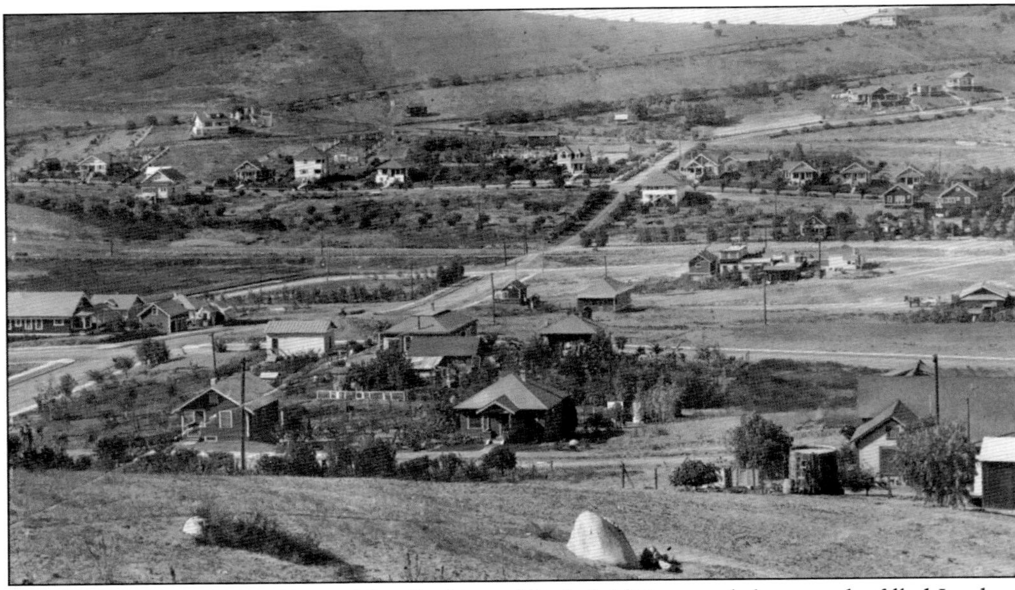

SOUTH CITY, VIEW WEST, 1910s. The Grable and Park Additions and the yet-to-be-filled Lookout Park tract on Mount Nebo are in view. Finley Avenue, named for pioneer and first city treasurer K. B. Finley, bisects the image. Date Avenue is filling with new homes, and the paved Pasadena and Summit Drives climb Mount Nebo awaiting homes.

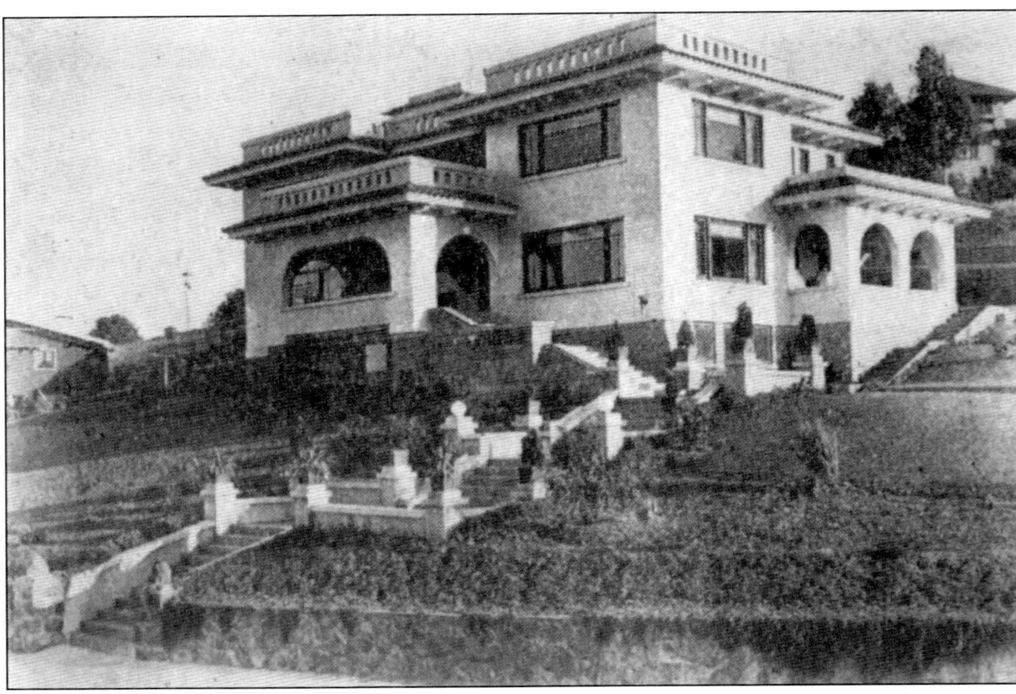

HODGSON HOUSE, MOUNT NEBO, AROUND 1915. One of the first of many beautiful and impressive Mount Nebo homes was the Hodgson House on Pasadena Avenue near Vista Drive. Built for the Hodgson sisters, this Prairie-style-influenced home reflects the progressive nature of the young city and its architectural interests.

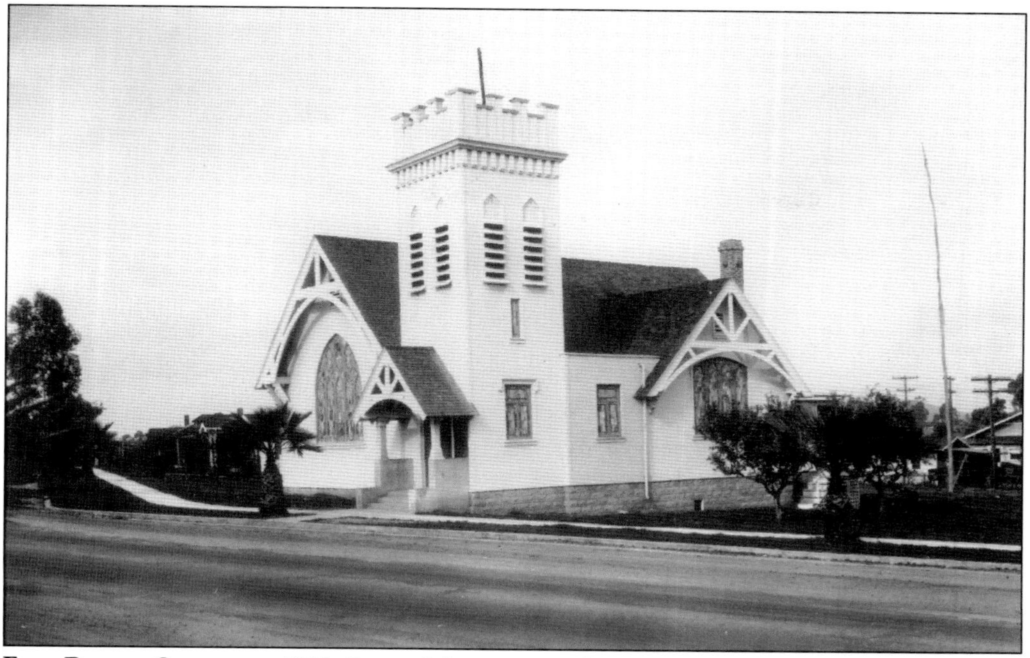

First Baptist Church, c. 1920. Some of the young city's most iconic architecture was found in its churches. The First Baptist Church was built in 1912 at the northwest corner of Lookout and Acacia Avenues (shown here). Moved one block north to Orange Avenue across from La Mesa Grammar School in 1927 and remodeled in 1952, this building remains a community landmark.

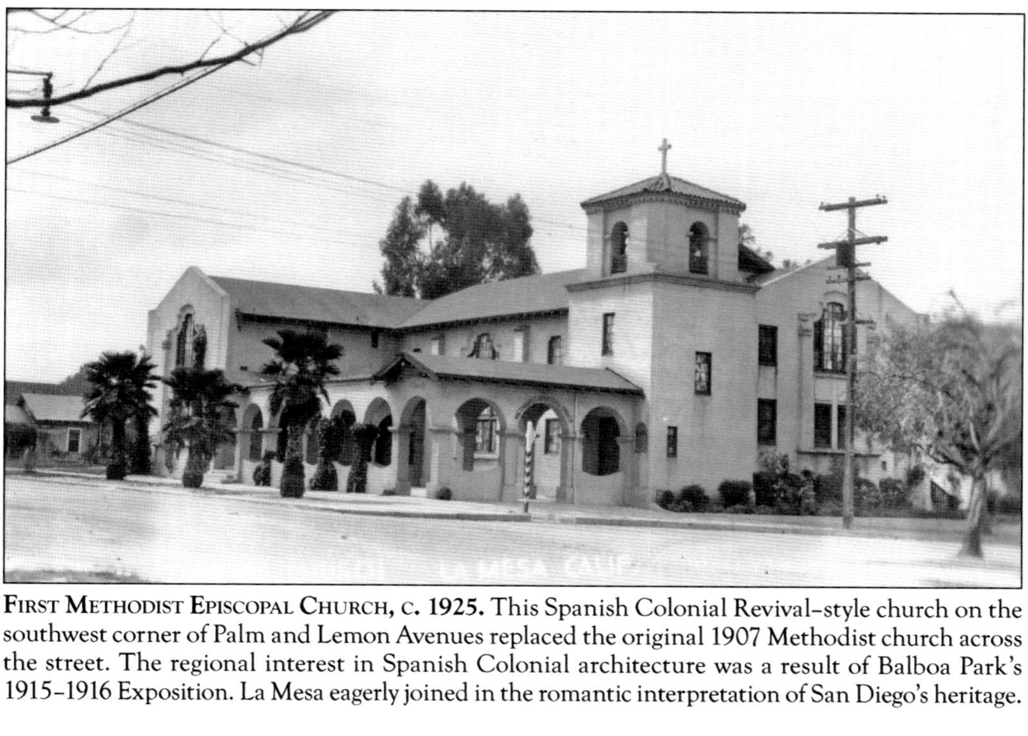

First Methodist Episcopal Church, c. 1925. This Spanish Colonial Revival–style church on the southwest corner of Palm and Lemon Avenues replaced the original 1907 Methodist church across the street. The regional interest in Spanish Colonial architecture was a result of Balboa Park's 1915–1916 Exposition. La Mesa eagerly joined in the romantic interpretation of San Diego's heritage.

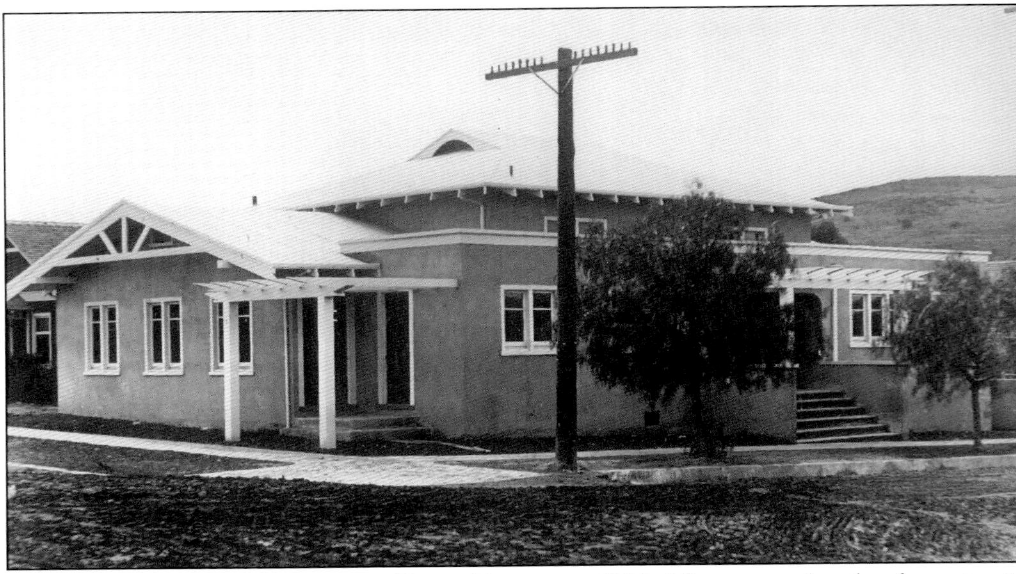

WOMEN'S CLUB BUILDING 1915 AND YOUTH RECITAL C. 1916. After over a decade of meeting in private homes, local churches, and the opera house, La Mesa Women's Club built this handsome clubhouse at the southwest corner of Third Street and Lemon Avenue in 1913. The club raised much of the $5,418.70 cost through a concert by world-renown contralto Ernestine Schumann-Heink—a new resident of Ed Fletcher's nearby Grossmont Colony. The women's club became a center of local civic and community events, such as the recital by youngsters below. The clubhouse featured an elaborate rosewood baby grand piano donated by famous composer and Grossmont resident Carrie Jacobs Bond.

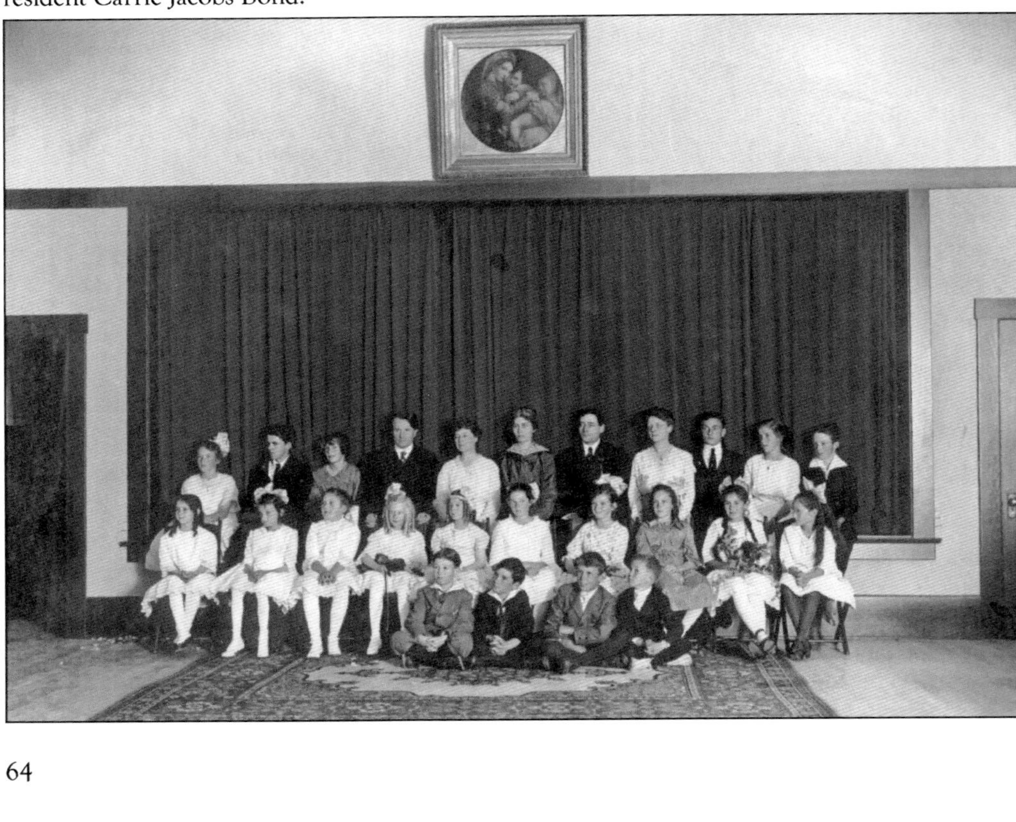

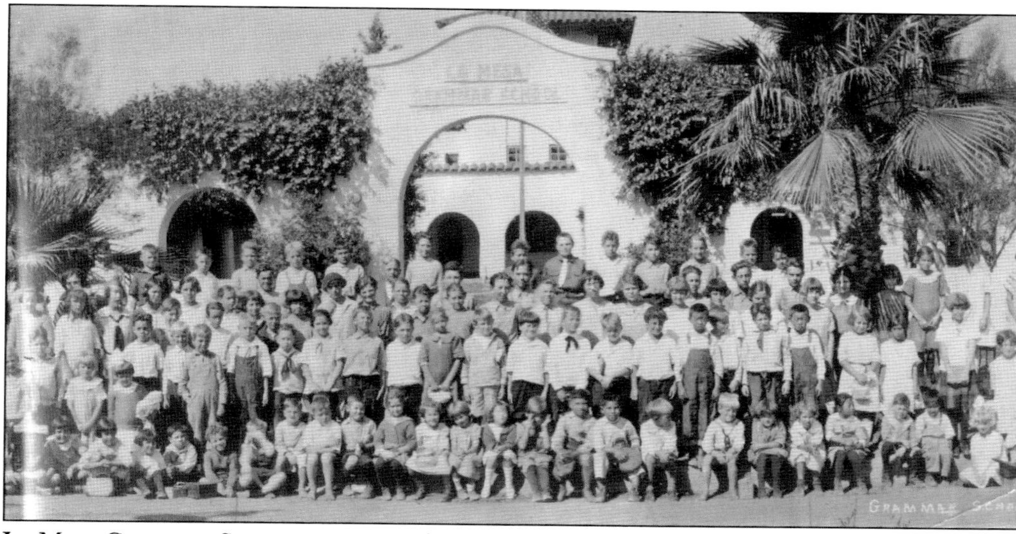

La Mesa Grammar School, c. 1918. The 1914 grammar school was another architectural gem. Designed by noted San Diego architects Richard Requa and Frank Mead, the Mission Revival–style building replaced the 1895 Allison School. All La Mesa and Spring Valley school-age children attended through the eighth grade, including those of the small but active Japanese American and Hispanic communities, as seen here.

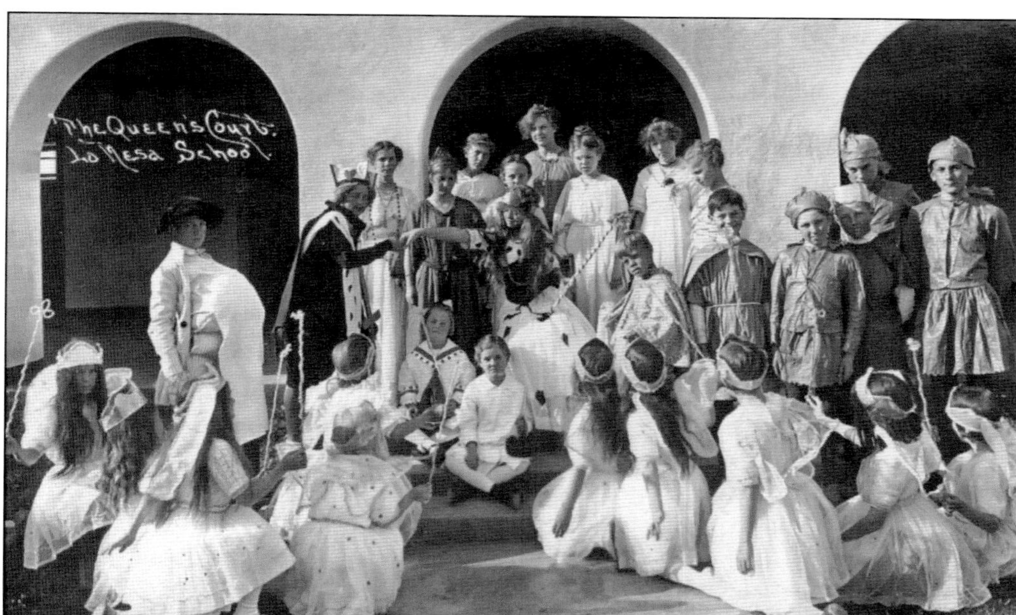

Grammar School Play Cast, 1916. The grammar school served not only as an educational institution but as an important site for local entertainments and social gatherings with the largest performance space in town in its auditorium. The school band, choir, sporting events, and performing arts productions, such as the one undertaken by these student actors, made the school an important community venue.

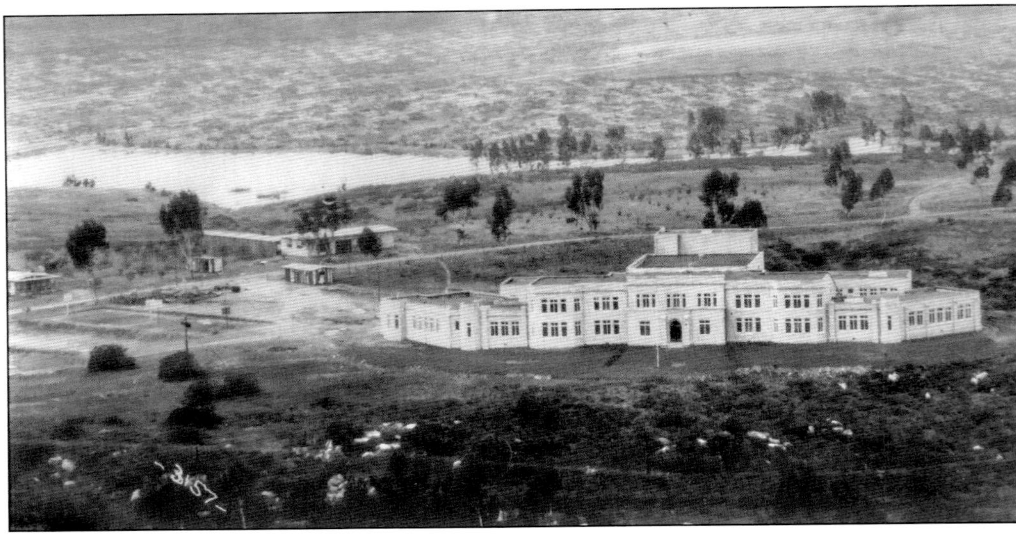

GROSSMONT HIGH SCHOOL, 1923, AND TACKY DAY, 1925. After incorporation, San Diego High School refused new La Mesa enrollees. Small El Cajon Valley High School, opened in 1893, also realized that La Mesans would be served without paying district taxes. Negotiations between the elementary districts from Lakeside to La Mesa Heights resulted in the Grossmont Union High School District in 1920. Students used Lakeside's new Riverview High School (1916–1920) until both schools were incorporated into the new Grossmont High School, opened in 1922 on land donated by Ed Fletcher above the Murray Hill Reservoir. Fletcher also provided the granite from his quarry for the Theodore Kistner–designed "castle." Grossmont traditions such as student Tacky Day and the annual Christmas Pageant quickly established Foothillers spirit.

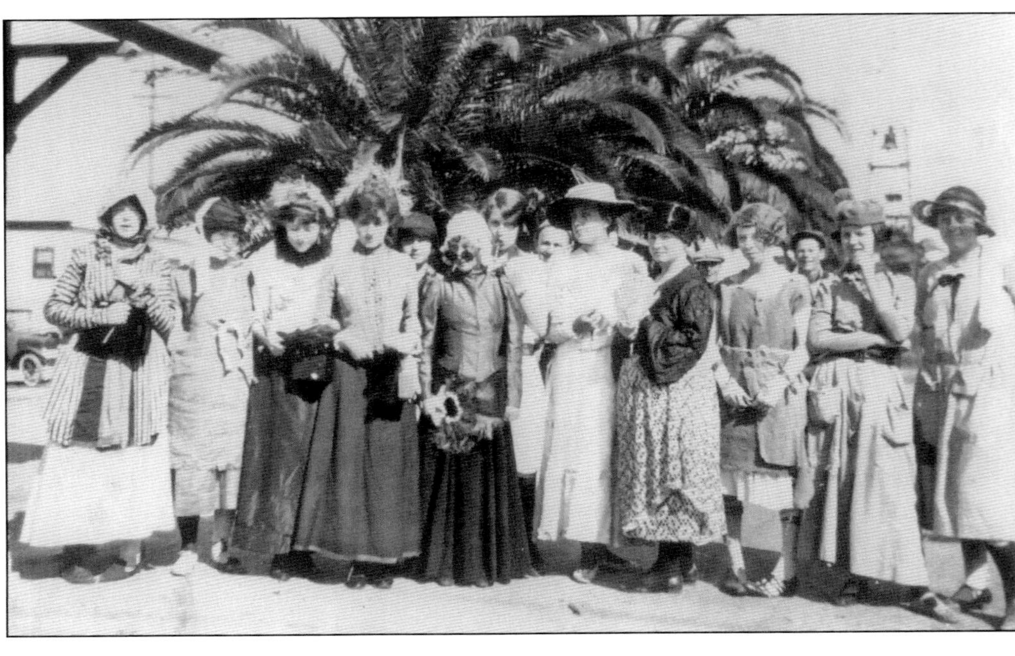

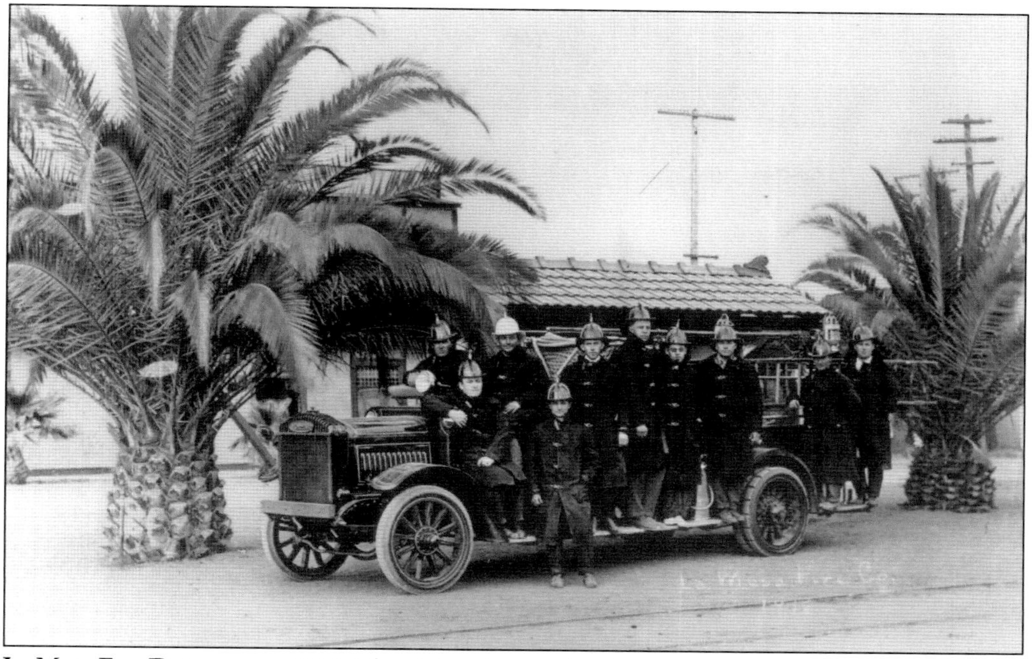

La Mesa Fire Department, 1916. The city's volunteer fire department poses with its new fire truck. Chief Harry Smith (third from left) led this crew of local men, most downtown businessmen who could respond immediately to alarms. Their finest hour was a November 1919 fire along the north side of Lookout Avenue between Palm Avenue and Spring Street that they kept from spreading through downtown.

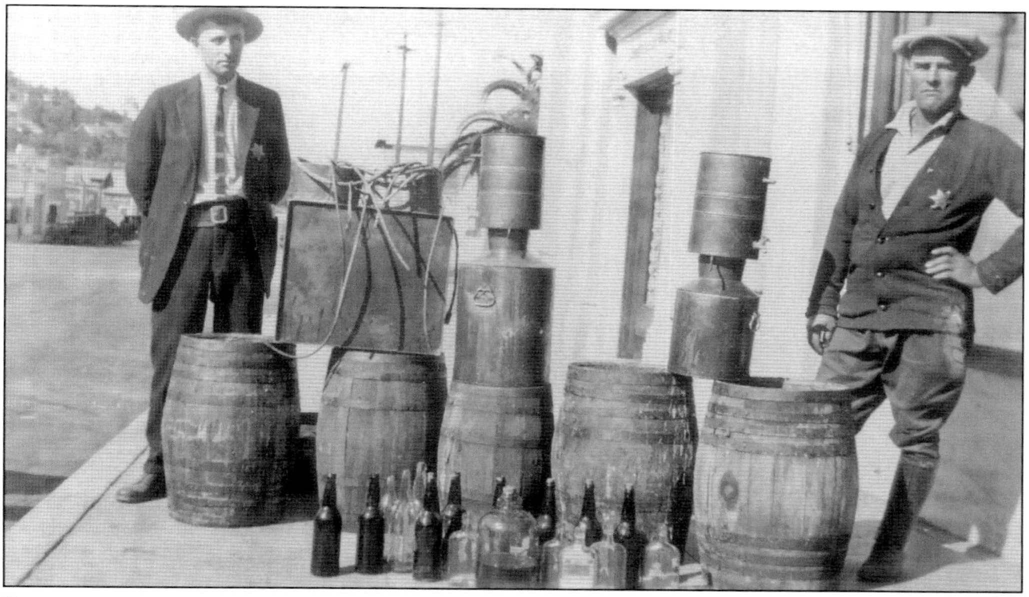

Prohibition Raid, c. 1925. The 18th Amendment made it illegal to make, sell, or transport alcoholic beverages in the United States, burdening law enforcement. City Marshal Jack Mercer (left) displays evidence recovered during a local raid. Mercer became marshal in 1921, overseeing the office's growth into a police department through the 1920s and 1930s.

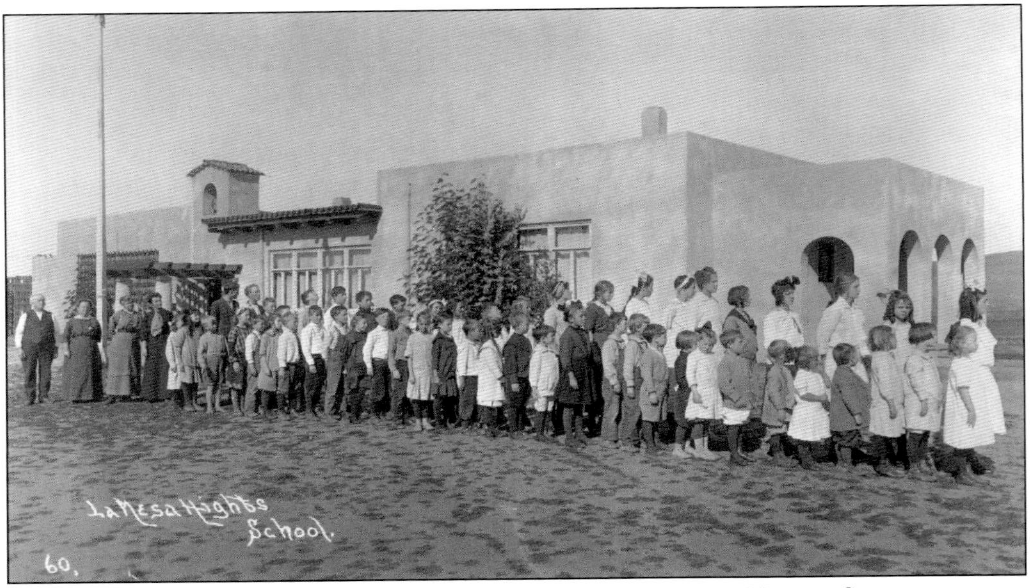

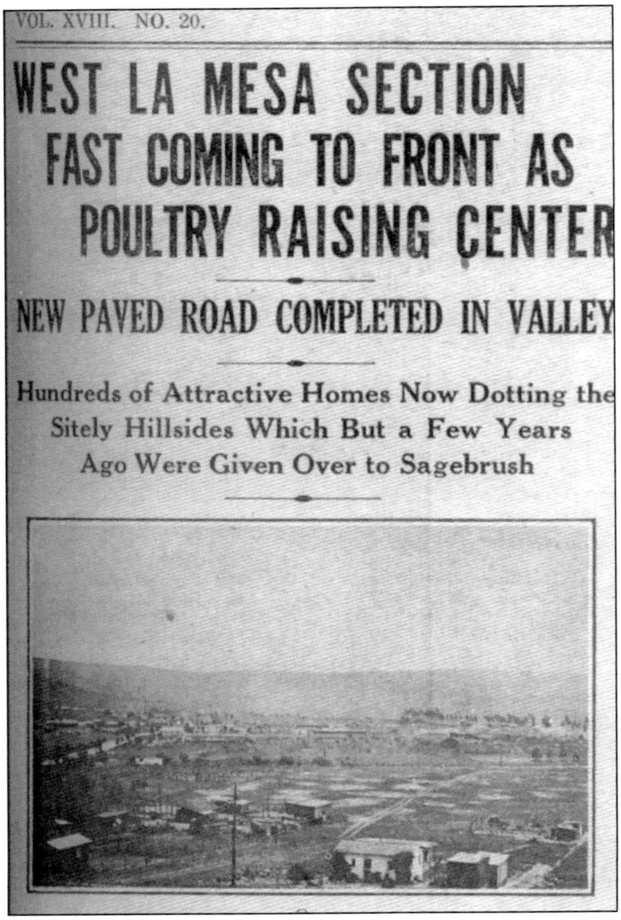
VOL. XVIII. NO. 20.

WEST LA MESA SECTION FAST COMING TO FRONT AS POULTRY RAISING CENTER

NEW PAVED ROAD COMPLETED IN VALLEY

Hundreds of Attractive Homes Now Dotting the Sitely Hillsides Which But a Few Years Ago Were Given Over to Sagebrush

La Mesa Heights School c. 1912 and Scout Article 1922. By 1910, the La Mesa Colony and Townsite had been begrudgingly renamed La Mesa Heights, formally changing its school district name as well. In 1911, La Mesa Heights residents banded together to replace the original 1891 La Mesa School. Iconic architect Irving Gill designed this school, which served the rural community for two decades. La Mesa Heights would continue to grow along with its west-side neighbors, including Maryland Heights to the north of Alvarado Canyon near the reservoir. By the early 1920s, citizens of the two heights and in the neighboring old 19th-century West La Mesa tracts, now within the city limits along the Chollas Road (University Avenue), would find success in poultry farming.

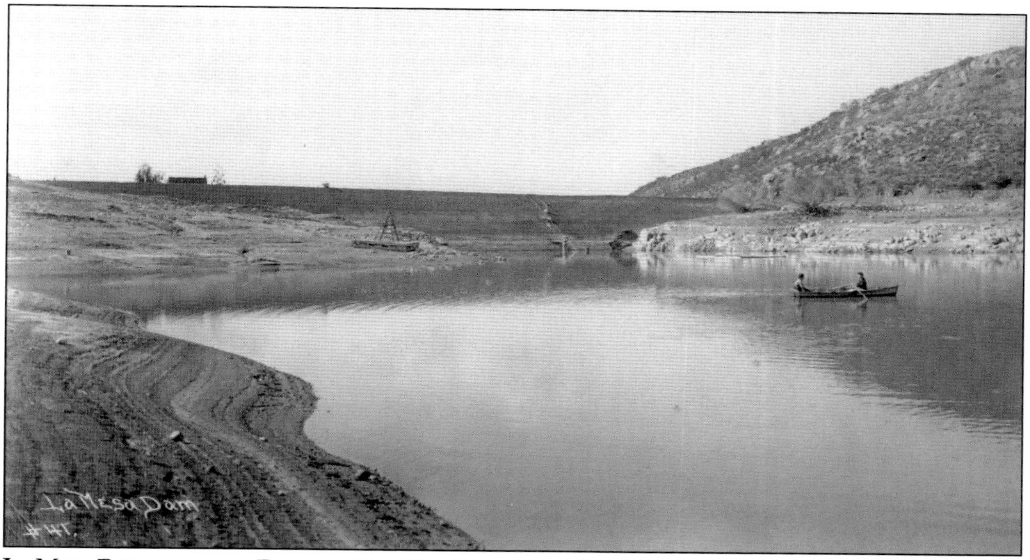

La Mesa Reservoir and Dam, c. 1915. The Cuyamaca Water Company's reservoir and earthen dam were showing signs of wear, especially after the historic January 1916 floods, during which it took the heroic efforts of the dam keeper's wife, Christina MacQuarie (in boat with daughter Annie), risking her life opening the flood gates at the dam's base to preventing its cresting and failure.

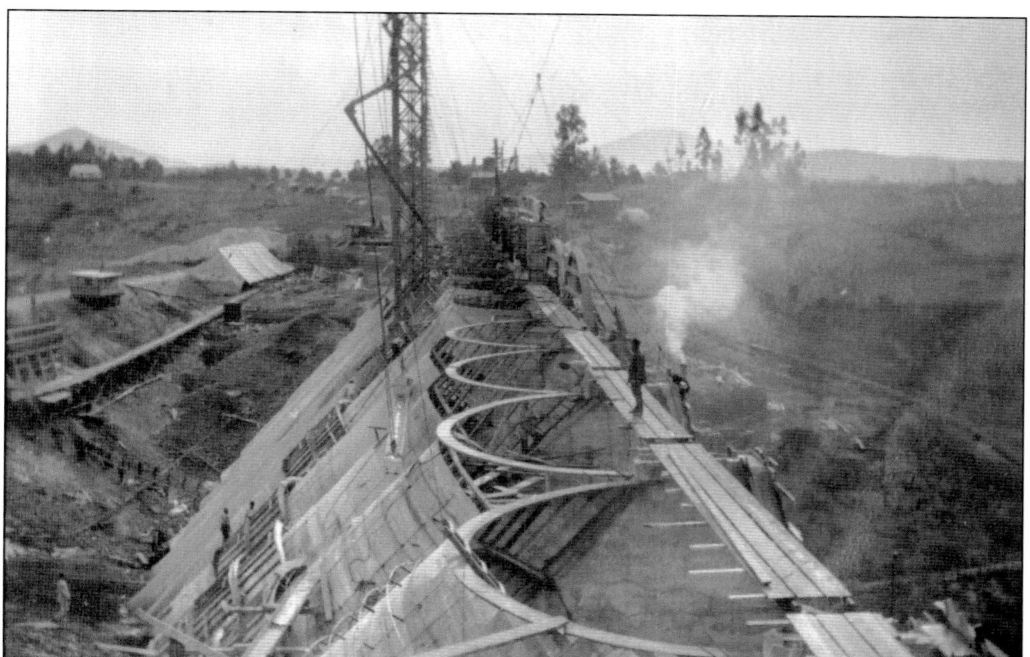

Constructing Murray Dam, 1917. The events of 1916 convinced Cuyamaca owner Ed Fletcher to replace the aging earthen dam. He hired innovative engineer John Eastwood to design and build one of his then-controversial multiple-arch concrete dams. This cutting-edge structure replaced the original dam (submerged under Lake Murray) with a safer and less costly structure, significantly increasing the reservoir's capacity.

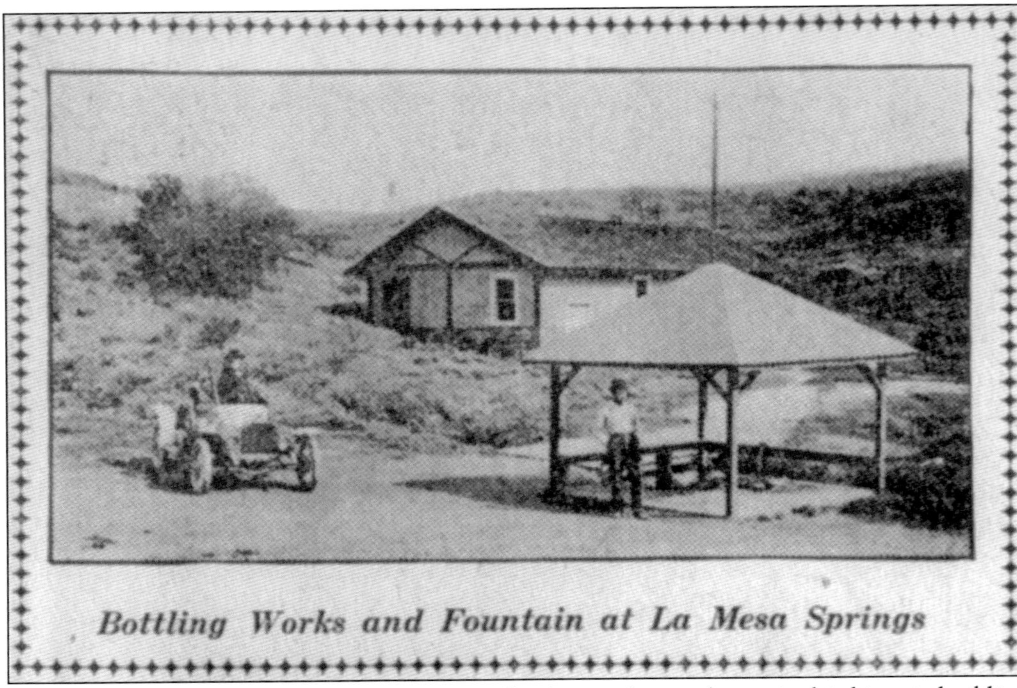

Spring House, Collier Park, 1912. D. C. Collier's most lasting legacy is this historic building and accompanying namesake park. This early image from the *La Mesa Scout* features Collier's improvements used to tap the springs, an effort started by Andrew Crowder in the 1890s. Although planned, commercial bottling never came to fruition.

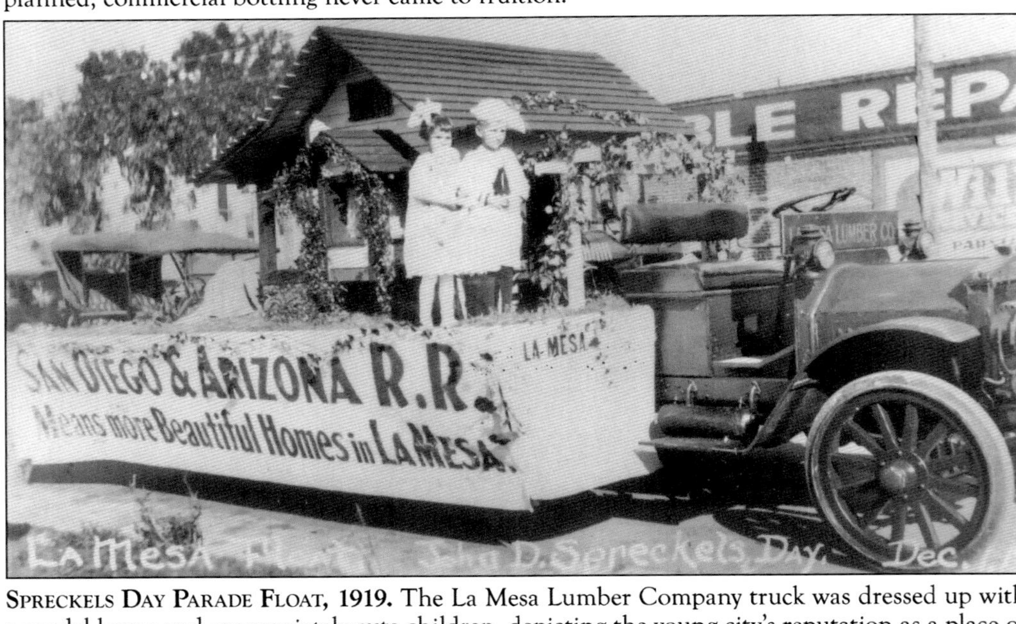

Spreckels Day Parade Float, 1919. The La Mesa Lumber Company truck was dressed up with a model home and appropriately cute children, depicting the young city's reputation as a place of domestic bliss. This float was for a parade to honor the regionally significant opening of the direct line of capitalist John Spreckels's San Diego and Arizona Railroad (SD&A) through the Carrizo Gorge east to Imperial County.

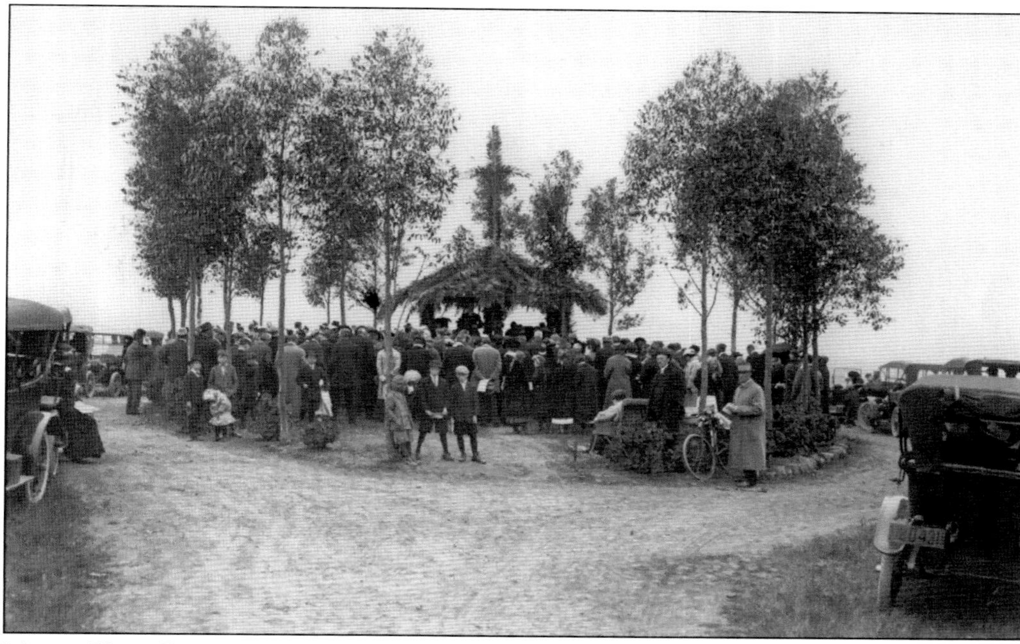

Mount Nebo Easter Celebration, 1915. The area's longstanding tradition of hilltop sunrise services began at Prospect Point Park atop Mount Nebo in the Lookout Park tract. Park and Grable had built a small pavilion there and landscaped the circular park, which they later deeded to the city, to take advantage of its 360-degree views. Services were held here again in 1916.

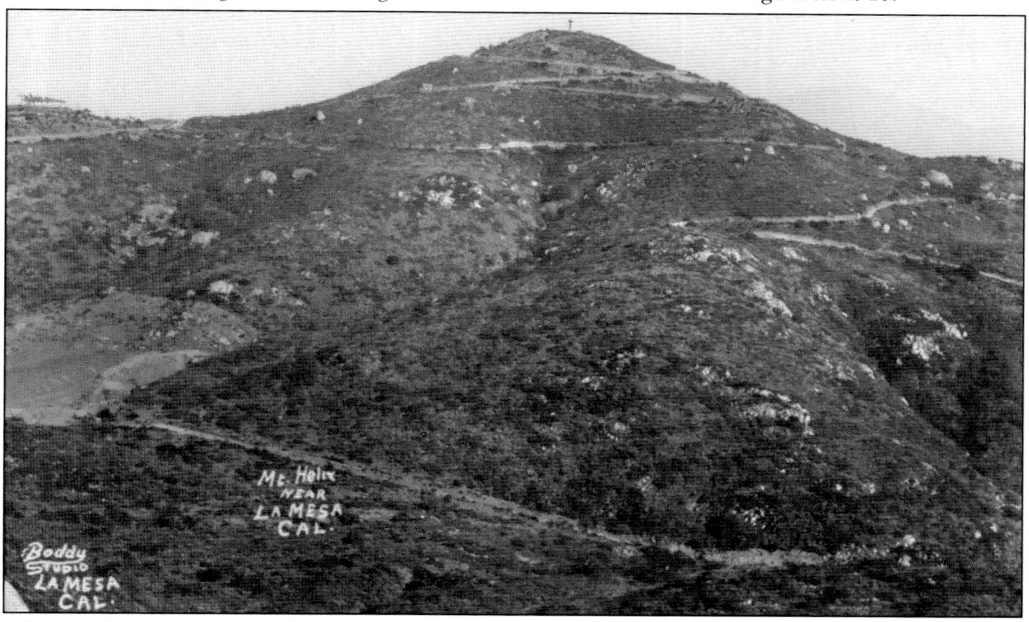

Mount Helix, c. 1917. The Easter sunrise services outgrew Prospect Park. Starting in 1917, Grossmont developer Ed Fletcher, who had acquired most of adjacent Mount Helix, allowed the San Diego Advertising Club to host the annual event. Early sojourners trekked up the steep switchback trail to the top, where attendees sat atop boulders or on crudely erected platforms near the peak's landmark wooden cross.

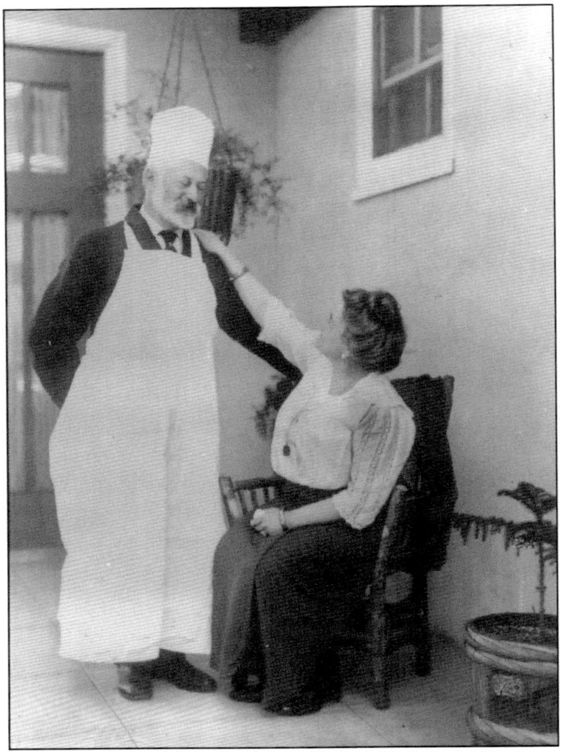

GROSSMONT'S WILLIAM GROSS AND MADAME SCHUMANN-HEINK, C. 1914. Ed Fletcher and noted actor Gross began their development partnership with purchase of the Alta Ranch in 1902. Fletcher was the development's visionary, while Gross lent his name and financing. Fletcher's vision looked to create a hilltop artist's colony featuring residents such as the world-famous operatic singer Schumann-Heink, who built a home there in 1912.

GROSSMONT INN AND RESIDENCES, 1915. Fletcher and his family lived at the Villa Caro ranch house while he planned and subdivided his Grossmont Park tracts, which opened in 1910, with a well-publicized steep and crooked peak road constructed in 1913. That year, Fletcher also opened the inn (at right) where lots could be purchased or a lovely tea or dinner obtained, served for many years by renowned Greenwich Village restaurateur Grace Godwin-Sperry.

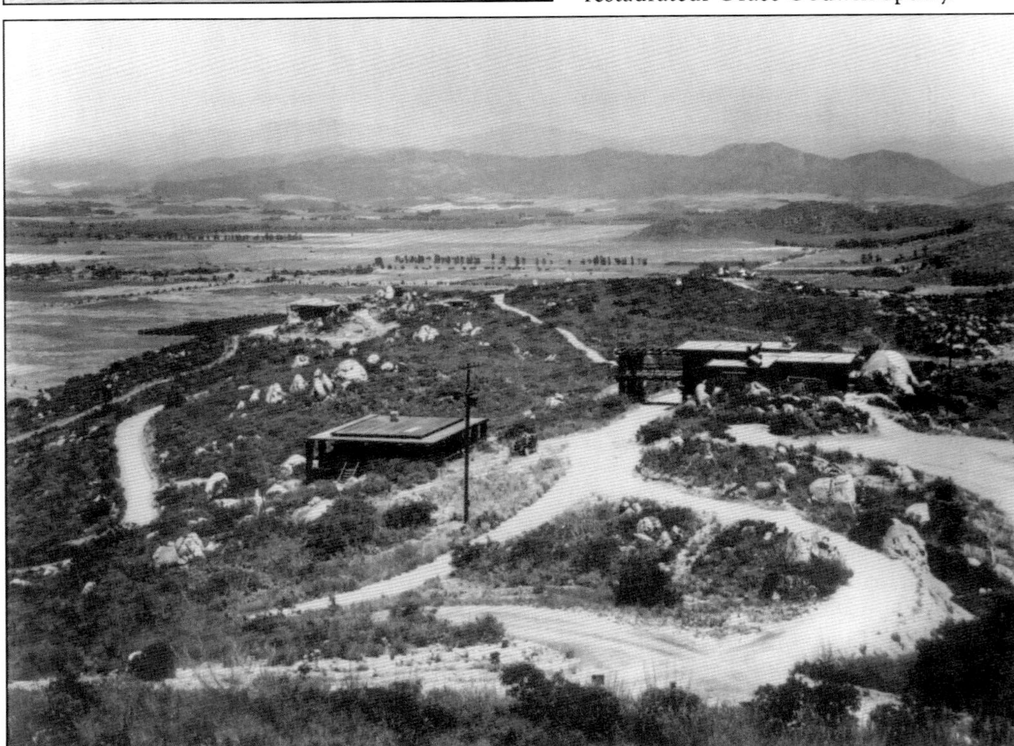

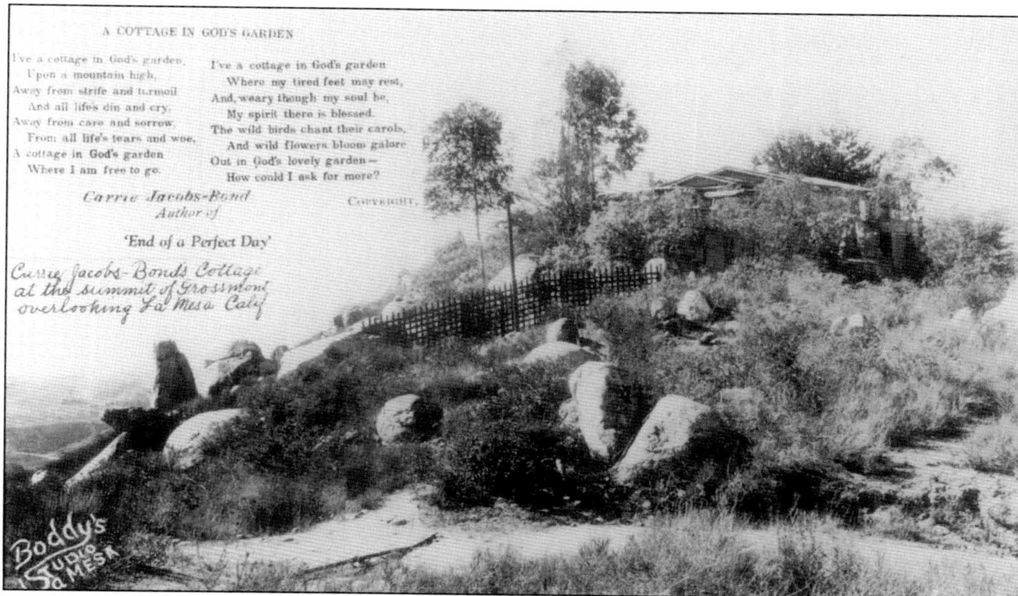

Carrie Jacobs Bond's Nest-O-Rest, c. 1918. Grossmont continued to attract artist and celebrity residents. Carrie Jacobs Bond, a noted poet and lyricist, built this inspirational home. Other noted colony residents included pianist Theresa Carreno; singer Johanna Gadske; Owen Wister, author of *The Virginian*; poet John Vance Cheney; and San Diego horticulturalist Kate Sessions.

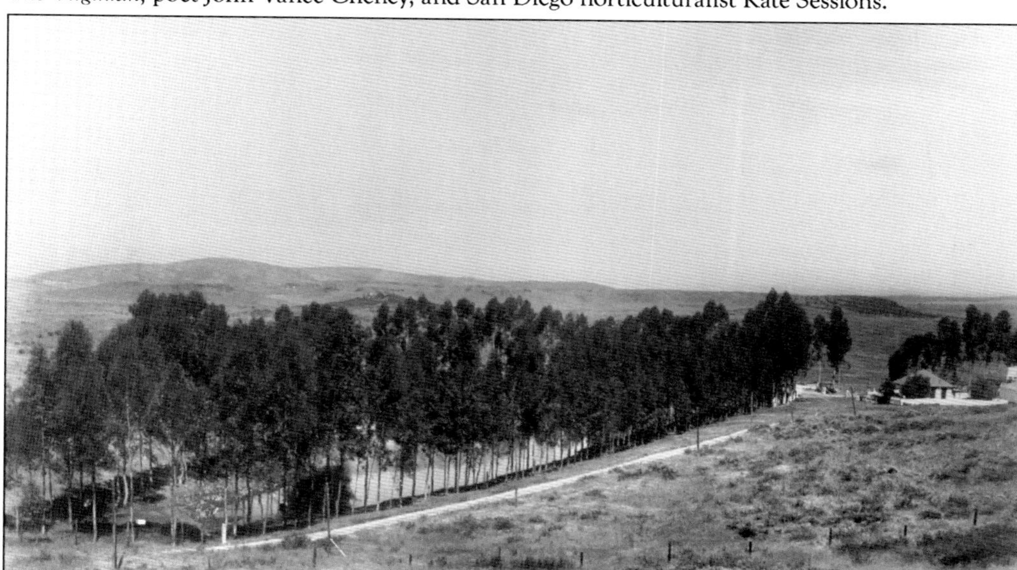

Eucalyptus Reservoir, c. 1915. Ed Fletcher recognized that roads and water were key to developing San Diego County. The importance of water to his and James Murray's La Mesa properties led to their purchase of the San Diego Flume Company, improving its infrastructure such as this holding reservoir at the site of today's Briercrest Park.

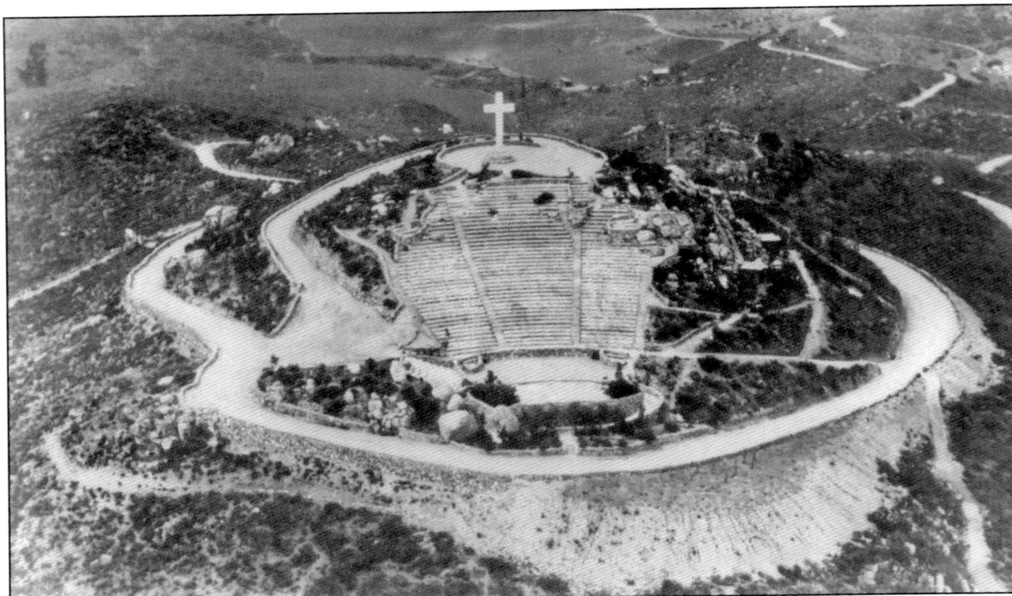

Mount Helix Nature Theatre and Easter Service, 1925. Grossmont residents and Mount Helix investors Fred and Mary White are responsible for what is arguably the region's most notable landmark. In honoring their deceased mother, Mary Carpenter Yawkey, Mary White and lumber magnate Cyrus Yawkey of Wisconsin worked with Ed Fletcher to build a permanent theater on Mount Helix. They hired architect Richard Requa to design to the contours of the rugged site. Ed Fletcher Jr. helped oversee the construction, which cost over $100,000, included a new electrically illuminated concrete cross, and was finished in time for over 7,000 to attend the 1925 services. After Mary White's passing in 1928, her husband, Fred, deeded the property to the county as a park.

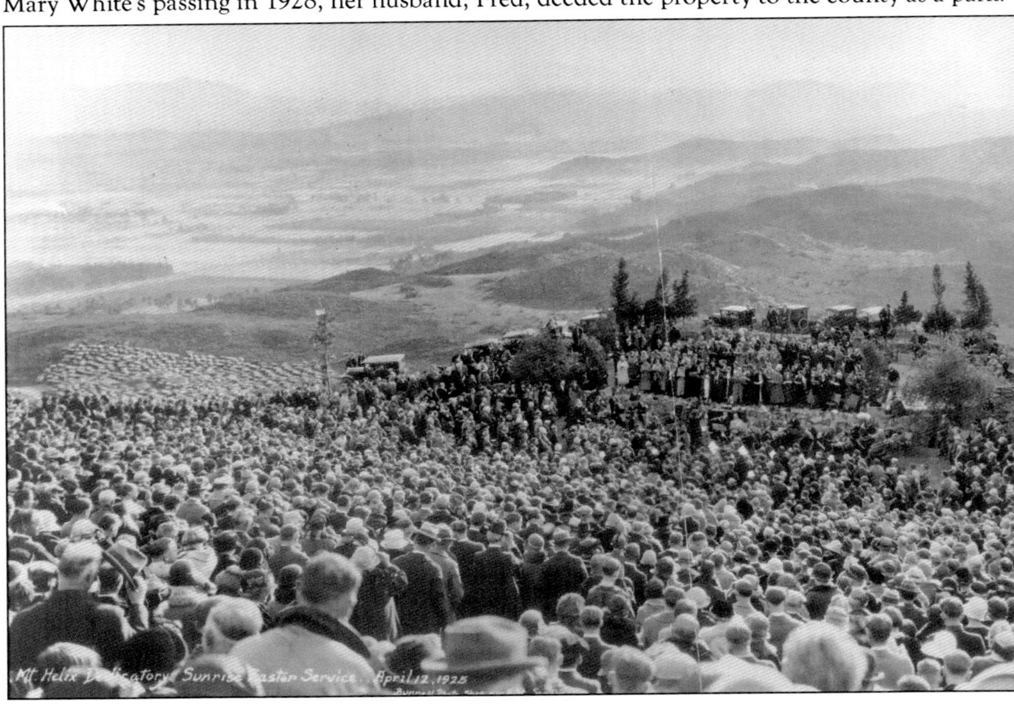

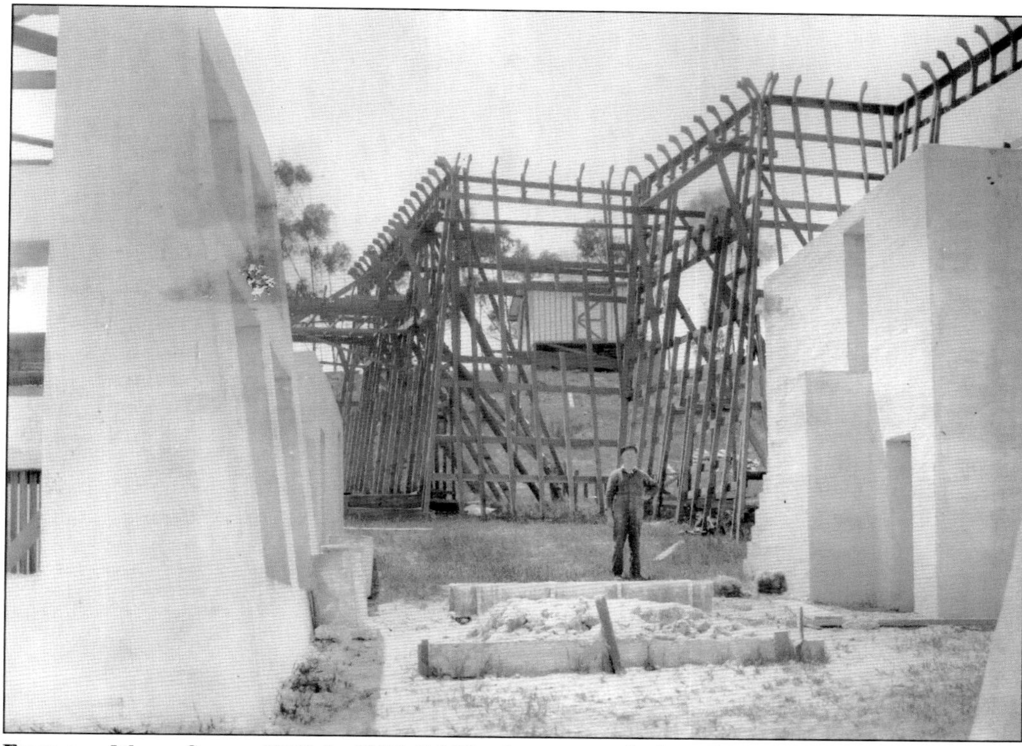

Egyptian Movie Set, c. 1925. In 1922, Ed Fletcher approached producer Arthur Sawyer, offering land for a new movie venture, the S-L Studios. Sawyer built a large studio building on Murray Drive a half mile west of Water Street. Mismanagement forced Fletcher and the shareholders to reorganize as Grossmont Studios. It too struggled. The former studio later served as a roller rink and nightclub until a destructive 1934 fire.

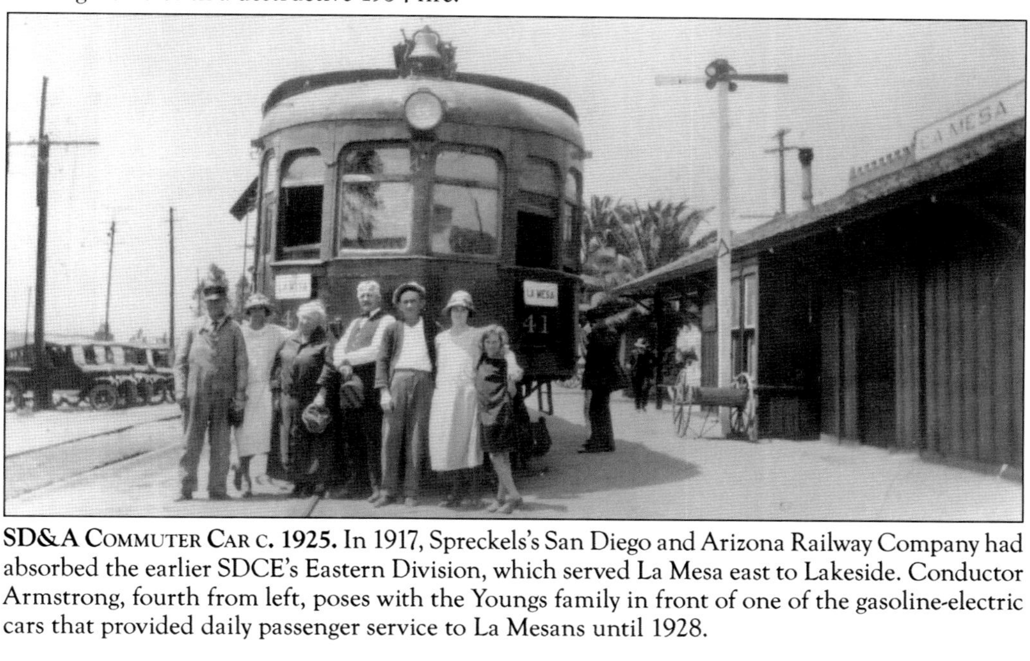

SD&A Commuter Car c. 1925. In 1917, Spreckels's San Diego and Arizona Railway Company had absorbed the earlier SDCE's Eastern Division, which served La Mesa east to Lakeside. Conductor Armstrong, fourth from left, poses with the Youngs family in front of one of the gasoline-electric cars that provided daily passenger service to La Mesans until 1928.

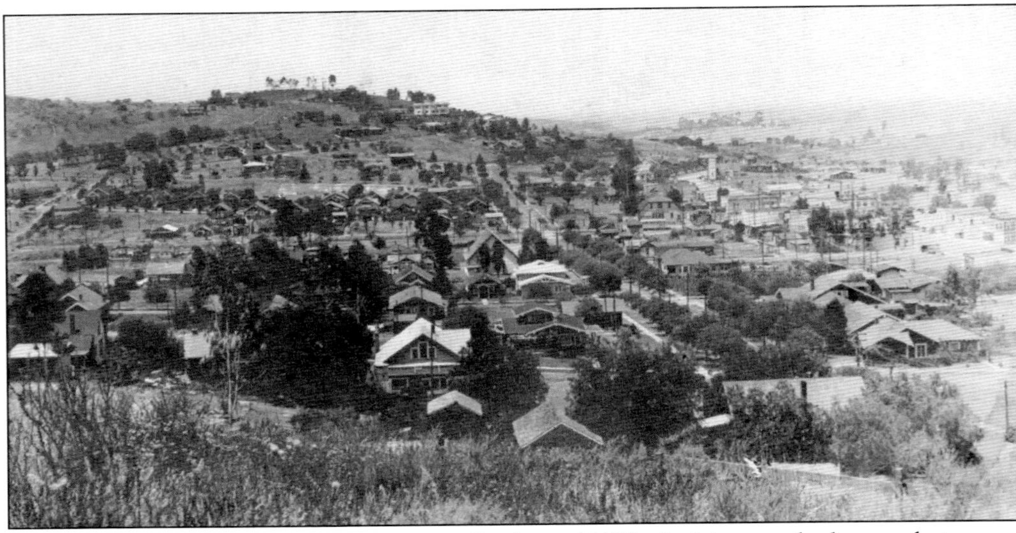

View West from Boulder Heights, 1920s. By the mid-1920s, La Mesa reached a population near 2,000. Its chamber of commerce and civic organizations crafted a reputation as a premiere homeland. With a new high school, modern electrical and telephone infrastructure, and federal funds to convert the state highway into U.S. 80, the young city was primed to fulfill its long-touted promise.

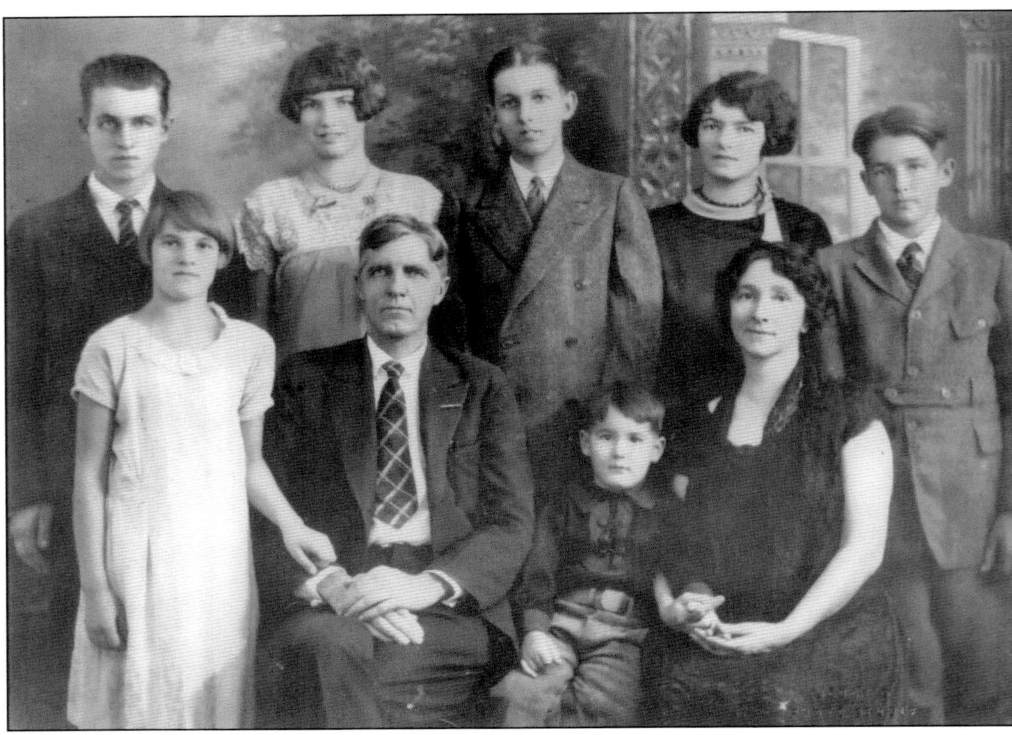

Garfield Family, c. 1925. Attorney Wade Garfield moved his wife and seven children to La Mesa in 1921, purchasing the Lyster House at Boulder Heights' crest on Sunrise Avenue. Mary, an accomplished artist of the California plein air landscape style, was inspired by the view shown above to write a poem that aptly described their new hometown titled, "La Mesa, Jewel of the Hills."

Four

Jewel of the Hills 1925–1945

As San Diego rode the 1920s Southern California real estate boom, La Mesa was positioned to fulfill its reputation as Jewel of the Hills. The La Mesa, Lemon Grove, and Spring Valley Irrigation District, formed back in 1912, was the key to securing future civic independence. In 1924, while the City of San Diego's legal challenges to the Cuyamaca Water Company's San Diego River rights continued, *La Mesa Scout* owner C. O. Smith promoted a campaign that banded together La Mesa, Lemon Grove, and Spring Valley interests to pass a $2.5-million bond to purchase the Cuyamaca system. This essential act placed the irrigation district and manager Chet Harritt in a favorable negotiating position for securing city river water in exchange for the district's Lake Murray and river dam sites, ensuring annexation independence from their western neighbor. With water secured, the suburban boom roared through La Mesa, as new banks and suburban speculators joined established developers in subdividing new high-end tracts such as Mount Nebo's Windsor Hills and Fletcher and William Thum's Fletcher Hills. Improvements to El Cajon Boulevard (now U.S. 80) and the new University Avenue extension from East San Diego prompted the creation of auto-oriented suburban developments such as the west end's Rolando, Vista La Mesa, and University Park. The city also moved east of downtown into the foothills with Boulder Heights and La Mesa Highlands. Soon Mount Helix and neighbors Casa de Oro and Calavo Gardens would open new, avocado-fueled gentleman's ranch developments. The Great Depression would temper these 1920s developments, leaving many tracts vacant until the economic recovery brought about by World War II. Still the maturing city had grown steadily through the rough times. In 1927, the trustees became the city council, adding a planning commission the next year that considered the future development leaders were sure would come. Already established community associations witnessed the addition of new service organizations and community events, while mature institutions and businesses retrenched during the lean Depression years, then rode the beginnings of exponential growth that World War II foreshadowed for their future.

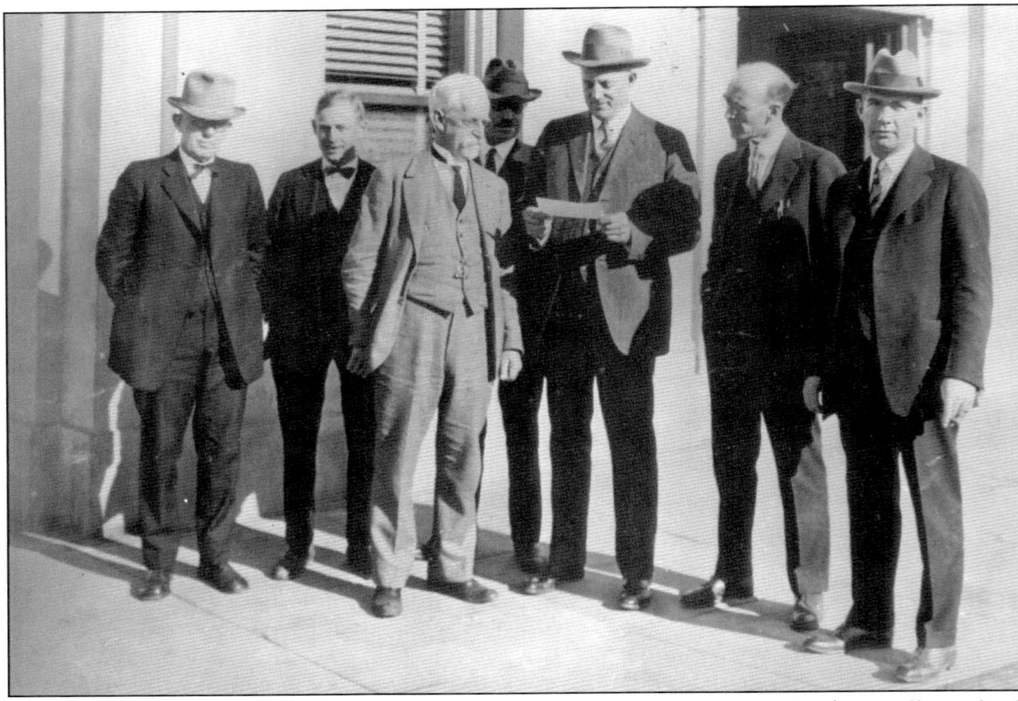

Handing over the Check, 1926. On January 4, 1926, Fletcher received a $1.2-million check finalizing the Cuyamaca water system's sale to the Irrigation District. Longtime district manager Chet Harritt, fourth from left behind Fletcher, negotiated the final sale of Lake Murray and the district's river dam sites to San Diego in 1932, guaranteeing the district's customers water.

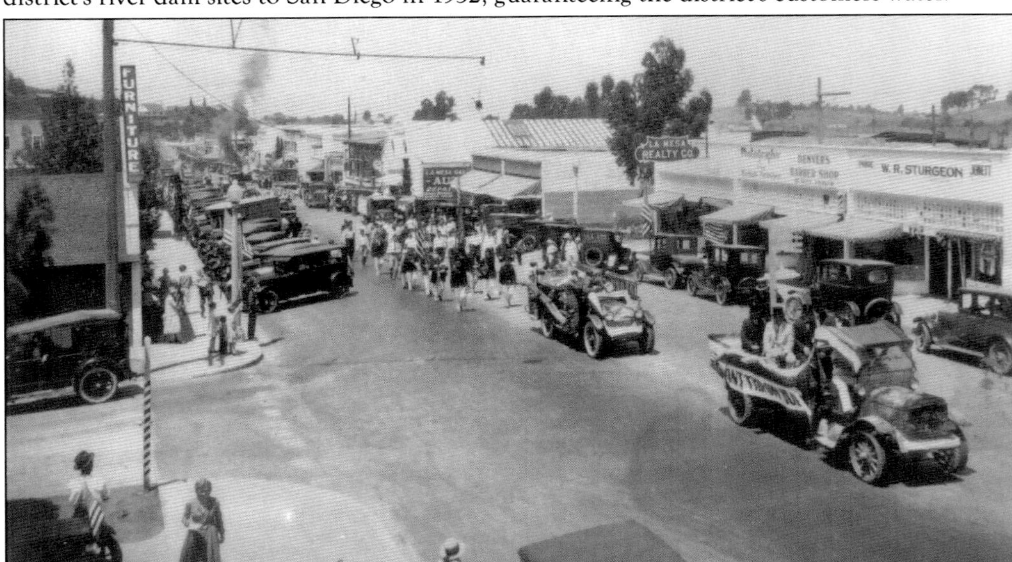

Fourth of July Parade from Third Street, 1927. Lookout Avenue continued to be a center of regional commerce and social activity. Changes can be seen, with scaffolding still on the new bank building that replaced the old opera house. The few empty lots still seen would soon be filled as new businesses and residents came to join the boom of the 1920s.

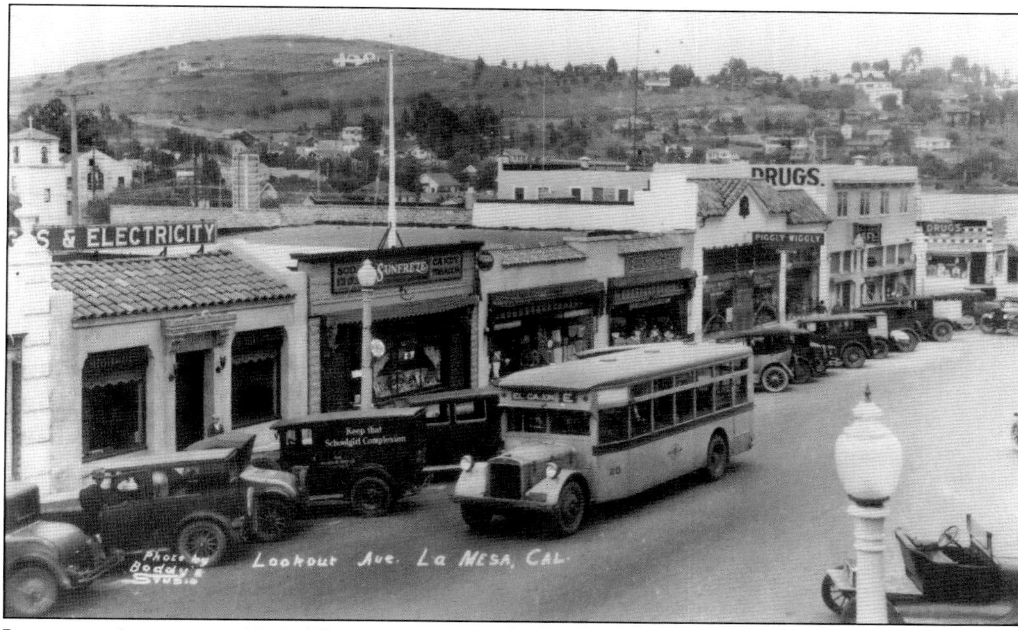

Lookout Avenue, c. 1929. The growing population reached 2,500 by 1930, and it demanded the latest in services, necessities, and conveniences, including utility offices, restaurants, domestic stores, and a Piggly Wiggly supermarket. This image shows the newly platted Windsor Hills on the top of Mount Nebo and the local transit buses that helped end passenger train service in 1928.

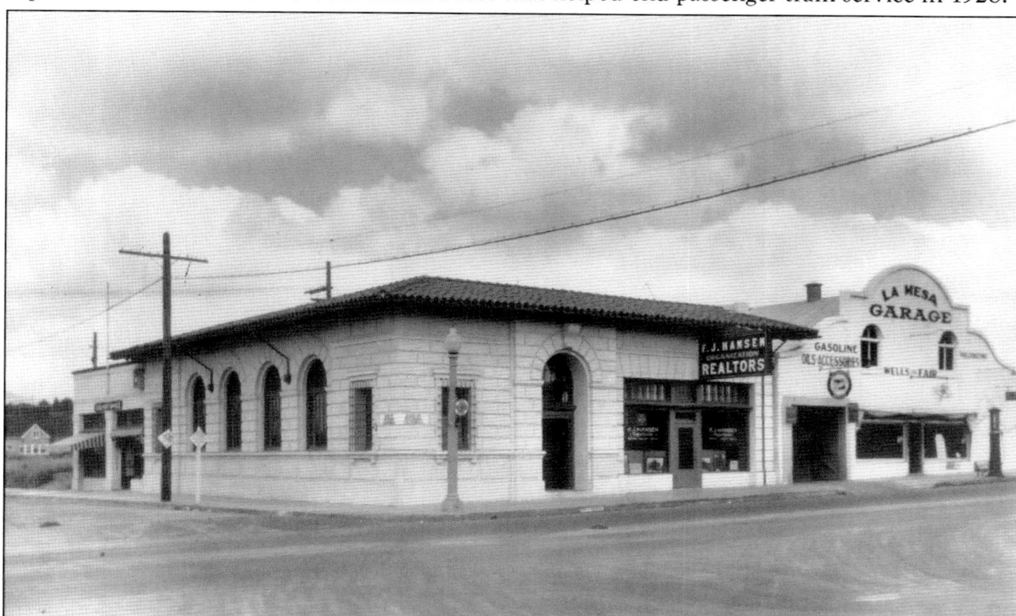

Bank of Southern California, 1927. This distinctive new commercial building is located at Palm and Lookout Avenues and also housed Helix developer Fred Hansen's office. The new Mediterranean Revival–style bank reflected the classical strength of traditional bank architecture with popular regional influences. The La Mesa Garage (right) catered to travelers, providing gas, repairs, and a wall-mural county highway map.

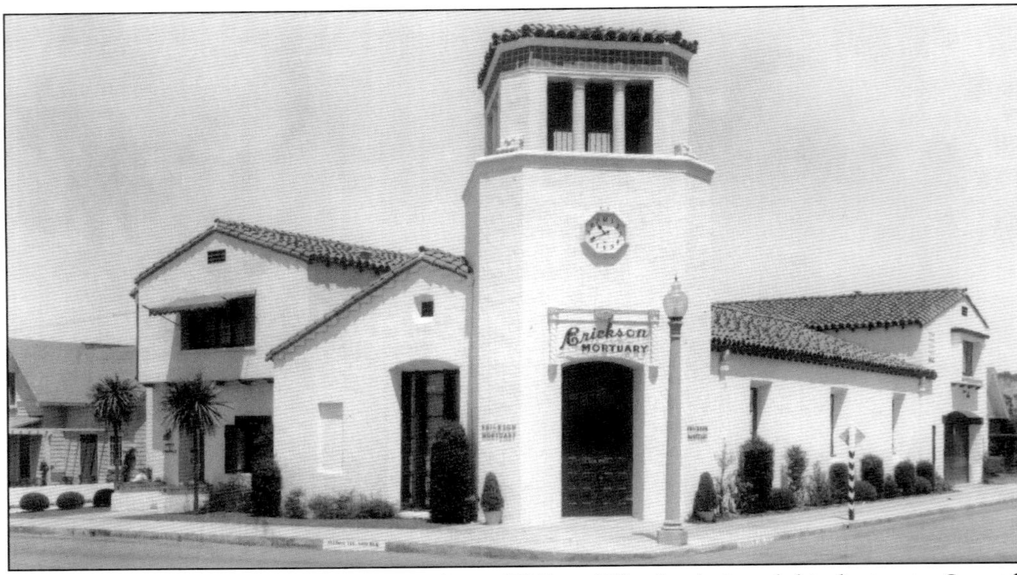

ERICKSON MORTUARY, 1930. San Diego architect William Wheeler designed this distinctive Spanish Colonial Revival building for Fred Erickson at Allison Avenue and Cypress Street. Erickson had purchased the local mortuary business in 1921. He later partnered with Enoch Anderson as manager and part owner. Anderson served two terms on the city council and was mayor from 1948 to 1950.

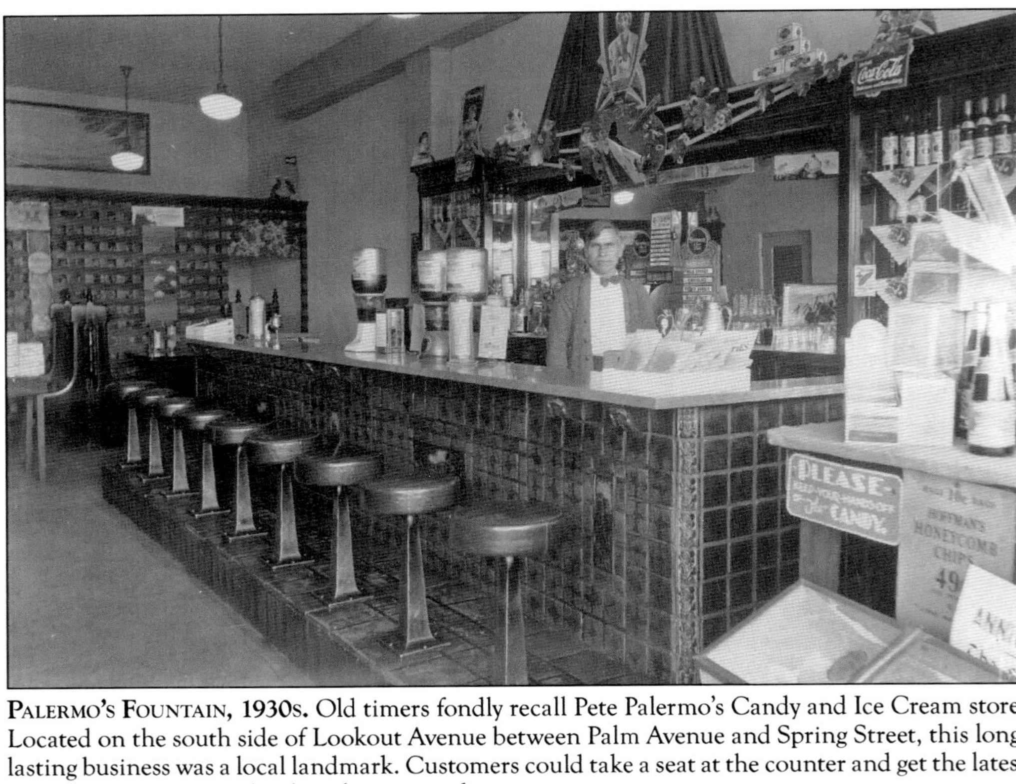

PALERMO'S FOUNTAIN, 1930s. Old timers fondly recall Pete Palermo's Candy and Ice Cream store. Located on the south side of Lookout Avenue between Palm Avenue and Spring Street, this long-lasting business was a local landmark. Customers could take a seat at the counter and get the latest in fountain treats, candy, chocolates, or sodas.

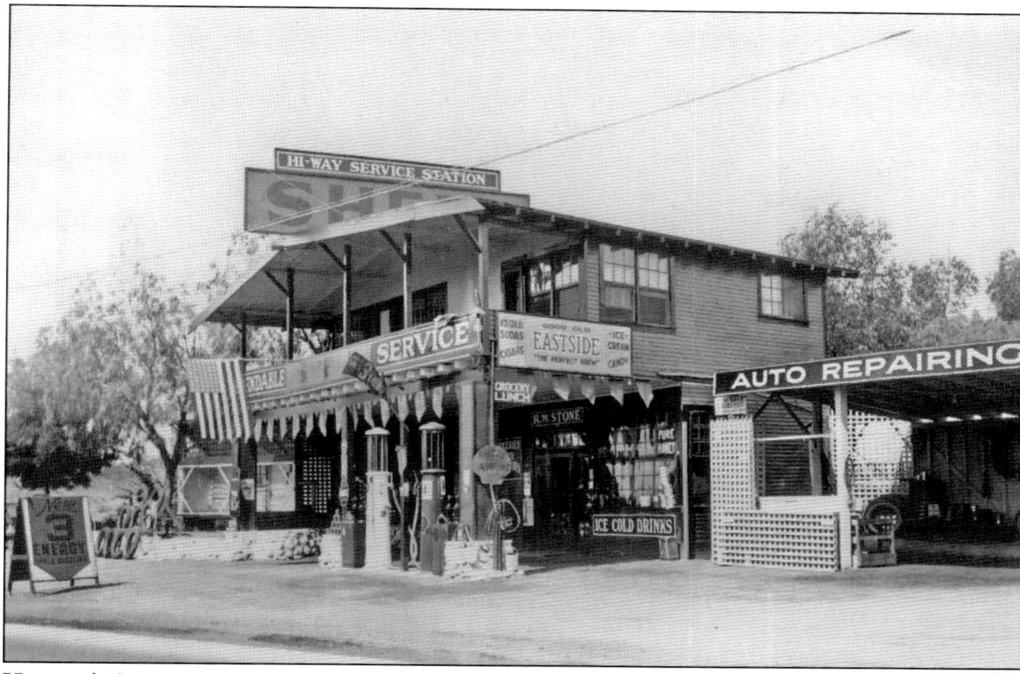

Hawley's Station, 1930s. Auto travelers on U.S. 80 east of La Mesa often stopped at Hi-Way Service. Arriving shortly after the beginning of the 20th century, the Hawleys purchased the land around Dan Manning's former road station. They farmed the area, currently near the Interstate 8 and State 125 intersection, and developed a fruit stand before opening this roadside stop within their Hawley Heights subdivision.

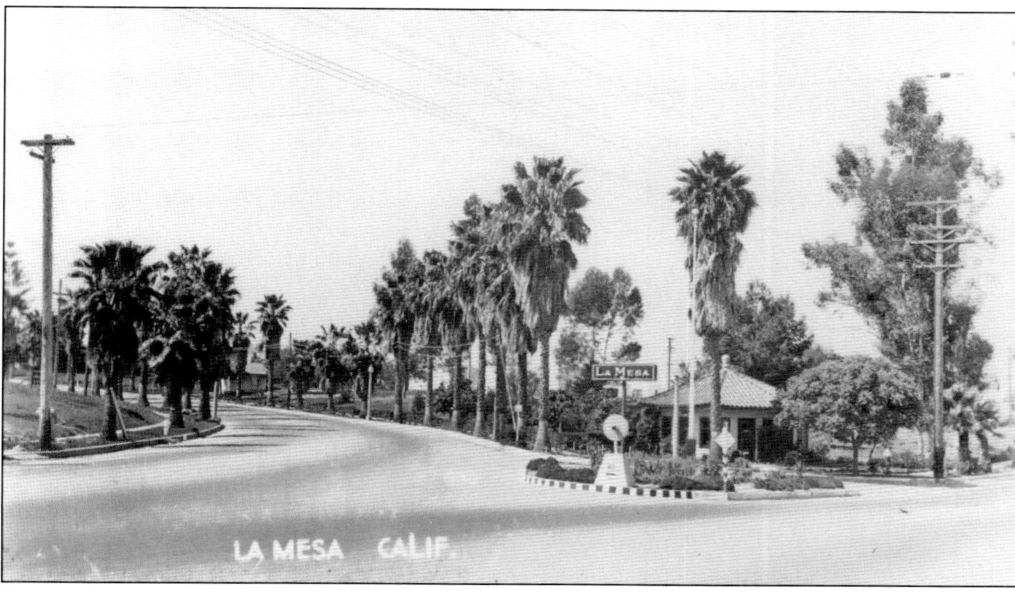

Porter Hall and Park, 1930s. James Porter donated the small Chinese-style building and property at the corner of Lookout Avenue and today's University Avenue to the city to honor his family. It served as the city library for many years before the 1957 library was built. Porter Hall was later moved across the street to make room for the city's senior center.

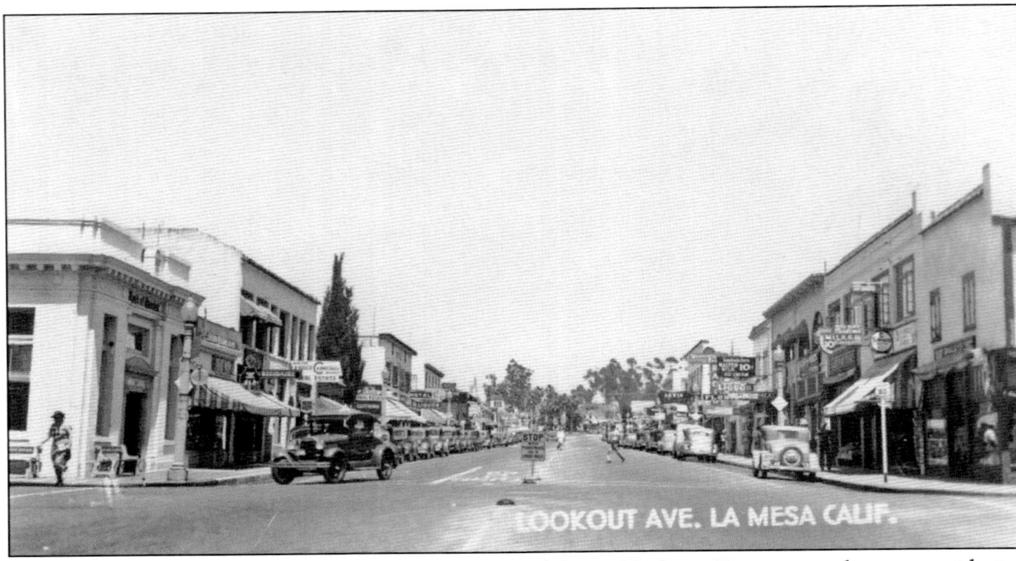

LOOKOUT AVENUE AND SPRING STREET, 1930s. The California Highway Department began considering bypassing downtown and adjacent El Cajon Boulevard's frequent stops with a high-speed highway down Alvarado Canyon as early as 1931, and the city and chamber moved to protect and promote local business presence by renaming Lookout Avenue "La Mesa Boulevard" in 1940.

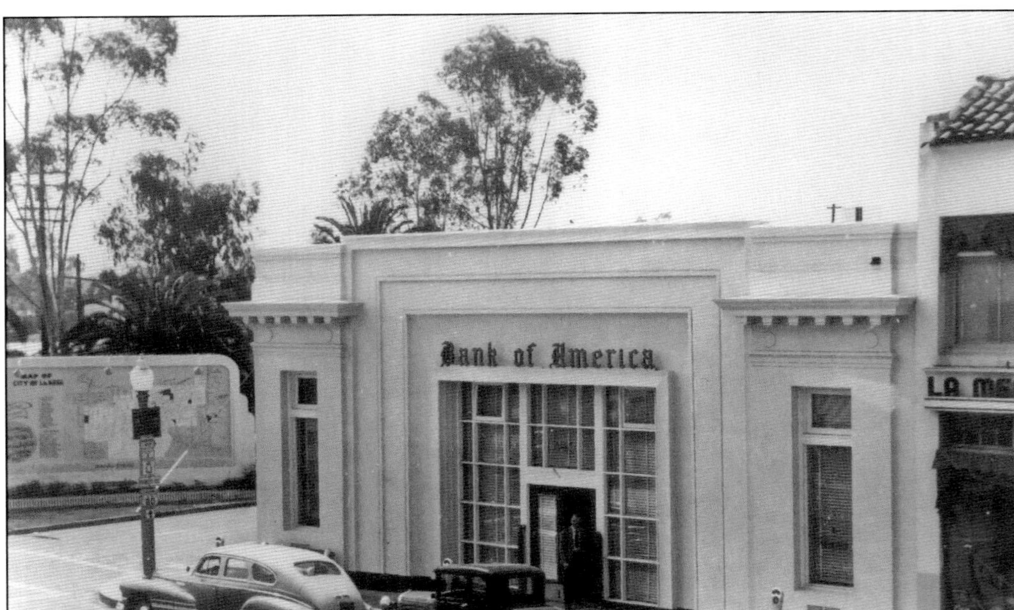

BANK OF AMERICA, 1940s. Shortly after the Bank of La Mesa constructed its new building at the corner of Spring Street and Lookout Avenue, it was purchased by the Bank of Italy, later Bank of America. The stately building held this corner for many decades before being replaced. The informative city map billboard lasted into the 1950s.

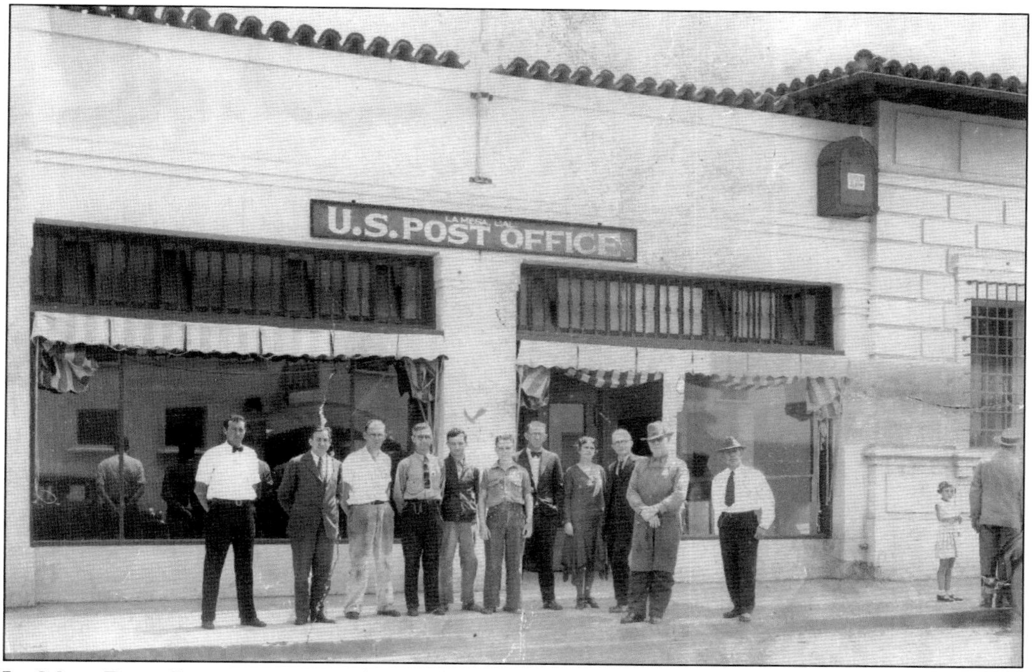

La Mesa Post Office, c. 1930. This building was attached to the rear of the Bank of Southern California building on Palm Avenue north of Lookout. It was the first built solely as a post office. In 1940, a new post office, funded by President Roosevelt's Public Works Administration, was built at Fourth Street and La Mesa Boulevard, replacing this Spanish Colonial–style building.

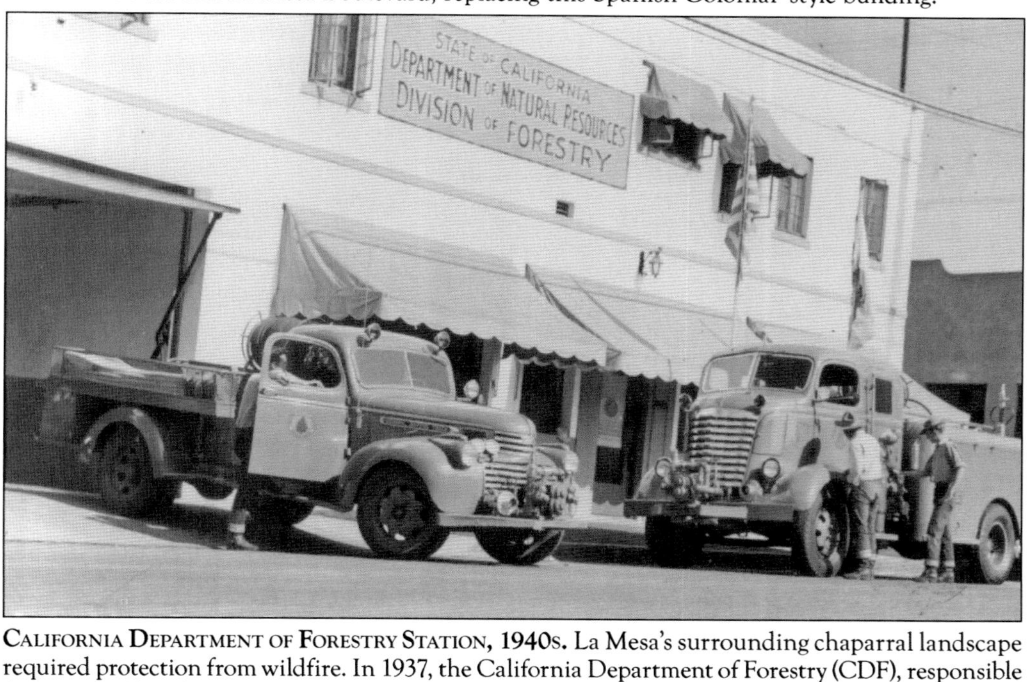

California Department of Forestry Station, 1940s. La Mesa's surrounding chaparral landscape required protection from wildfire. In 1937, the California Department of Forestry (CDF), responsible for state and local wildland fire protection, opened a new station and office on north Date Avenue. CDF was a constant presence in La Mesa until its 1980s move east to the more rural Jamacha area.

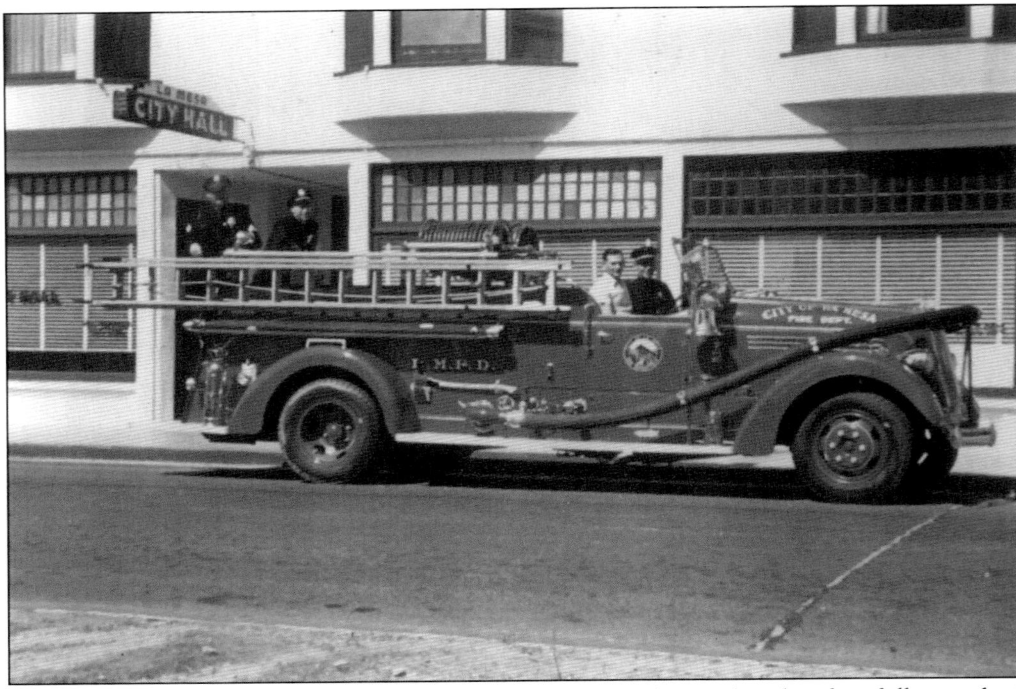

New Fire Truck, 1941. A year after this photograph, Ray Lyles was hired as first full-time chief. Lyles oversaw a staff of one paid and four volunteer firefighters, one of who was on duty at all times. The first permanent fire station was on Nebo Drive directly across the railroad tracks from the Spring Street city hall shown here, just north of Lookout Avenue.

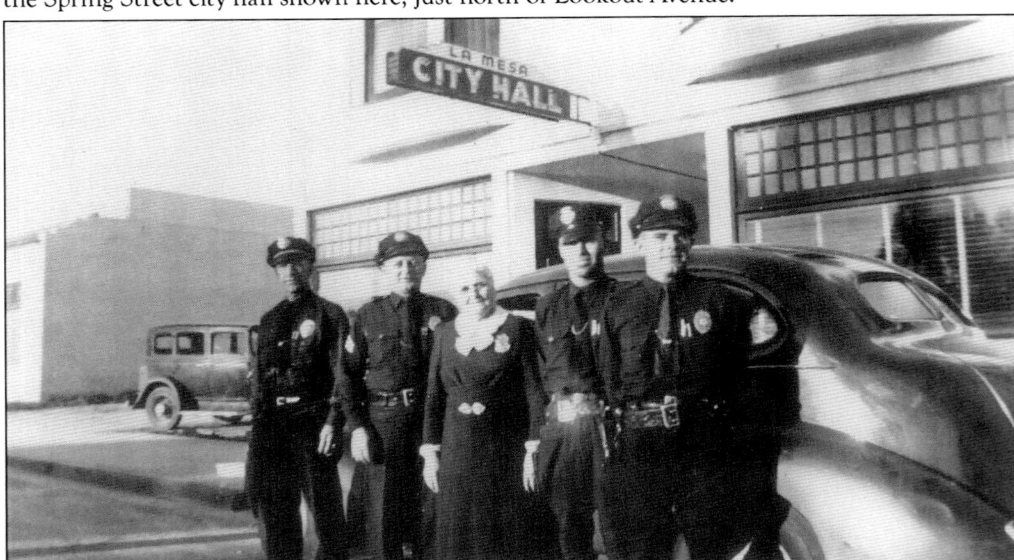

Police Department Officers, 1940s. Longtime marshal and police chief Jack Mercer retired in 1940. Amos Stuckey (second from left) served as chief during the war, giving way to the next chief, Glenn Adams (far right). Arvilla Beckman, the police matron, was a recognized community asset, watching out for the community's young ladies, especially when the town filled with servicemen during World War II.

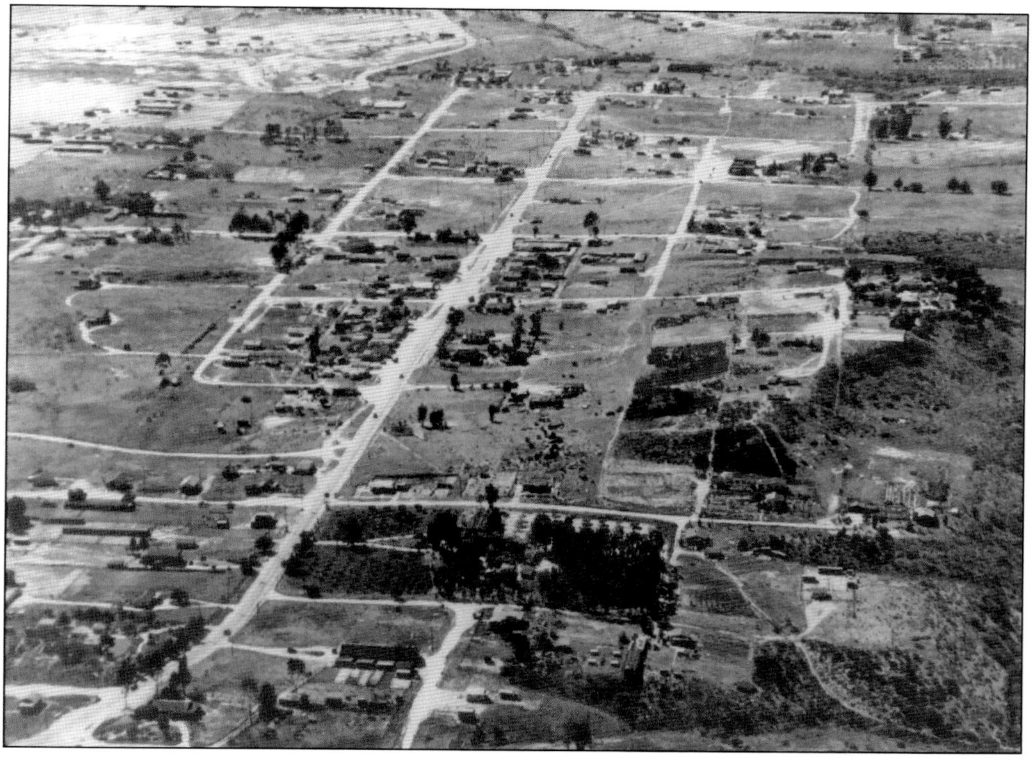

La Mesa Heights, c. 1929. The original town site street grid (Sixty-seventh to Seventy-third Streets) is centered on U.S. 80, with Rolando to the upper left. After San Diego State chose Montezuma Mesa for its new campus in 1928, the town site and lands north and west of Rolando were annexed to San Diego, with the school district annexed in 1932, giving rise to San Diego's College Neighborhoods.

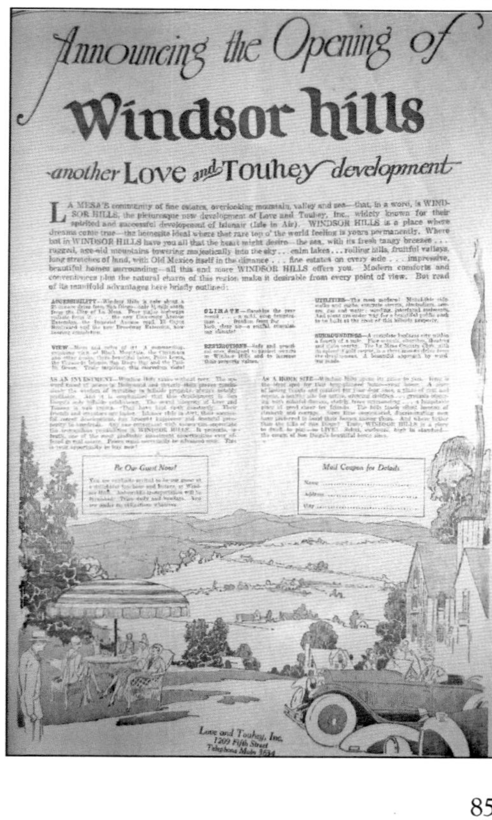

Windsor Hills Advertisement, 1927. La Mesa's new 1920s developments included several high-end suburban subdivisions, such as this Mount Nebo tract's legendary public pedestrian walkways between streets. Promotions featuring scenes of domestic bliss were joined with creative marketing programs including, in this case, the hiring of baseball great Babe Ruth for publicity photographs, creating unfounded rumors of Ruth's Windsor Hills home building.

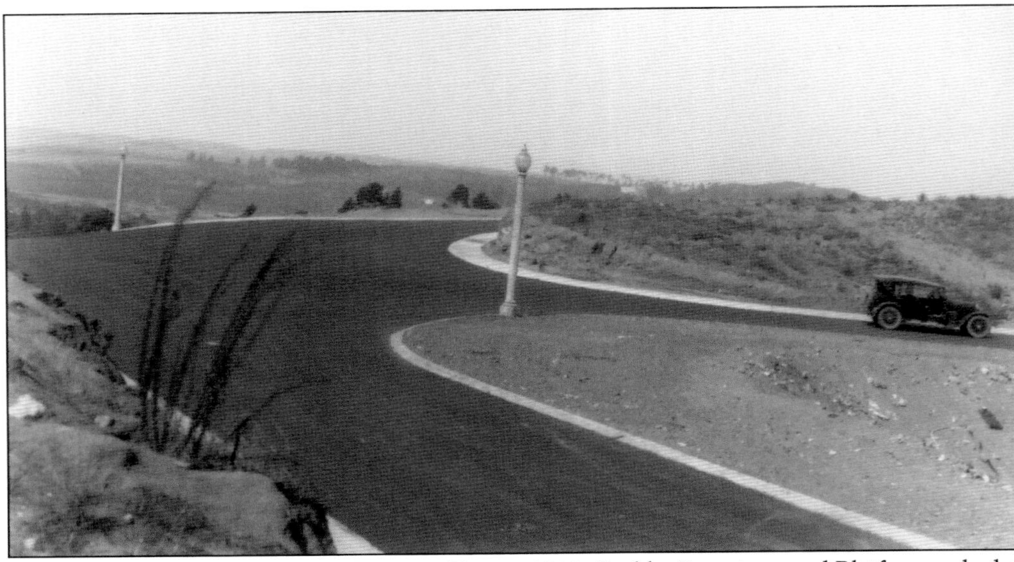

CORNER OF BOULDER PLACE AND BOULDER DRIVE, 1927. Grable, Francisco, and Bleifuss worked to add their own high-end tracts to the hills east of downtown. Boulder Heights, encompassing the old Lookout Ranch and Upland Tracts, provided another suburban development featuring sidewalks, in-place utilities, decorative streetlights, and wonderful views for prospective homebuilders.

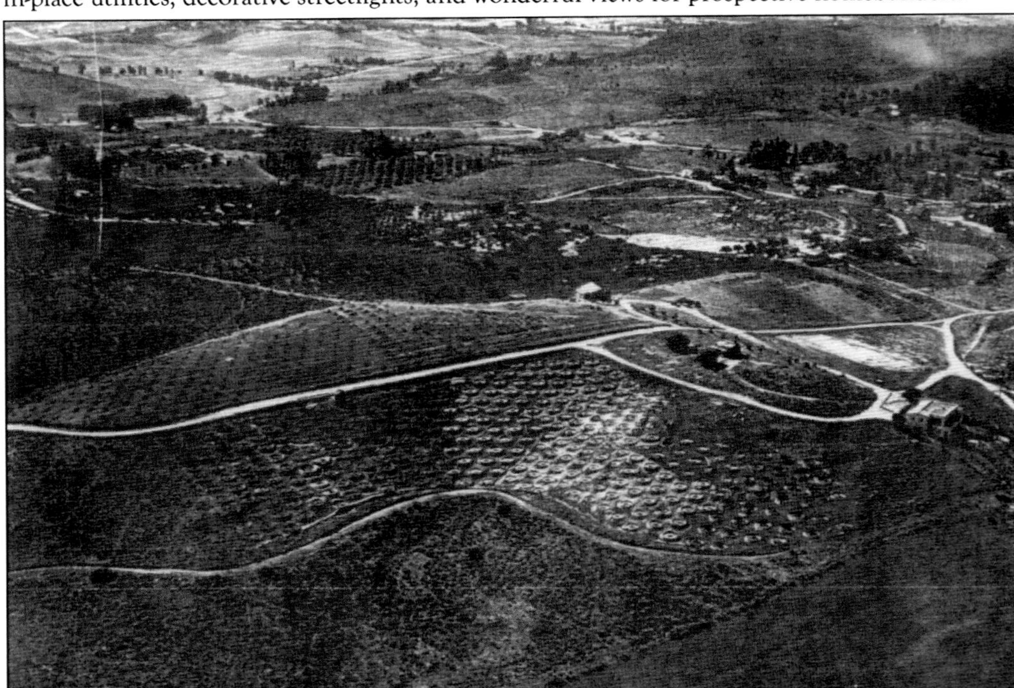

LA MESA HIGHLANDS, VIEW SOUTHWEST, C. 1935. East of Boulder Heights, this rural development stretched into the orchards and foothills east of Garfield and north and south toward Bancroft Drive. As with all of these pre–World War II tracts, homeowners bought lots from the developers and then chose a contractor to build in a style of their liking, creating eclectic neighborhoods of popular Revival-style homes.

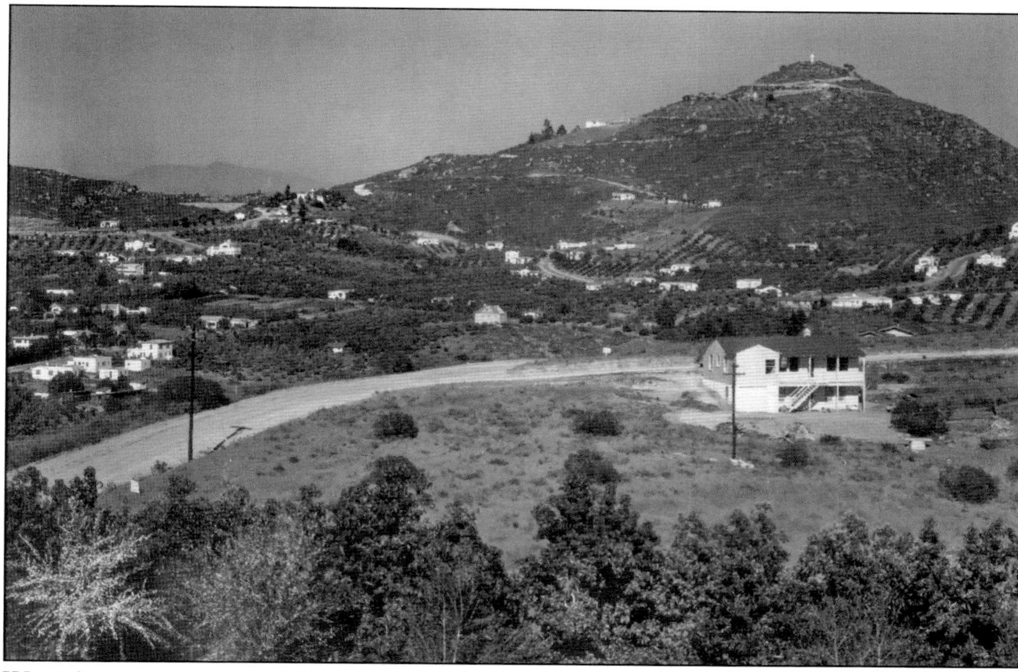

West Slope of Mount Helix, 1939. In the 1920s, Mount Helix began to see development. Newcomer Fred J. Hansen became a key promoter for the area. Hansen built his own elaborate Brittany-Spanish-style home there in 1925. Mount Helix would become popular for homebuilders working with innovative local architects in the following decades, with Hansen's Avocado Villas tract on a relocated Lemon Avenue cemetery later being annexed into La Mesa.

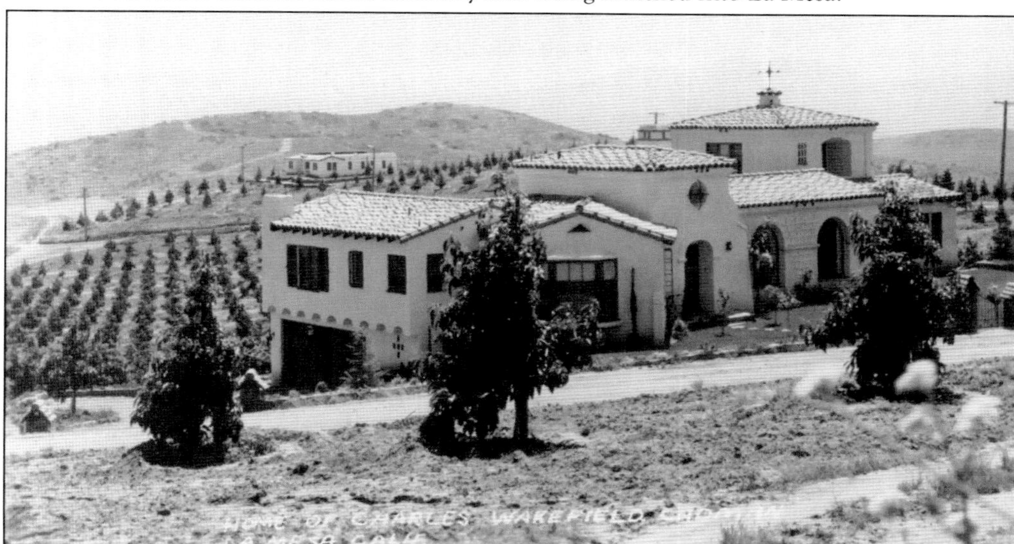

Cadman House, Mount Helix, c. 1930. Hansen's interest in avocados as an income crop for tract homeowners helped him promote his east slope Calavo Gardens and his Avocado Villas tracts and also inspired others, such as John Cornelius' Casa de Oro Avocado Estates. These gentleman's ranch developments attracted prominent residents like noted American composer Charles Wakefield Cadman to build in Calavo Gardens.

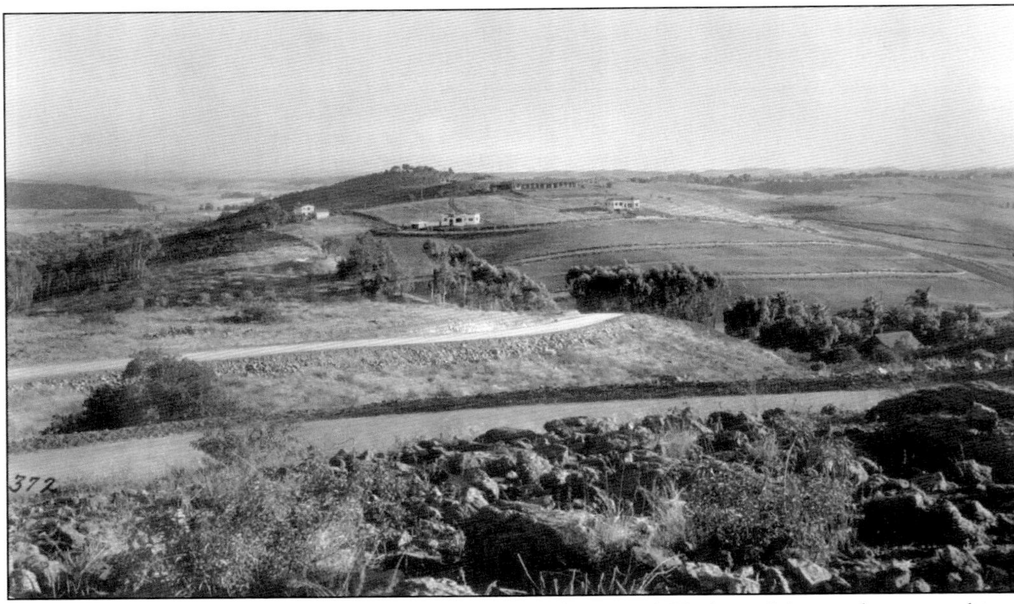

LA MESA COUNTRY CLUB, 1930s. South of today's Highway 125–Highway 94 interchange, architect Richard Requa adapted a former Bancroft residence with a large dining hall and ballroom to create a popular site for local social events. In 1928, the course was expanded to 18 holes, and in 1929, it was adapted from dirt to grass fairways. The club was sold to developers in 1950.

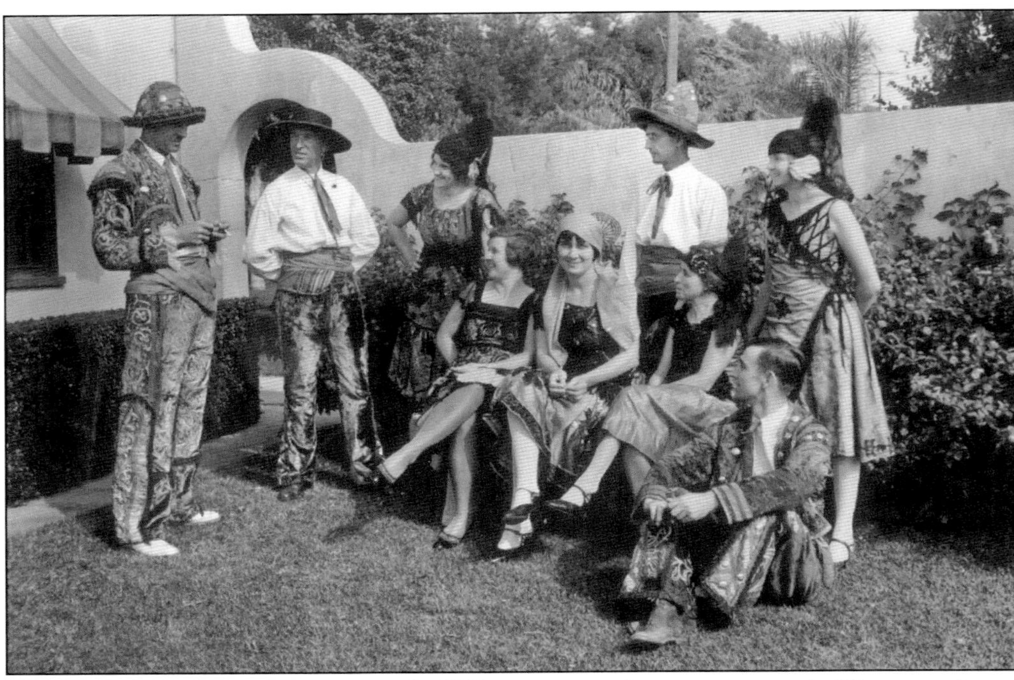

FIESTA DE LOS FLORES COMMITTEE, 1929. In 1928, a new annual civic event started a 29-year run (except during World War II). The La Mesa Chamber of Commerce sponsored the long-running fiesta, which took San Diego's love affair with its romantic interpretation of the region's Spanish heritage to heart. The event featured a flower show and concerts held in the grammar school auditorium.

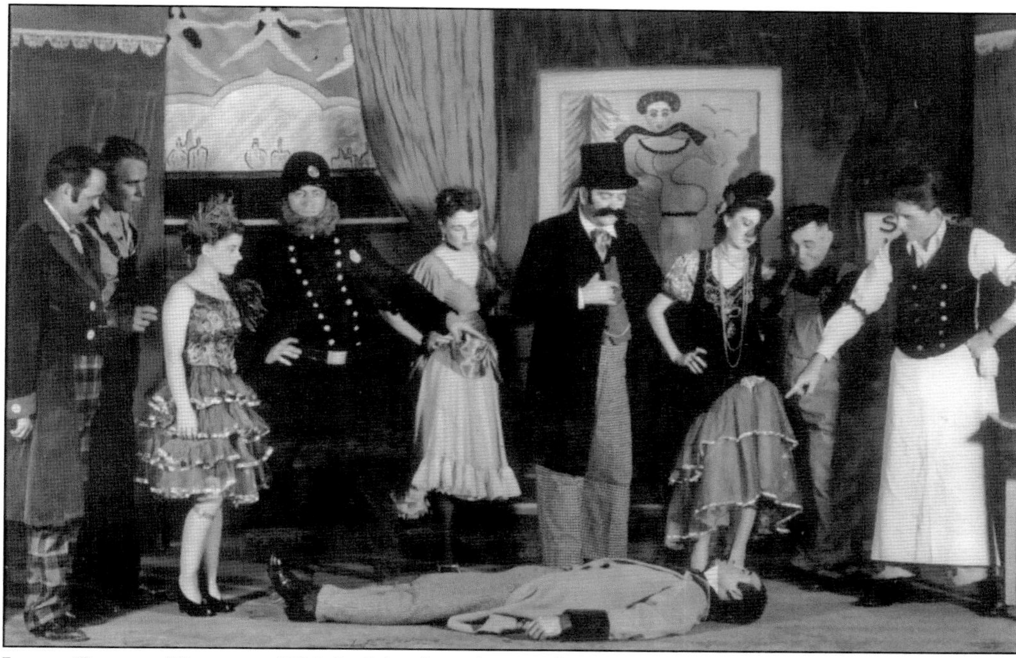

LITTLE PLAYERS THEATER, 1938. La Mesa's tradition of community theater formally began with this group of local thespians started by Olive Walker and Austin Cordtz. The Little Players continued on, eventually renamed the Lamplighters Community Theatre, and were housed in the city's Ben Polak Arts Center (1957–2006). This tradition has also inspired youth theater such as the Peter Pan Junior Theatre and CYT La Mesa.

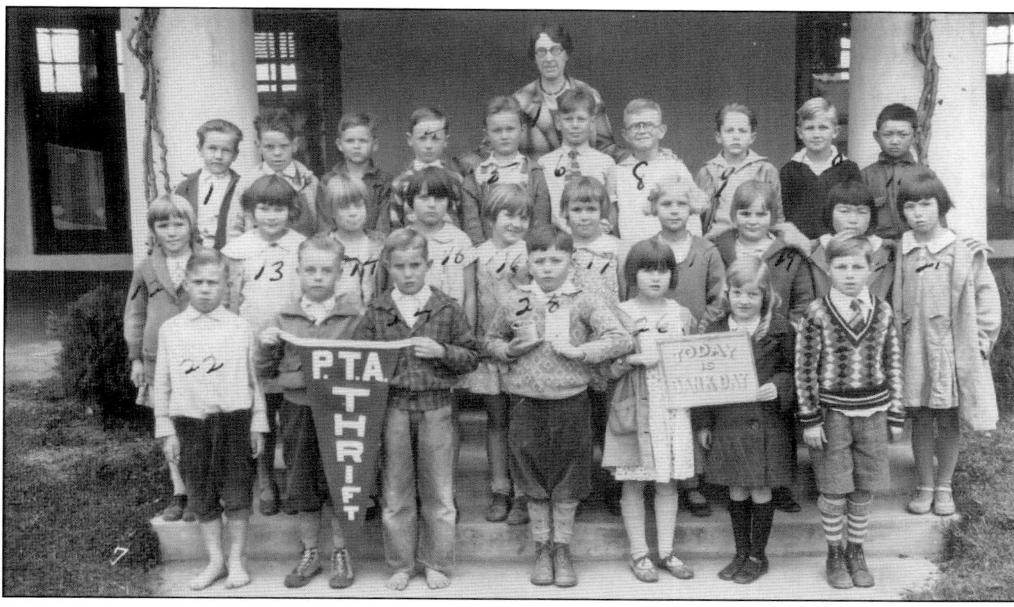

PTA BANK DAY, c. 1930. The Great Depression slowed growth. Newer tracts like Windsor Hills, Rolando, and Fletcher Hills were caught in pyramiding assessment districts that put them in foreclosure by 1930, with many other 1920s developments barely filled. The community still banded together, teaching frugality and thrift as well as providing support for struggling families.

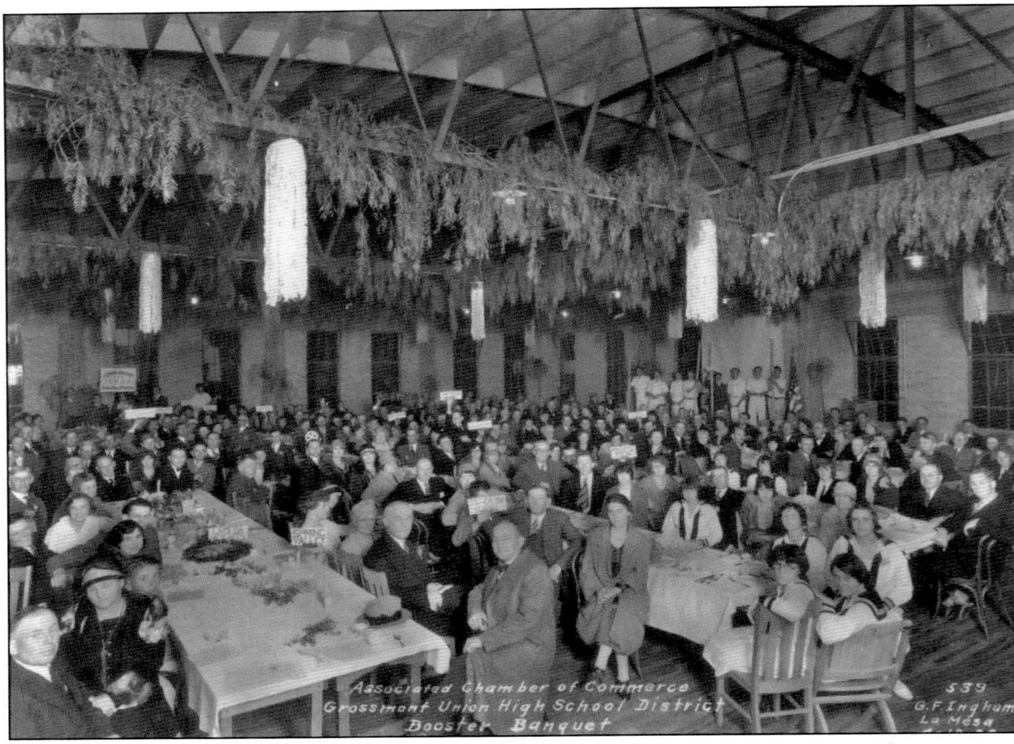

Grossmont High School Chamber Banquet, 1929. Grossmont High School served as a regional community institution for La Mesa and its neighbors. Here elementary school district representatives meet at the old auditorium. During the Depression, the school received WPA funding to expand its campus facilities, including a new gymnasium/auditorium in support of athletics and performing arts programs.

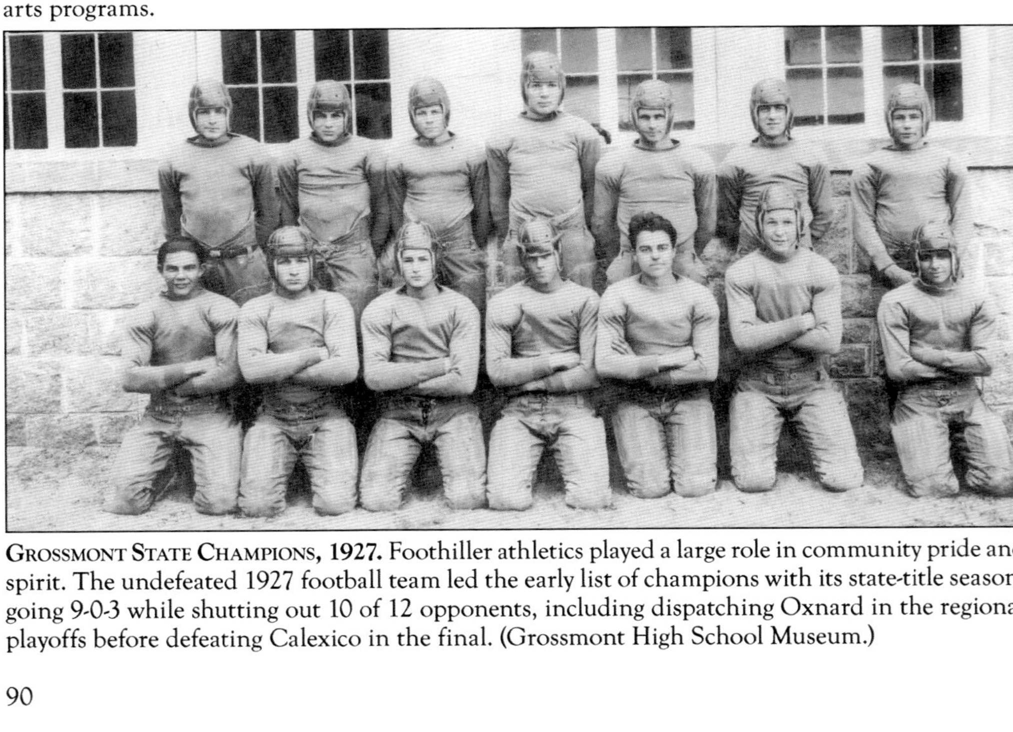

Grossmont State Champions, 1927. Foothiller athletics played a large role in community pride and spirit. The undefeated 1927 football team led the early list of champions with its state-title season, going 9-0-3 while shutting out 10 of 12 opponents, including dispatching Oxnard in the regional playoffs before defeating Calexico in the final. (Grossmont High School Museum.)

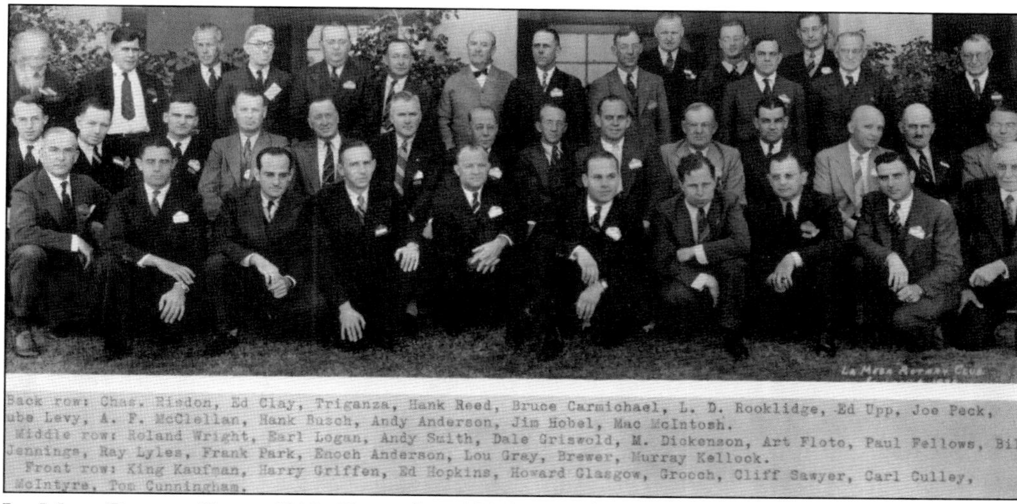

La Mesa Rotary Club, 1939. Formed in 1925, one of La Mesa's oldest service clubs annually raises funds for community events and programs. This photograph features many of the interwar community leaders, including mayors Frank Park (1932–1934), Enoch Anderson (1948–1950), water district board president Harry Griffin, and numerous businessmen, all of whom supported Mayor Ben Polak's (1936–1948) leadership during the Depression and World War II years.

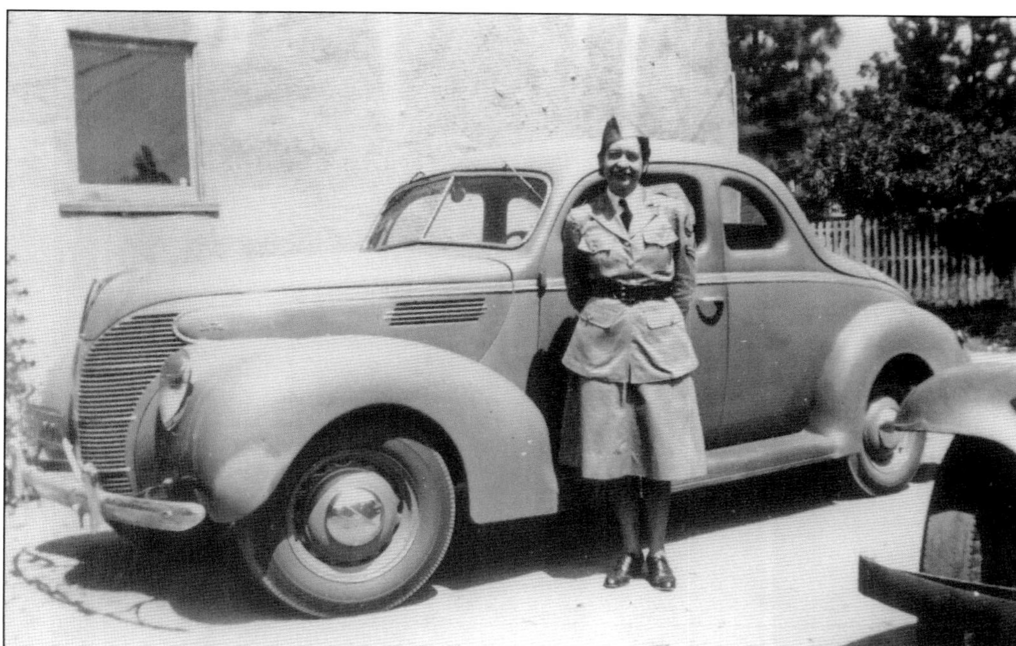

Hazel Ogle, Women's Cadet Corps, 1940. La Mesa ambulance driver Hazel Ogle represents the "all-in" commitment of the home front in support of overseas servicemen and the national war effort. The downtown USO club was a wartime amenity for those U.S. Army and U.S. Navy personnel on leave from training at Camp La Mesa, the converted prewar Fletcher Hills CCC Soil Conservation Service camp, opened from 1939 to 1941.

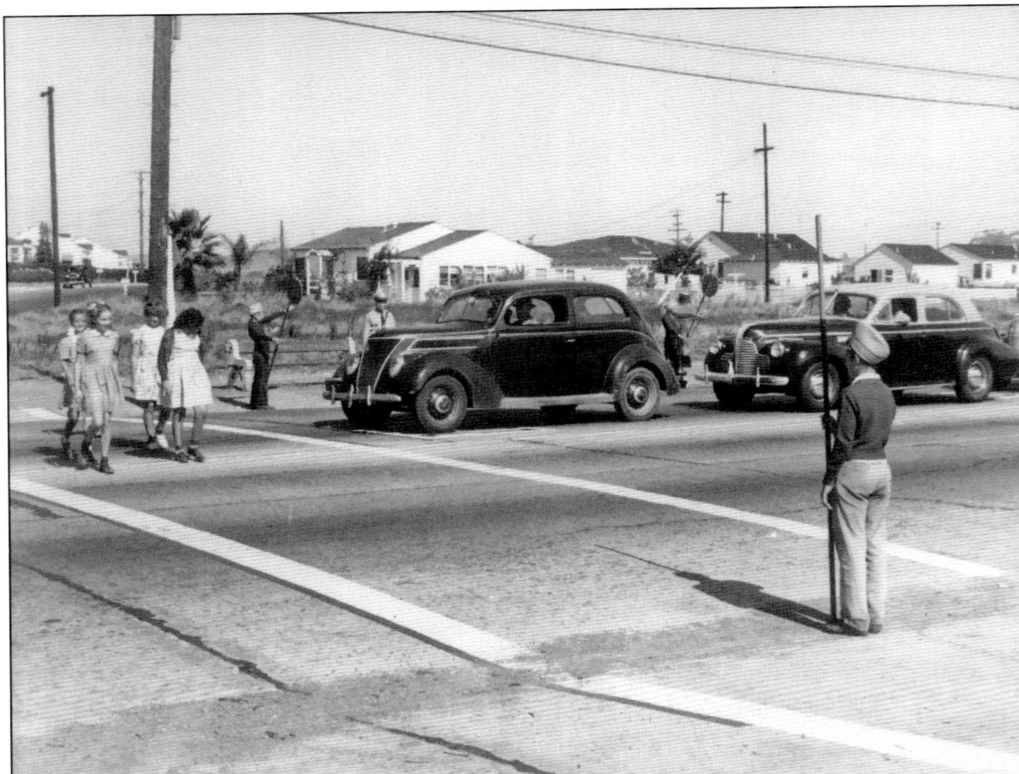

Crossing U.S. 80 at Old Jackson Drive (Glen Street), 1944. The slow growth of the 1930s rapidly increased prior to and during World War II. Relatively empty tracts such as the east end's Boulevard Addition began to fill with the popular FHA-funded minimal traditional–style small homes to meet the demand. The school district also realized the coming impact, opening new schools, including the tract's Lemon Avenue School in 1942.

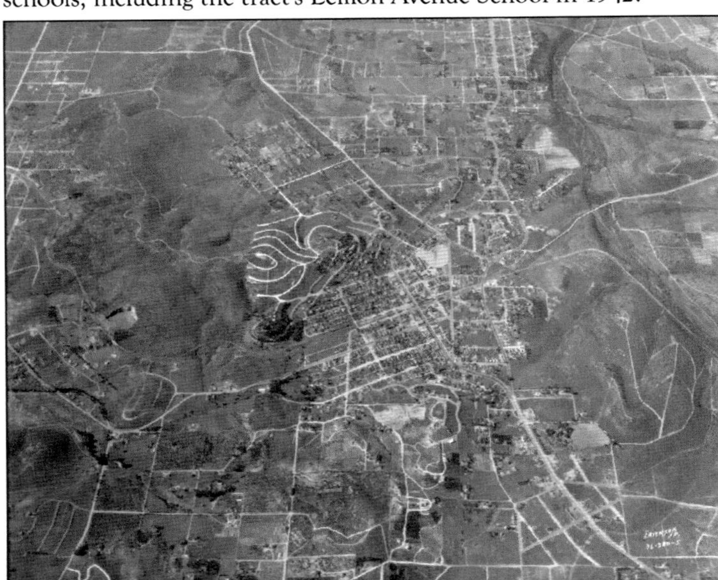

La Mesa Aerial, November 1936. Many of the 1920s tracts are still awaiting homes, but the landscape for future suburban growth is visible here. Established early tracts such as Vista La Mesa, La Mesa Dale, University Park, Windsor Hills, Boulder Heights, and Boulevard Addition are soon to be joined by the sprawling north city, all prepped for the coming exponential population growth. (San Diego Historical Society.)

Five

Postwar Suburban Boomtown 1945–1980

La Mesa came out of World War II primed to fulfill its destiny as a suburban homeland. The federal government's efforts connected the county to Southern California's Metropolitan Water District in 1947, allowing for the city and region's expansive urbanization. The La Mesa, Lemon Grove, and Spring Valley Irrigation District also responded, first by annexing El Cajon and improving their storage and distribution system before changing their name to Helix Irrigation District, then Helix Water District, reflecting its primarily urban customer base. City and school district planners, having just experienced the county's wartime population-doubling boom, recognized and implemented massive infrastructure expansion programs. With some earlier tracts in place, La Mesa became a prime location for early postwar tract developers, especially in the west end and at Fletcher Hills. With completion of the new Alvarado Freeway and U.S. 80 bypass, land to the north in old Maryland Heights and along Lake Murray Boulevard soon caught the eye of community-scale developers, who rapidly created new neighborhoods with massive suburban developments of prebuilt, affordable tract houses to meet the postwar demand. These new neighborhoods filled quickly and were annexed to the city to gain necessary services. Far-sighted city planners also quickly moved to annex the area just west of Fletcher Hills when San Diego's Marston Company announced creation of a regional shopping mall next to the new Grossmont Hospital and the new and proposed freeways. This essential economic engine would require a relook at the aging downtown business district, challenging the rapidly growing city and leading to a new city civic center and redevelopment plans. City services would also trigger annexation of adjacent neighborhoods and tracts such as at Mount Helix's Avocado Villas, south La Mesa Highlands, Fletcher Hills/Severin Manor, Rasonia, Rolando Knolls, and Vista La Mesa. Although the city added new neighborhoods, new schools, and thousands of new residents, it would still support its venerable civic organizations, community institutions, and many long-standing businesses and celebrate its many notable sons and daughters as San Diego's recognized suburban "City of Champions."

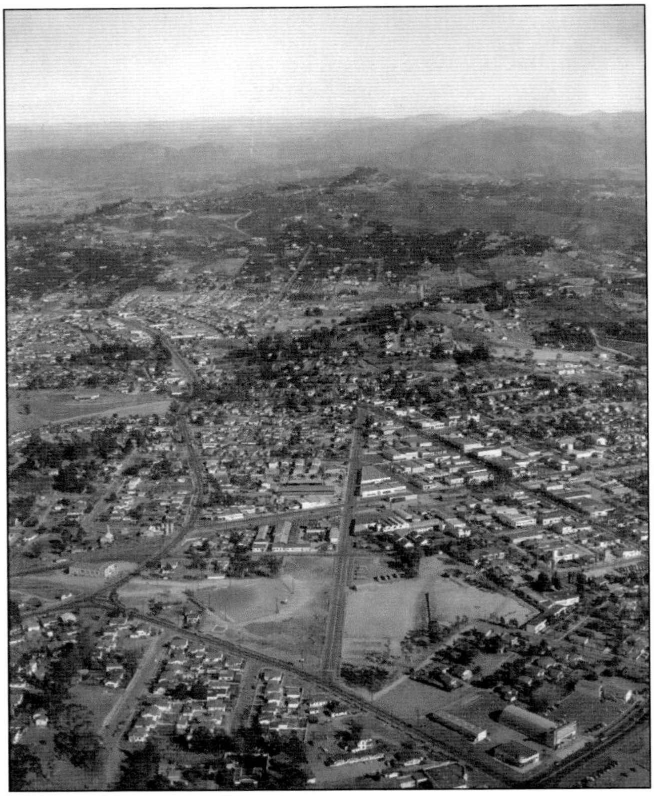

LA MESA AERIAL, 1949. This east view shows a city ready to grow. U.S. 80 is still routed on El Cajon Boulevard, splitting the now filling Boulevard Addition and Porter Hill tracts to the east. Home seekers were also making their way to Mount Helix and the Highlands to convert the remaining citrus and avocado orchards into new homes.

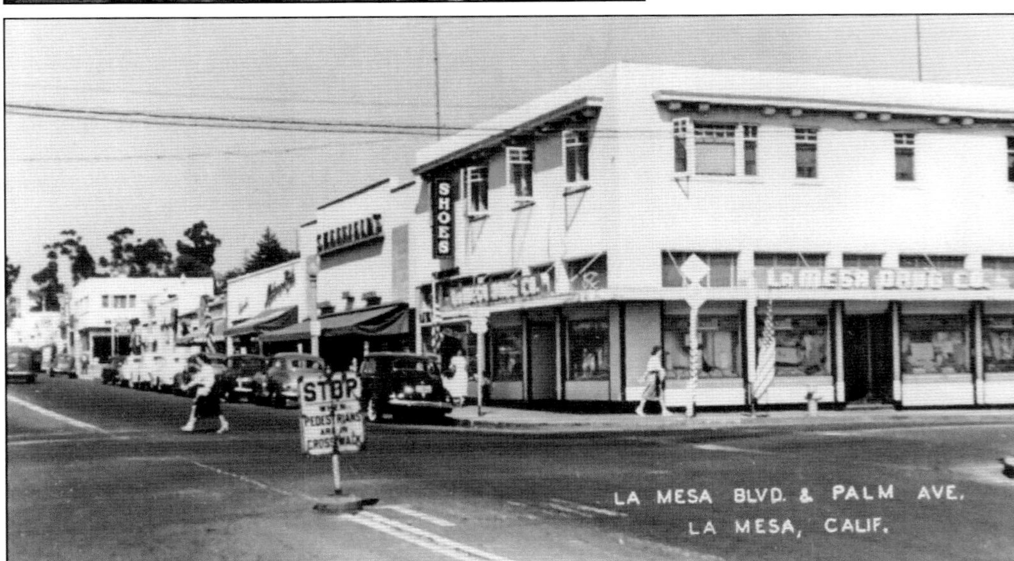

LA MESA BOULEVARD, C. 1949. By 1950, the city had nearly 11,000 residents, most still shopping in the old business district. As the city population spread into the growing suburbs and with the opening of the Alvarado Highway and State Route 94 in the early 1950s, the downtown would soon experience competition to its commercial dominance from new suburban retailers with auto-friendly access and ample parking.

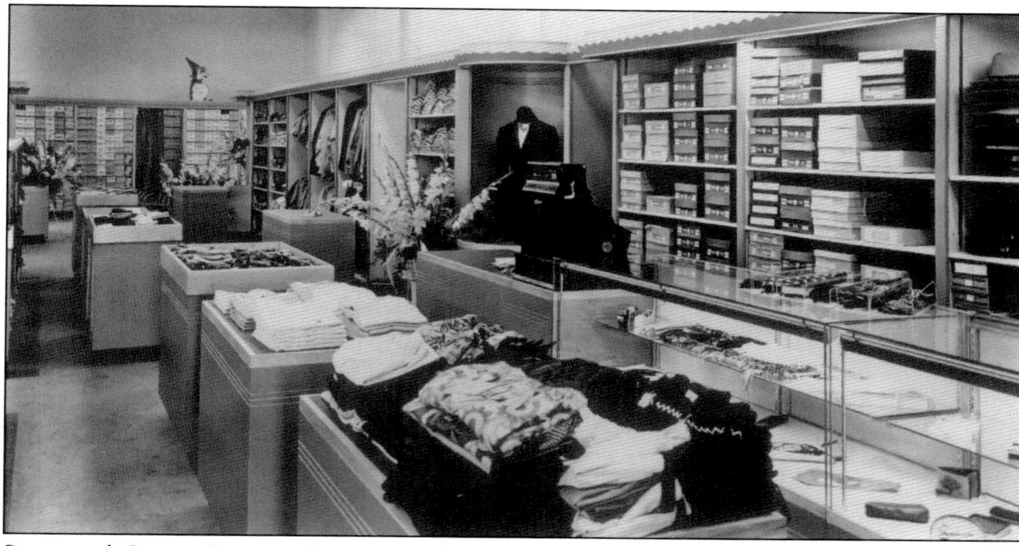

SHEFFIELD'S STORE, OPENING DAY, 1946. Sheffield's clothing store at 8315 La Mesa Boulevard was one of the business district's newest stores. Seen here on its opening day, it provided both men's and women's apparel for the growing city. Such full-service specialty stores provided the latest in fashions for postwar La Mesans.

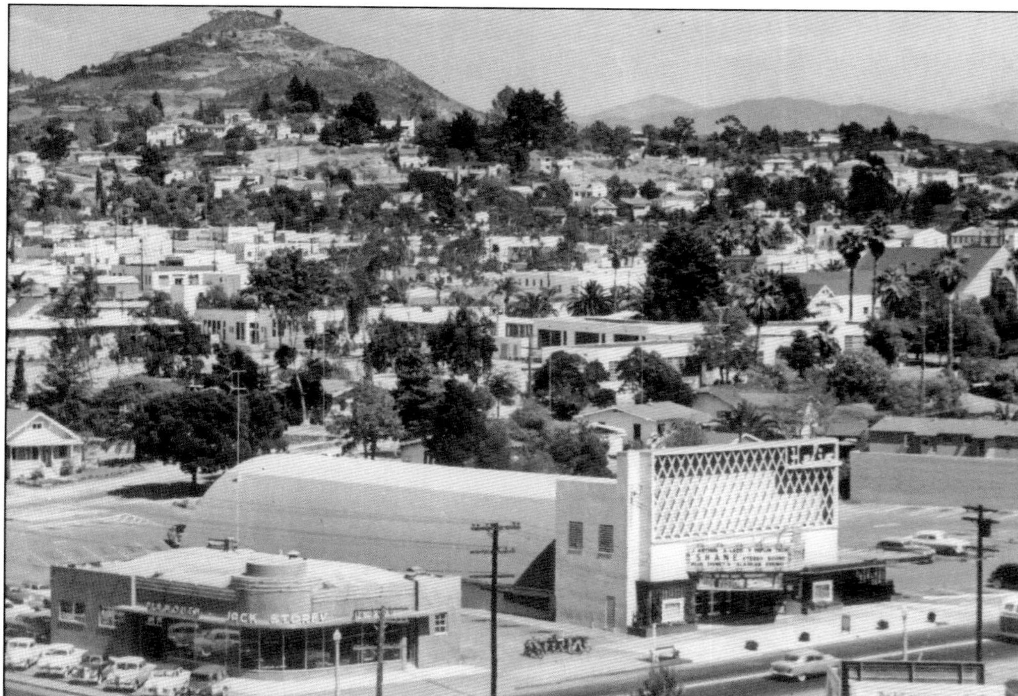

HELIX THEATER, 1954. A warmly remembered La Mesa business was this movie theater near the corner of La Mesa Boulevard and University Avenue. Renowned movie theater architect S. Charles Lee designed the Helix, opened in 1948, providing La Mesans with first-run movies in their own modern movie palace. Later competition from mega-theaters and multiplexes helped bring the Helix down for the La Mesa Springs Shopping Center in the early 1980s.

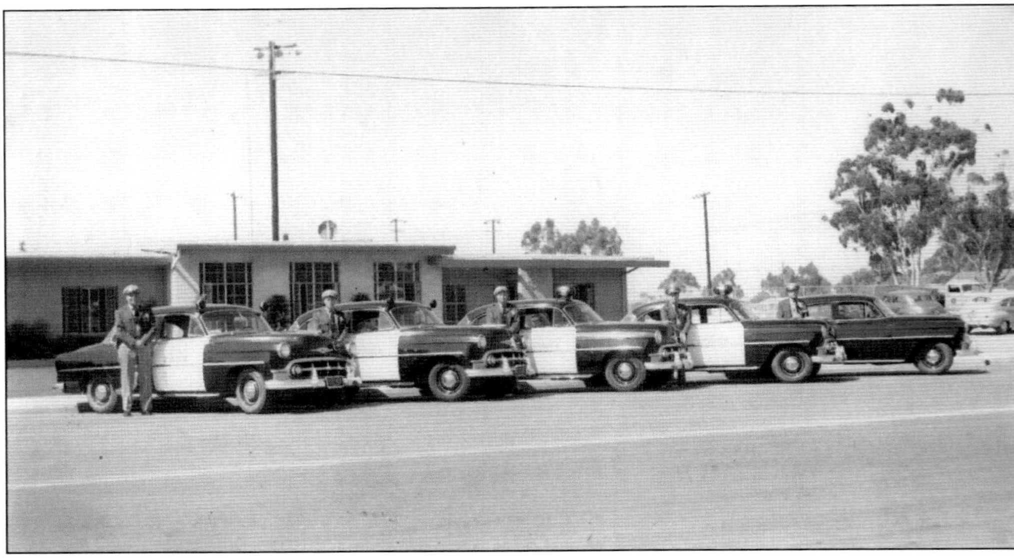

Police Force and New Station, 1954. The police department finally got its own station in 1952 on the north side of Allison Street. Chief Glenn Adams (far left) oversaw a growing force that would soon need an even larger station. In 1967, the city dedicated another new station, designed by local architects DesLauriers and Sigurdson on the south side of Allison Street at Date Avenue.

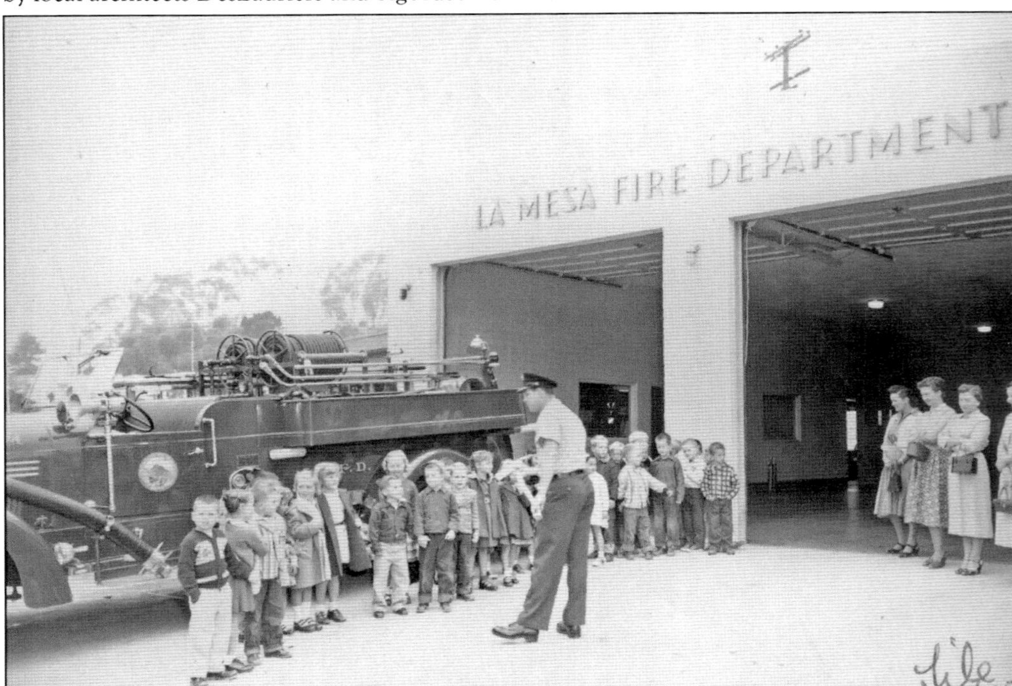

Fire Station School Tour, c. 1955. The fire department also experienced rapid growth. By 1962, the department would have over three-dozen full-time professional firefighters at three new stations: Station No. 1, shown here next to the new police station near the corner of Allison Street and University Avenue; Station No. 2 in the growing suburbs north on Dallas Street (opened 1955); and Station No. 3 on Grossmont Boulevard (opened 1962).

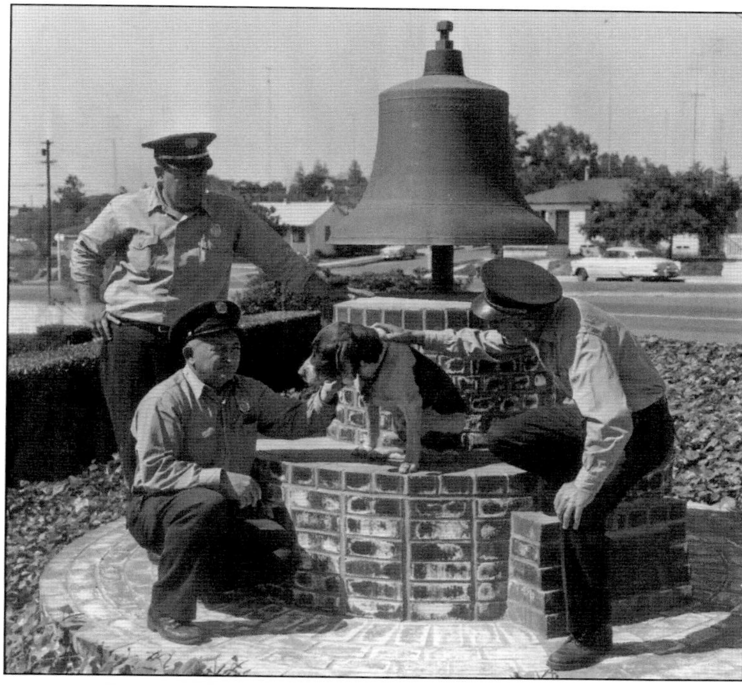

Blaze, the Fire Dog c. 1960. Possibly the most beloved city employee was Blaze. Chief Ray Lyles (kneeling) assigned the springer spaniel–pointer mix gifted to the department in 1948 the official title of "Fire House Greeter." Erma Lyles, the chief's wife, trained Blaze in all necessary skills for his job welcoming Station No. 1 visitors. Blaze officially retired in 1959 and passed away in 1962.

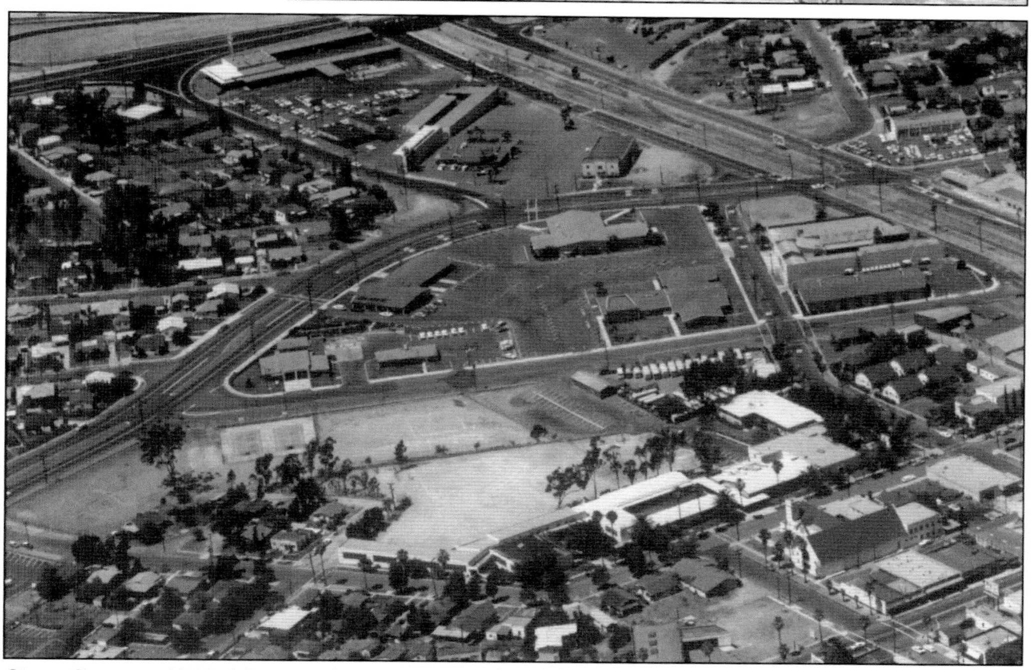

Civic Center, 1962. Meeting the growing city's public service needs required new facilities. The city developed a plan to maximize its property between University Avenue, Date Avenue, and Allison Street. In 1958, the new city administrative building at Allison Street and Date Avenue, the Library and Polak Arts Center on University Avenue north of Allison Street, the Helix Water District building on University Avenue west of Date Avenue, and the Post Office at Allison Street and Nebo Drive opened.

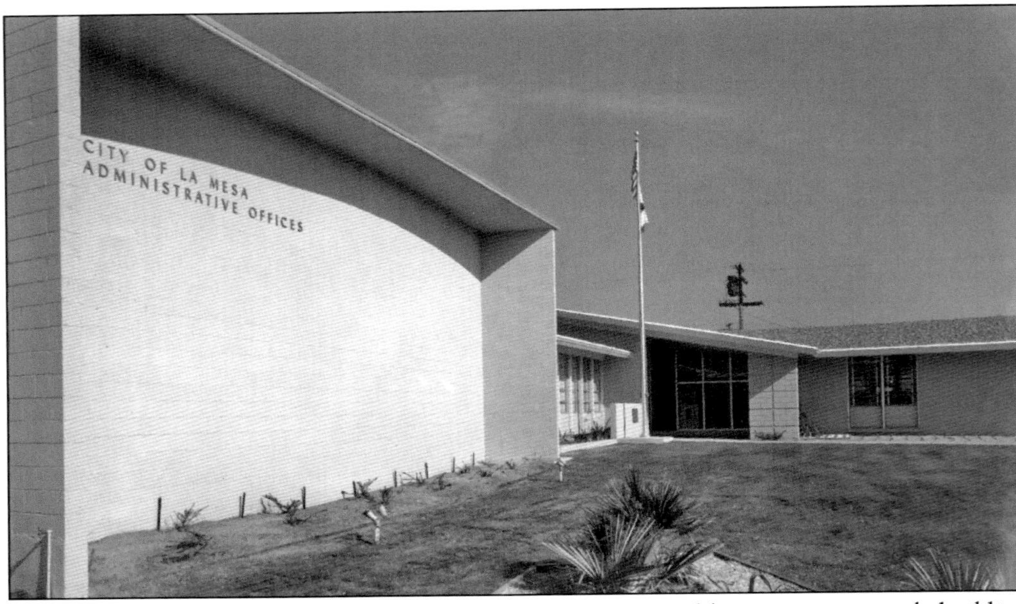

CITY ADMINISTRATIVE BUILDING (CITY HALL), 1958. George Hatch's contemporary-style building reflected the rapid growth of city government. In 1947, the city hired its first fulltime engineer, creating a public works department for its growing infrastructure two years later. Recognizing the growing workload, the city adopted a city manager form of government in 1952, hiring Lester Halcomb (1952–1957) as its first top executive.

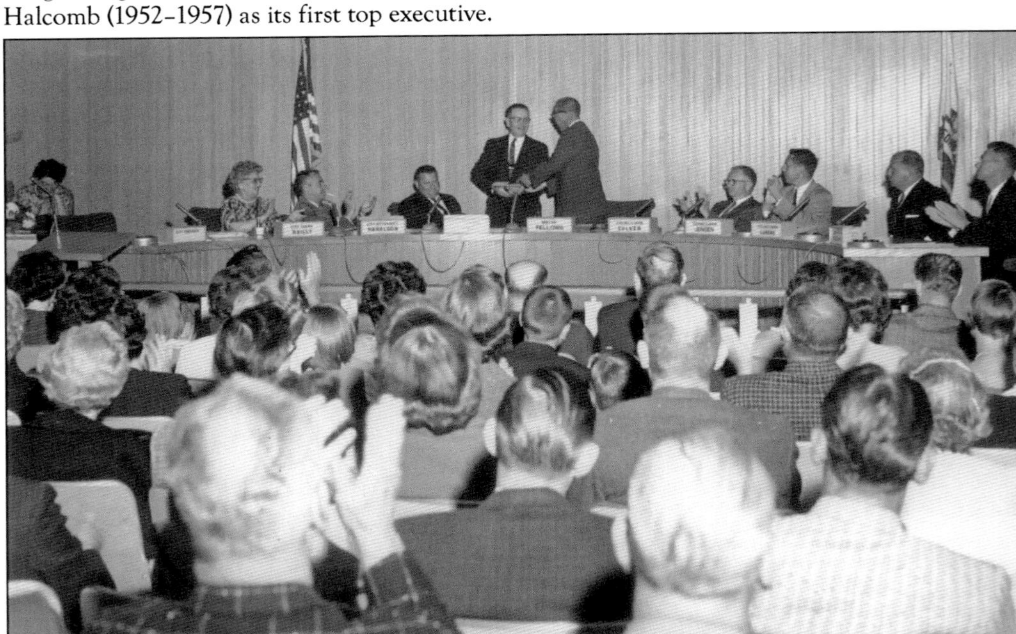

MAYOR FELLOWS TAKING OFFICE, 1962. A new city ordinance helped local son and insurance man Ray Fellows become the first publicly elected mayor. Fellows oversaw a period of great growth and activity during his two terms (1962–1970). He followed a series of councilmen mayors in the similarly expansive 1950s, including Miles Nagel (1950–1954), Earl Logan (1954–1956 and 1960–1962), Glen Crosbie (1956–1958), and Julius Acevez (1958–1960).

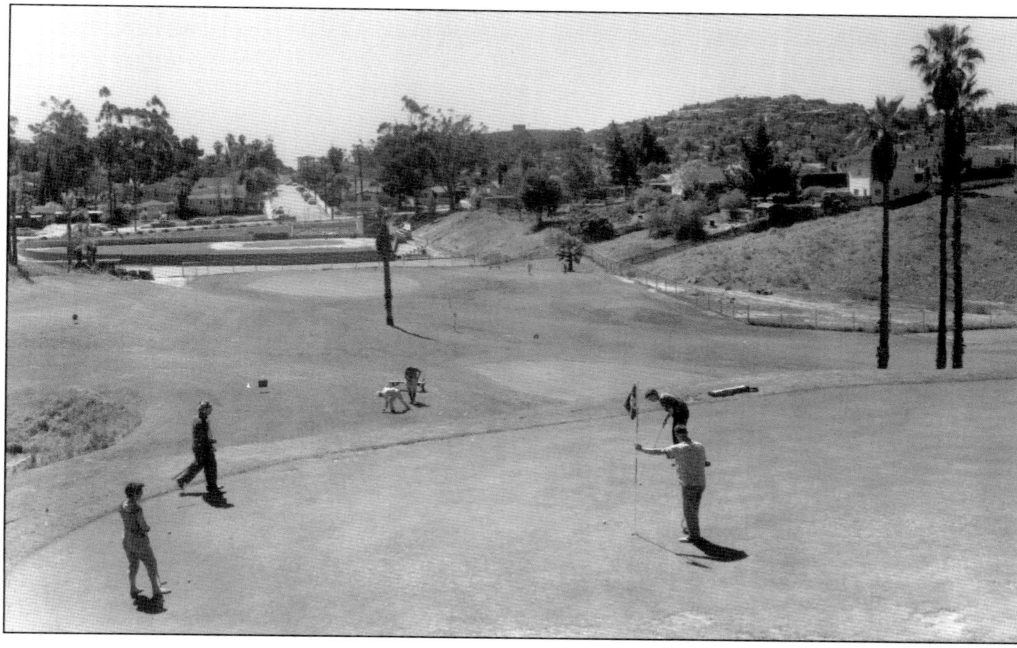

MacArthur Park Golf Course and Swimming Pool, 1959. The city expanded its public recreation facilities program into one of the county's best. MacArthur Park, first acquired in 1939 and home to today's Community Services Department, began its development with a youth recreation center in 1948, followed by the Nan Couts Girl's Cottage in 1956, named for a legendary local community service volunteer and organizer. That same year, the Khulken Ballfield for little league baseball and adult and senior softball was completed, replacing the historic diamond lost for the new civic center. Other key recreational facilities included the La Mesa Pool, opened in 1953 to replace the aging 1920s pool at Collier Park, and the nine-hole golf course opened in 1958 to fill the void left when the country club course was sold and converted to the Brookside Subdivision in 1951.

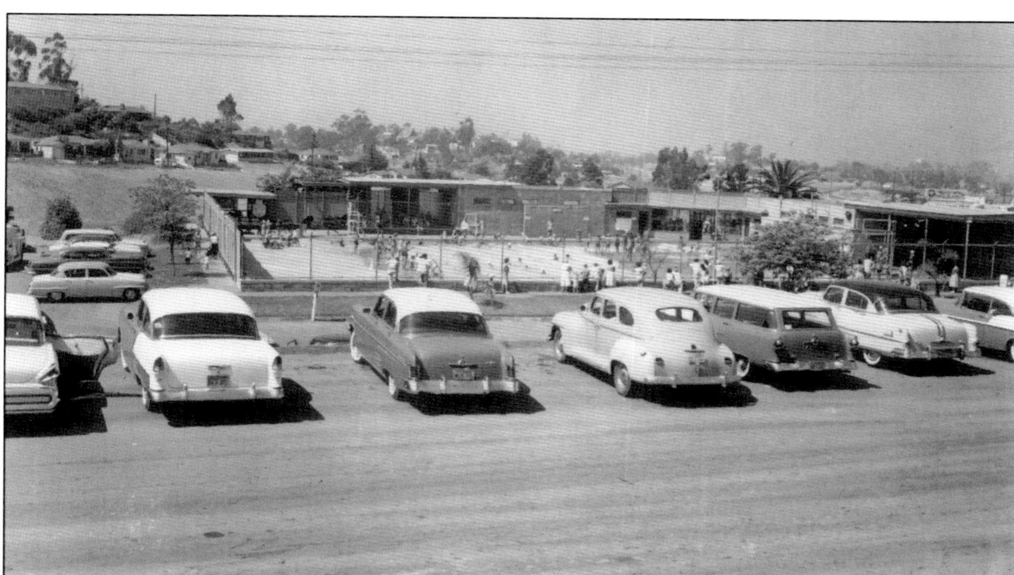

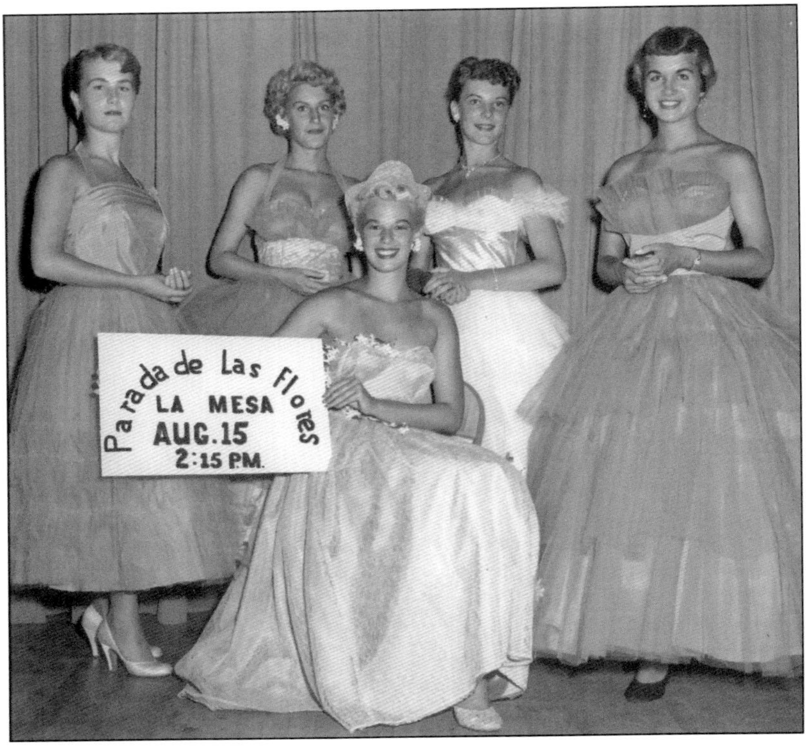

MISS LA MESA AND HER COURT, 1954. The annual Fiesta de los Flores peaked in size and popularity in the 1950s. By 1949, the flower competition awards included 75 trophies and 850 ribbons for 14 different categories. One attractive aspect of the civic celebration was the Miss La Mesa Pageant, an annual event that continues today.

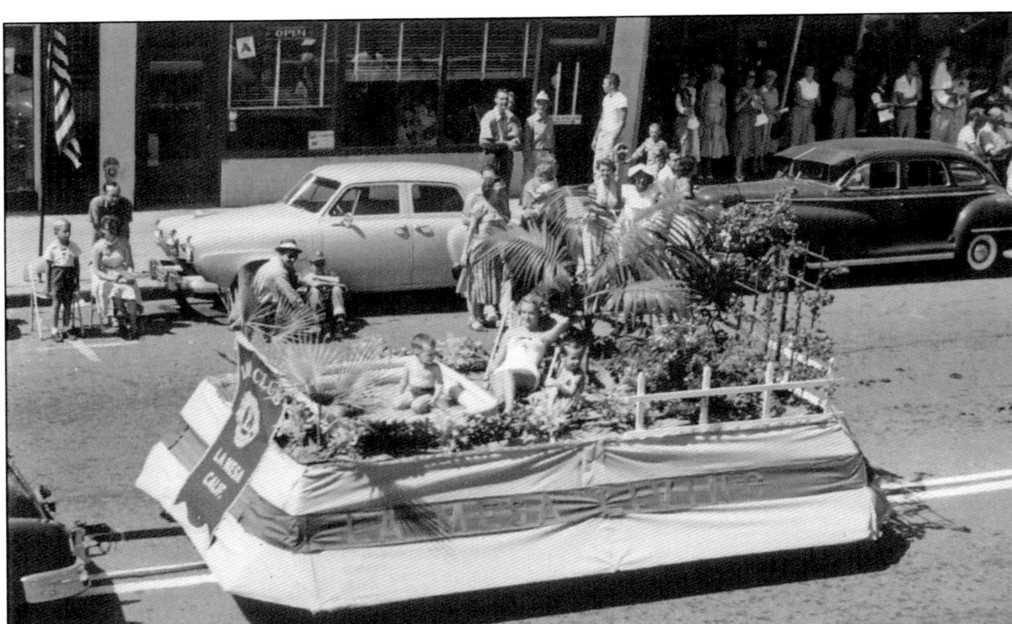

FIESTA PARADE FLOAT, 1955. Adding the parade made the event a regional draw. In 1953, the parade drew an estimated 100,000–125,000 spectators. The 1955 parade featured 18 floats representing local businesses, community, and service organizations, such as the Lion's Club float shown here, depicting a somewhat idealized vision of suburban life for La Mesa homemakers.

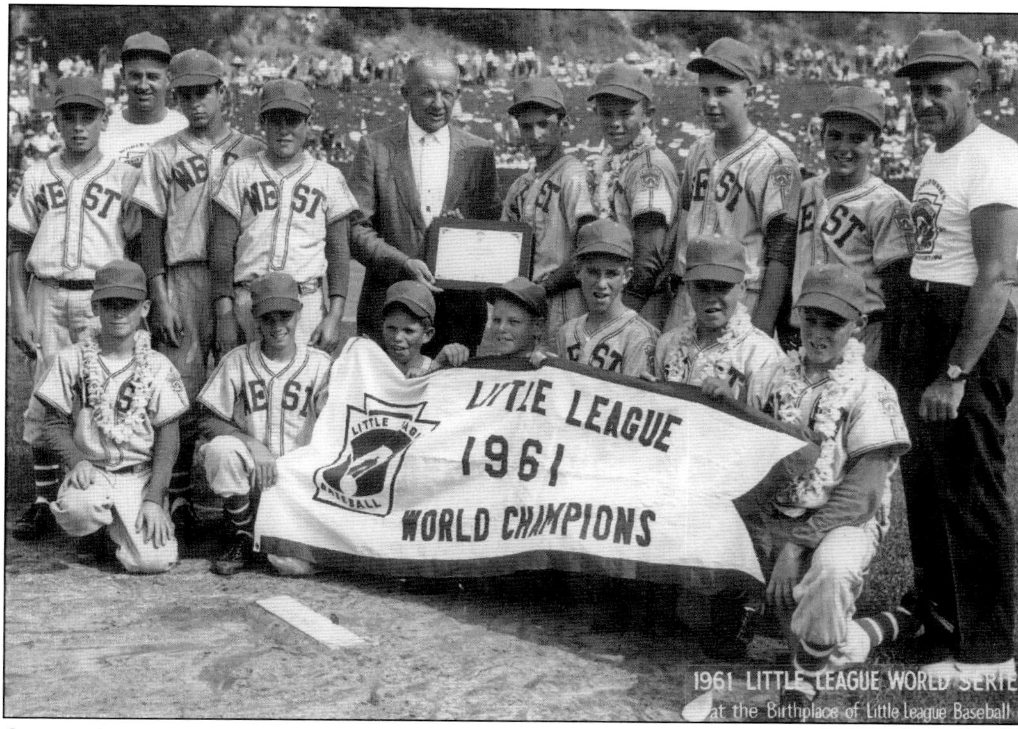

CITY OF CHAMPIONS, 1961. Fletcher Hills' Northern Little League's legendary 1961 championship run featured an amazing string of walk-off home runs and close wins in the single-elimination tournament. This followed several years of deep tournament runs by local teams, with 1957 being quite memorable as the Pony Leaguers won the Western Region, the Little Leaguers were U.S. title-holders, and the Colt League team became world champions. (Chico Leonard.)

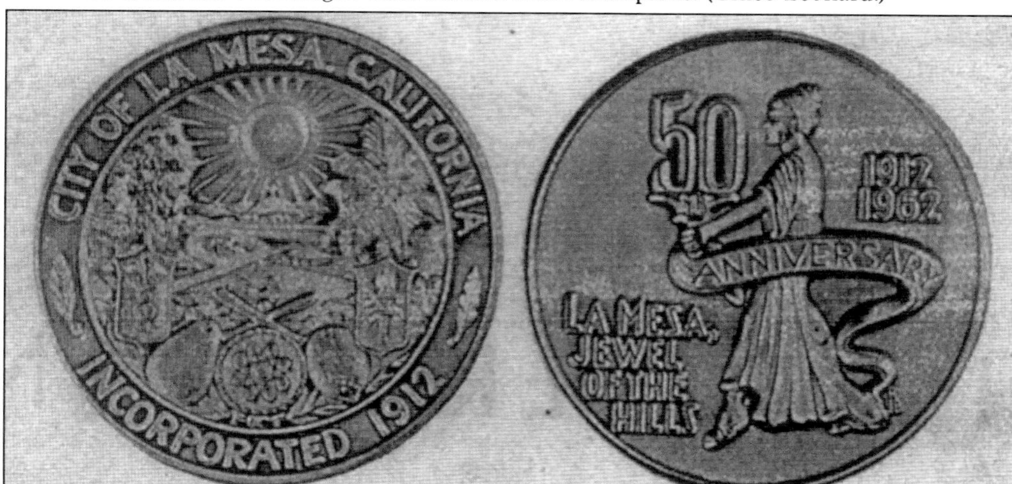

GOLDEN ANNIVERSARY MEDALLION, 1962. La Mesa went all out to celebrate the city's 50th anniversary. Riding community pride from the recent youth baseball success, the city declared itself the "City of Champions" for 1962. New mayor Ray Fellows led the yearlong festivities capping a decade of 300-percent population growth and sponsored by the chamber of commerce from its new Nebo Drive building.

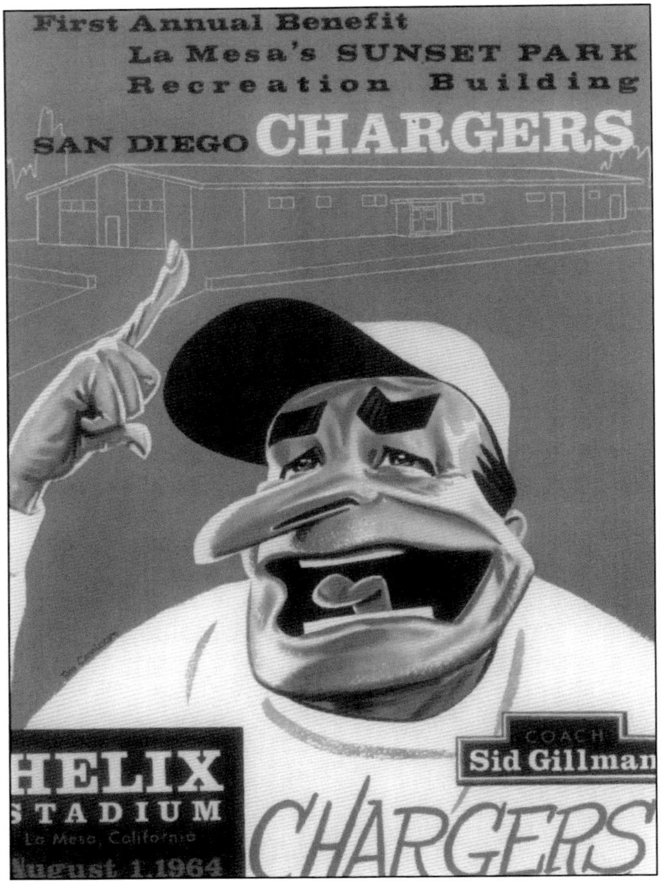

CHARGERS IN LA MESA, 1964. Another relationship providing a sense of pride in the 1960s was the association with San Diego's new professional football franchise, which spanned several years. The 1963 AFL champions first helped out with an inter-squad scrimmage at the Helix High School stadium to help raise funds for a new recreation building at the city's Sunset Park, which the team used as a practice facility.

TOWN CENTER PROJECT, 1960s. As the city grew outward, the old business district declined. From 1964 to 1966, the city joined with La Mesa businessmen to initiate the Town Center Project. Plans called for a pedestrian mall with covered sidewalks, new landscaping, and additional public parking. Citizen concerns over traffic rerouting and rising costs caused support to wane, shelving significant downtown redevelopment till the 1980s.

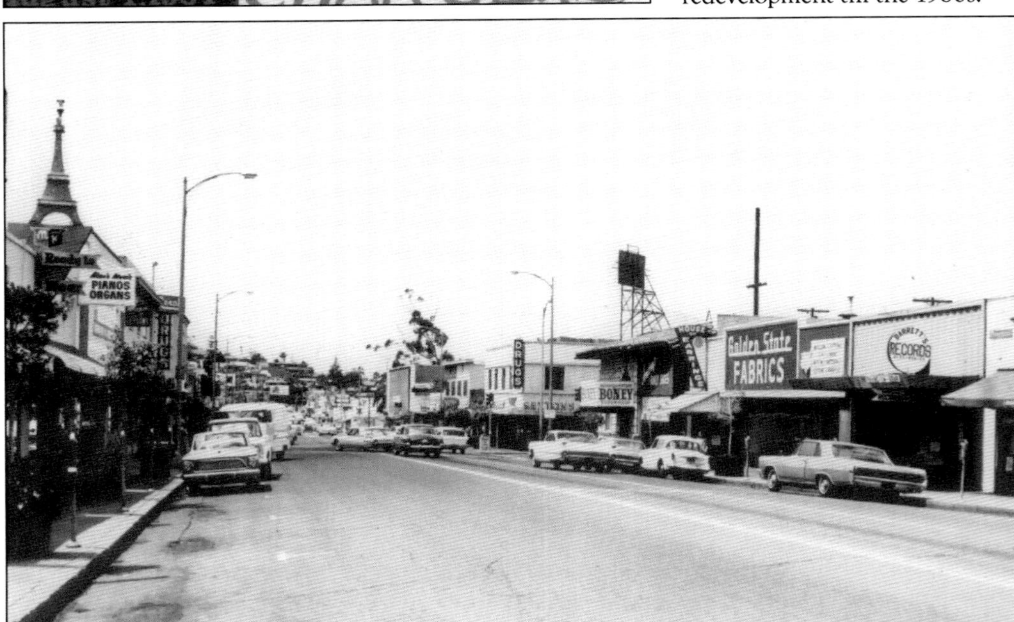

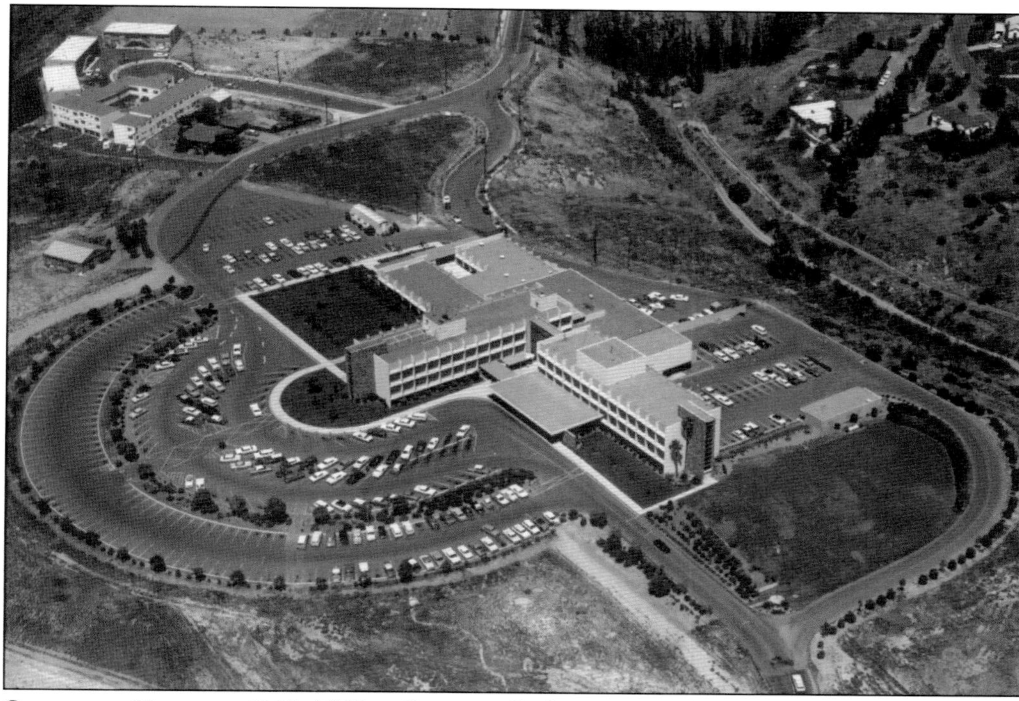

GROSSMONT HOSPITAL, 1955. All East County rallied to support the 1951 bond act used to match state and federal funds for a much-needed regional hospital. After obtaining land from the Fletcher Company, the newly formed Hospital District hired noted architects and planners William Perreira and Charles Luckman to design the original hospital complex.

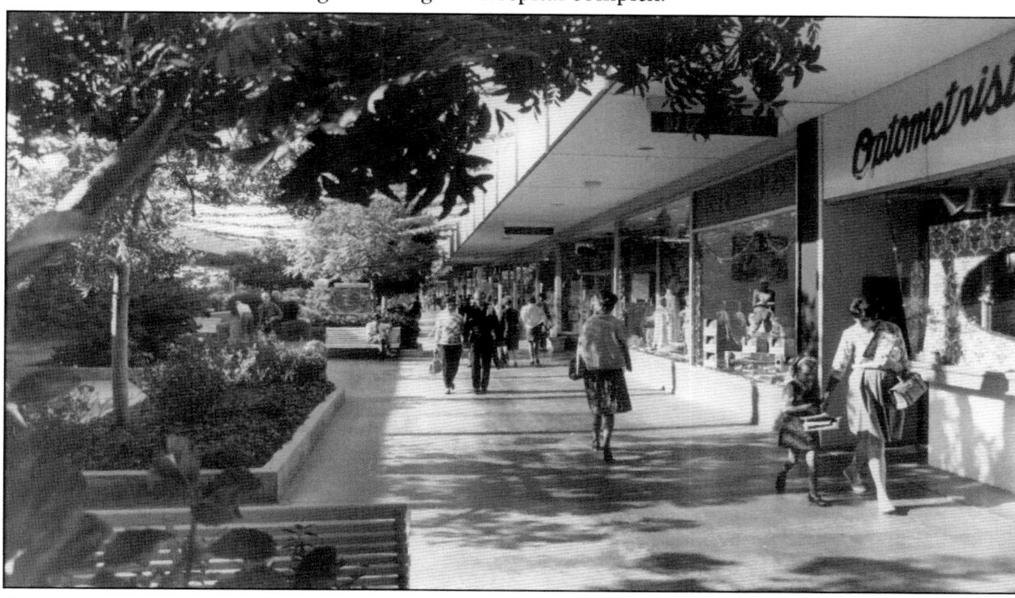

GROSSMONT CENTER, 1962. Opened in 1961 and only the third regional shopping mall completed in the county, this modern retailing center featured the local Marston's department store as its anchor tenant. In its half-century of retail service, the center is still an economic engine and community asset for La Mesa and the surrounding region.

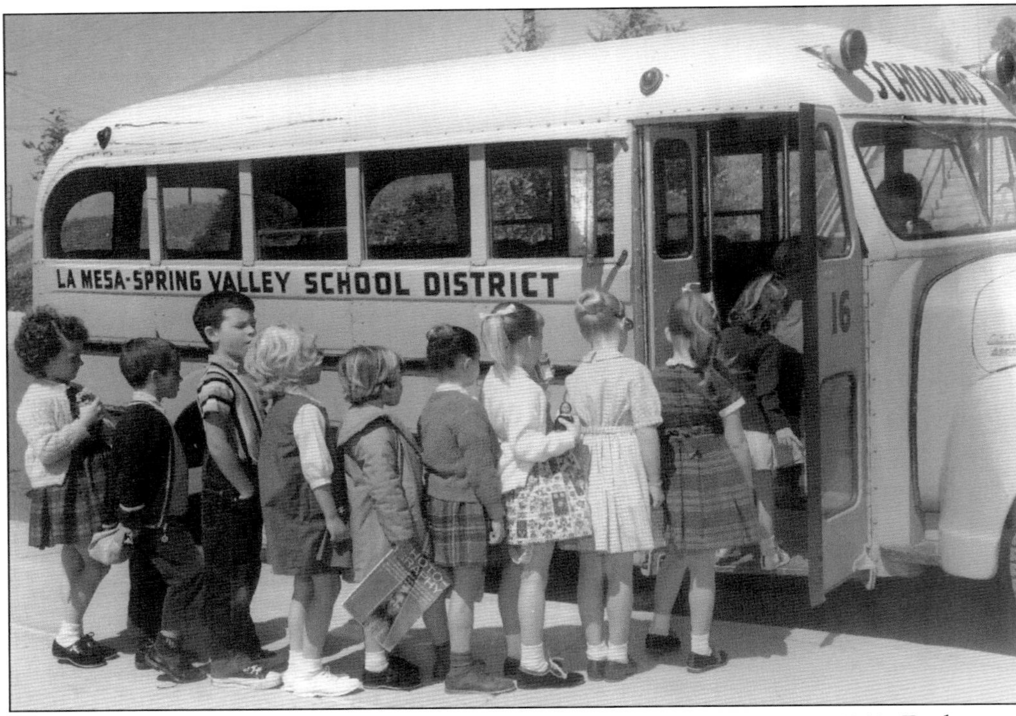

MURRAY MANOR KINDERGARTNERS 1963 AND LEMON AVENUE CLASSROOM C. 1958. Evidence of the area's exponential residential growth is found in the La Mesa–Spring Valley School District. Wartime growth required construction of Lemon Avenue and Spring Valley Elementary Schools, both opening in 1942. A district planning study outlined the need for many additional schools to meet the expected postwar growth. Enrollment did rise rapidly, going from 3,855 in 1950 to 10,459 nine years later and peaking near 15,000 by 1970. In response, the district built 18 elementary and 4 middle schools, including these in or adjacent to La Mesa: Rolando (1946); La Mesa Dale (1949); Fletcher Hills, Rolando Park, and La Mesa Intermediate (1951); Murray Manor (1954); Northmont (1957); Briar Patch and Maryland Avenue (1958); Parkway Middle (1961); and Murdock (1972). Lemon Grove District also built Vista La Mesa (1951).

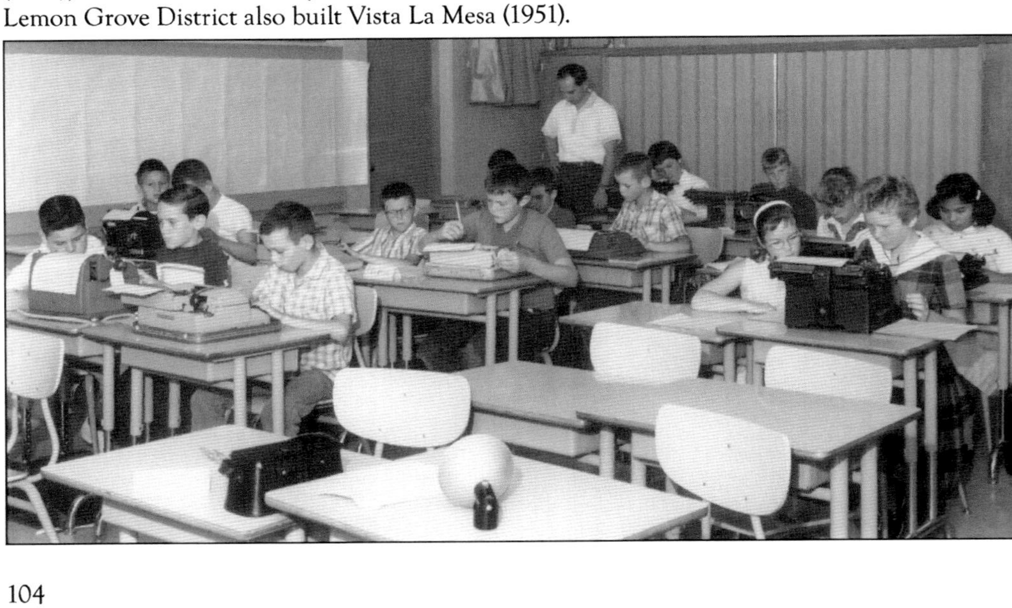

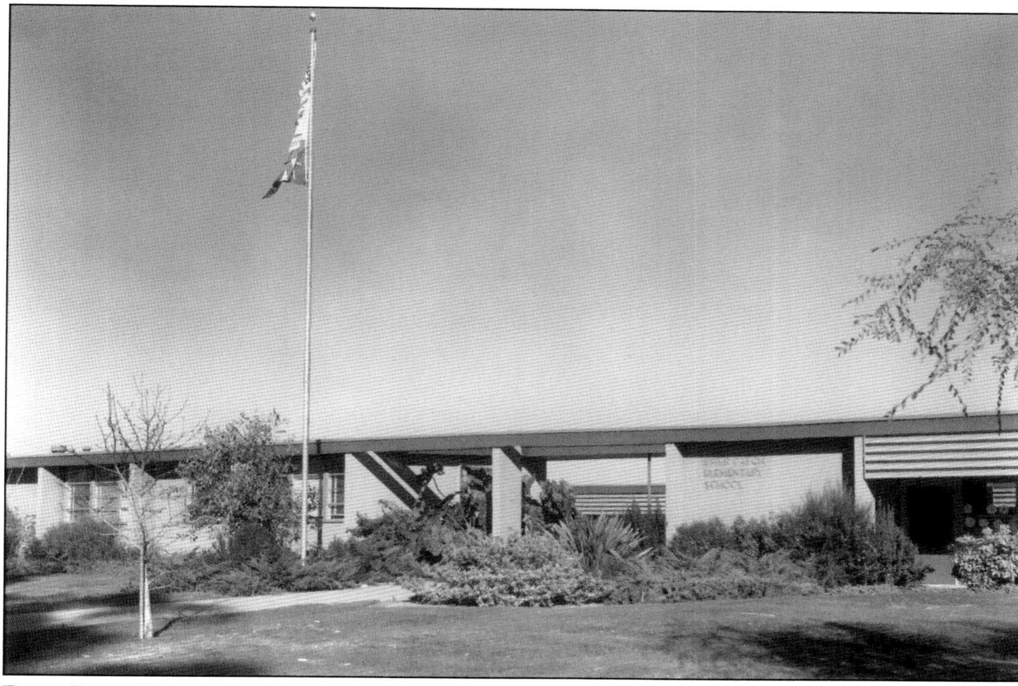

BRIAR PATCH ELEMENTARY C. 1964. La Mesa's new bond-funded schools reflected the latest in modern campus designs. Noted local architects such as Albert Treganza, Lloyd Ruocco, Sam Hamill, Clyde Hufbauer, and Robert DesLauriers designed schools and facilities for the district. The new school openings led to many attendance boundary changes and student shuffling—including the unique 1955 transfer of Rolando Park Elementary to San Diego City Schools.

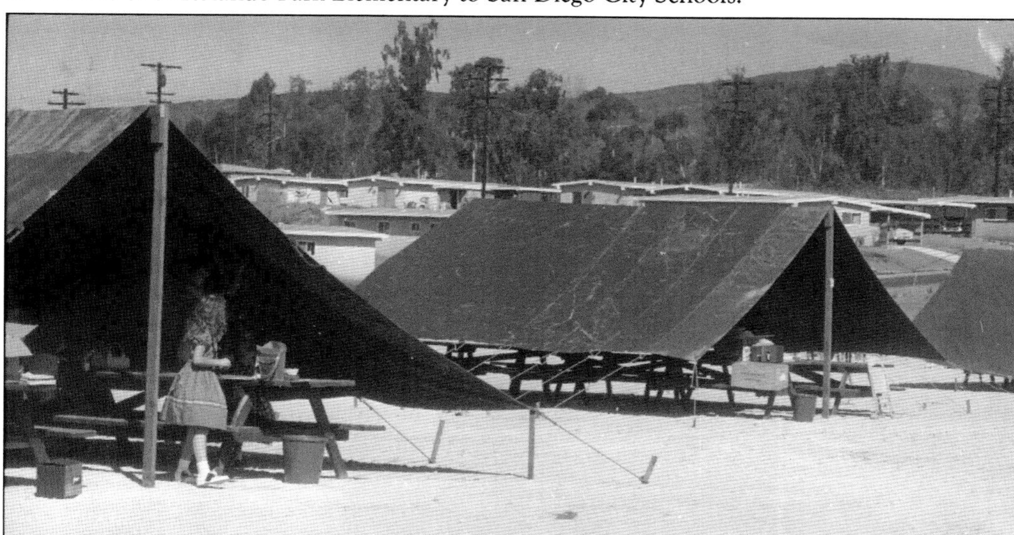

MARYLAND AVENUE TEMPORARY FACILITIES, 1958. Longtime district superintendent Glenn Murdock and his staff were constantly challenged in building and opening schools for new and growing neighborhoods, one example being these temporary facilities serving the school's first students. New modern schools and affordable tract houses proved attractive for thousands looking for the American Dream lifestyle available in La Mesa's new suburbs.

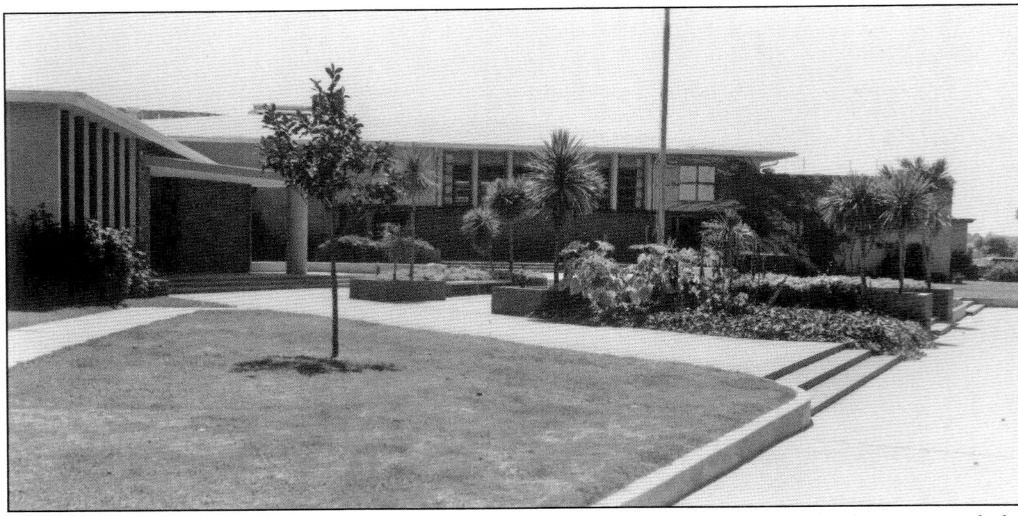

LA MESA JUNIOR HIGH 1955 AND PARKWAY JUNIOR HIGH 1961. The growth also required the establishment of middle schools. La Mesa Intermediate, as it was originally called, technically opened in the old grammar school, graduating its first class in 1949. The original Sam Hamill–designed junior high campus on Parks Avenue opened in 1952. The rapid growth of the north city and neighboring Fletcher Hills required building Clyde Hufbauer's Parkway Junior High adjacent to Fletcher Parkway and seen here in October 1961; Parkway was also opened before construction completion. The district would also build Spring Valley Middle (1954) and La Presa Middle (1963) to serve Spring Valley's elementary schools, including Casa de Oro (1948); Bancroft (1956); Avondale and Rancho (1960); Highlands (1962); La Presa Elementary and Kempton (1965); Loma (1978); and Sweetwater Springs (1993).

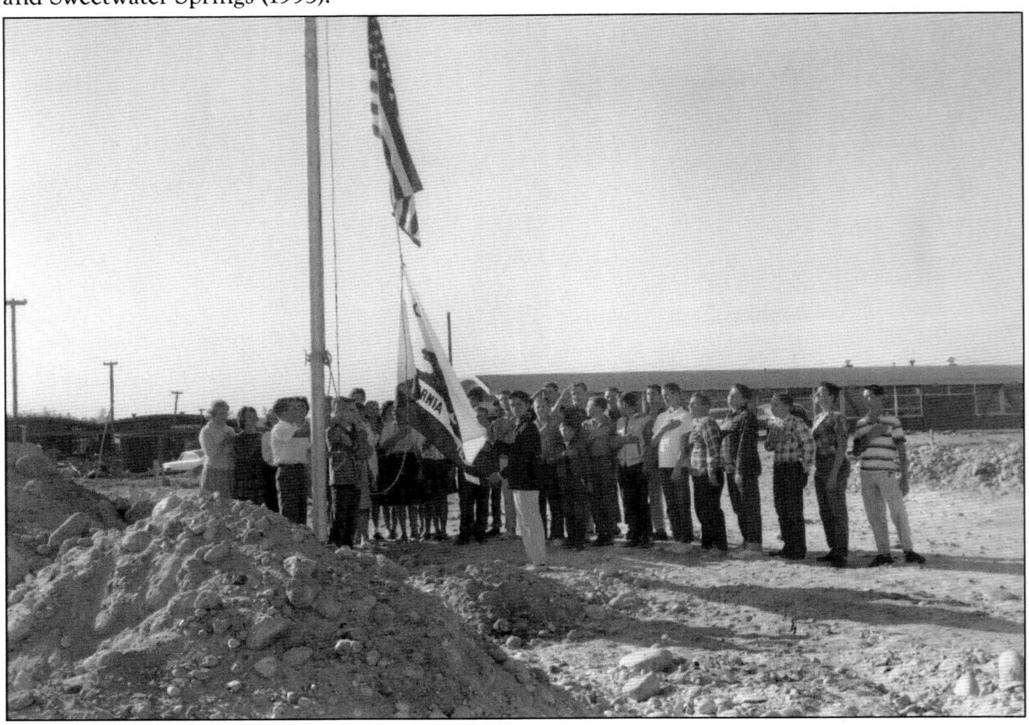

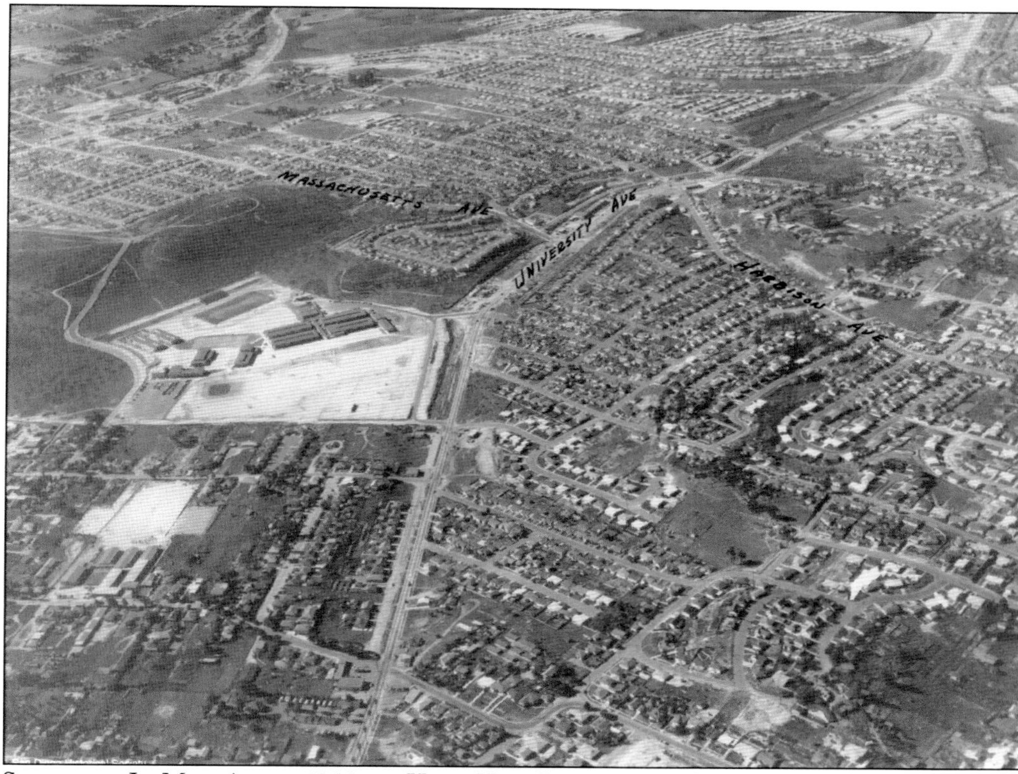

SOUTHWEST LA MESA AERIAL 1956 AND HELIX HIGH BAND C. 1953. Grossmont High School District was also impacted, opening its second school, Helix High, on James Murray's old west-end land, a finalist in the 1920s for the location of San Diego State and the inspiration for the University Park tract that provided the nearby college-named streets. After the World War II, those older west-end tracts along University Avenue including the renamed Academy Heights, Stanford Terrace and Rolando Knolls off Seventieth Street, and Vista La Mesa along Massachusetts Avenue, all filled in. Helix High held its first classes at Grossmont High in 1951 before moving into its new campus in 1952 under the guidance of longtime principal Benton Hart. Helix's Highlander Marching Band, including its Highland Pipe Band, became a staple at local civic events since its creation in 1952. (Above, San Diego Historical Society.)

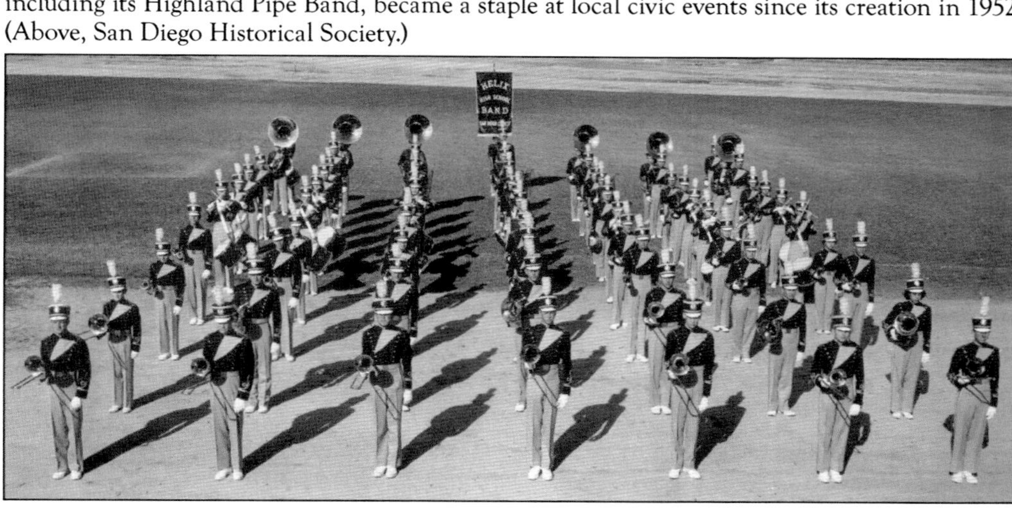

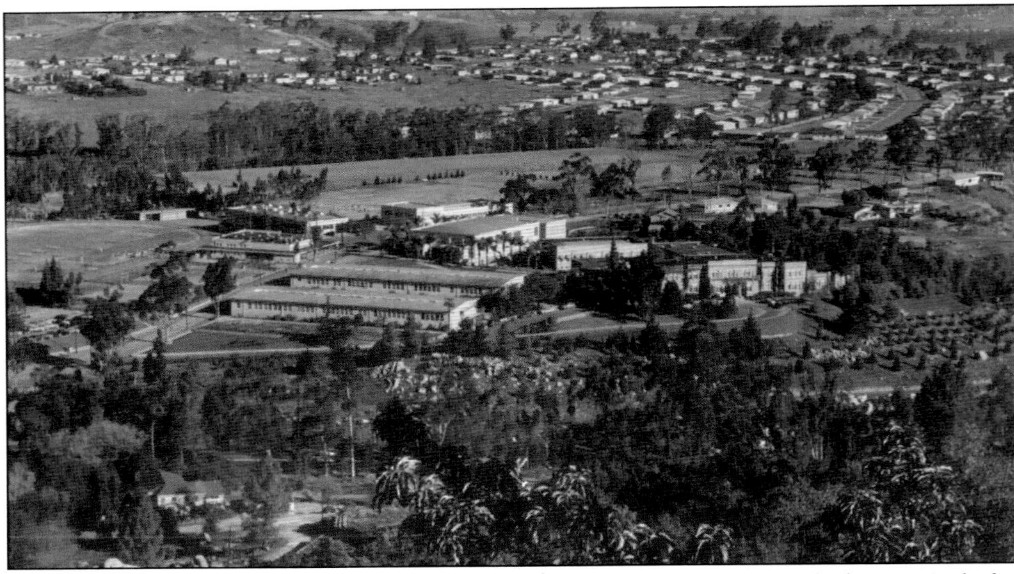

Grossmont High School, View East, 1953, and Pom Pom Girls, 1950s. By the late 1940s, before the opening of Helix High School, Grossmont High School's enrollment had risen to near 3,200. In the meantime, the campus grew with new buildings and facilities, keeping up with the surrounding Fletcher Hills neighborhood and East County areas seen beyond. Over the following decades, the high school district would respond with new high schools, including El Cajon's El Cajon Valley (1955) and Granite Hills (1960); Lakeside's El Capitan (1958); Spring Valley's Mount Miguel (1957) and Monte Vista (1961); Santee's Santana (1965); and Calavo Gardens' Valhalla (1974). After 28 years as the only high school, the opening of each of these schools tapped the original campus for students and faculty, but the prestige and spirit of the Foothillers continued both academically and athletically.

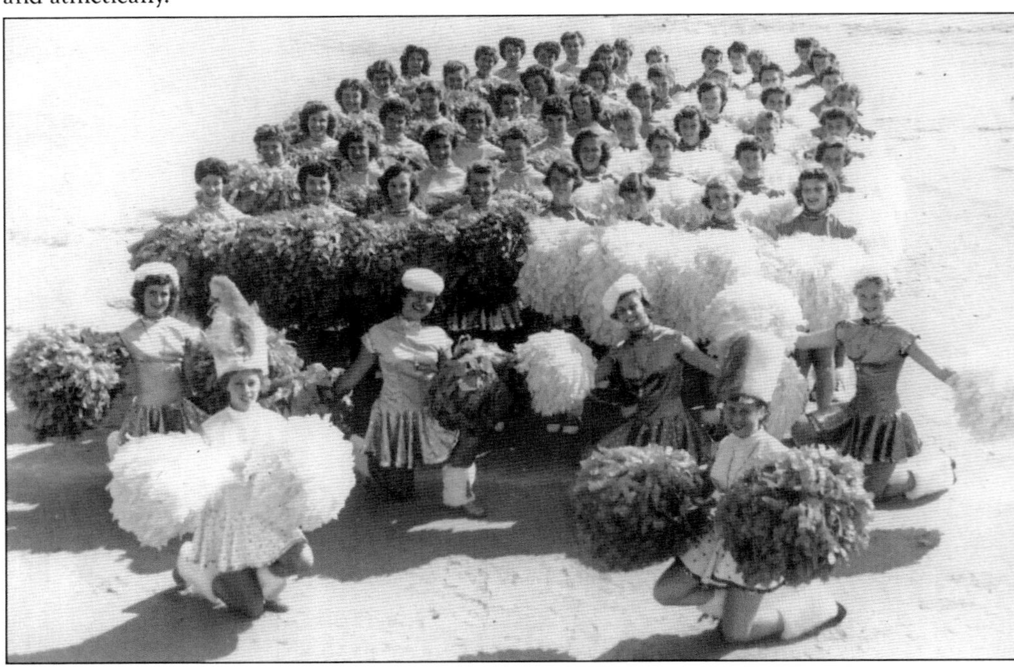

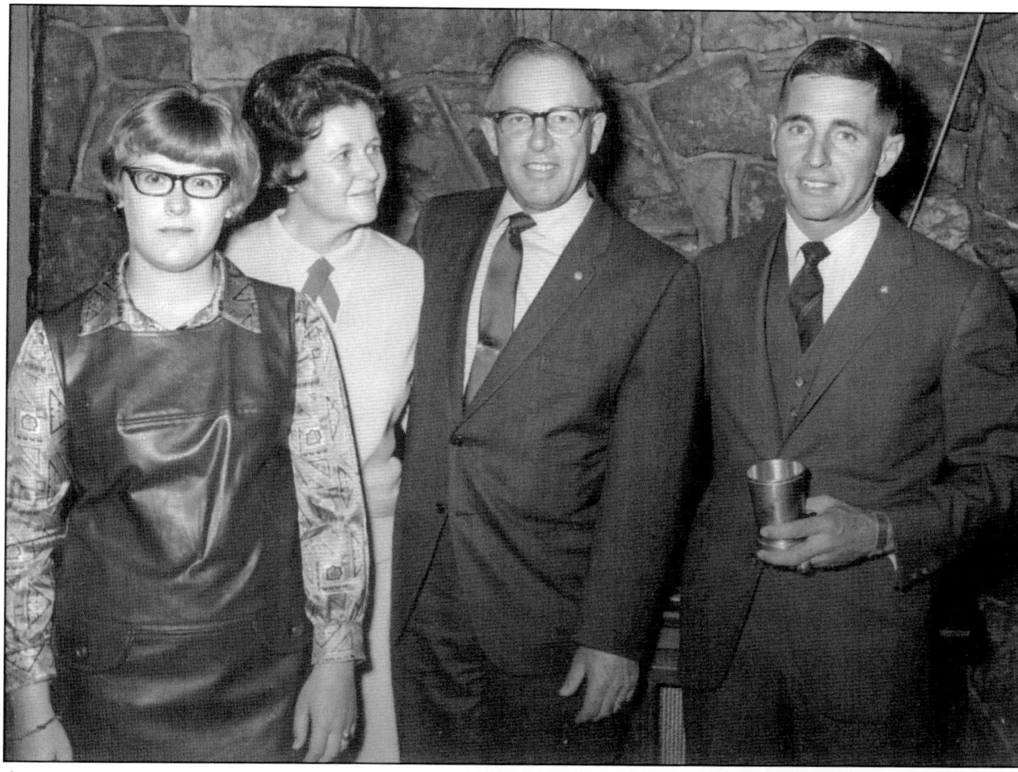

ASTRONAUT BILL ANDERS, 1969. William Anders, La Mesa native and Grossmont High alum, became one of La Mesa's most favored sons after earning immortality as an Apollo 8 astronaut, orbiting the moon in December 1968. Anders (holding cup at right) poses with Mayor Fellows along with his wife Hope and daughter Louann at a benefit honoring Anders's accomplishments, which later included a career in nuclear engineering and aeronautics.

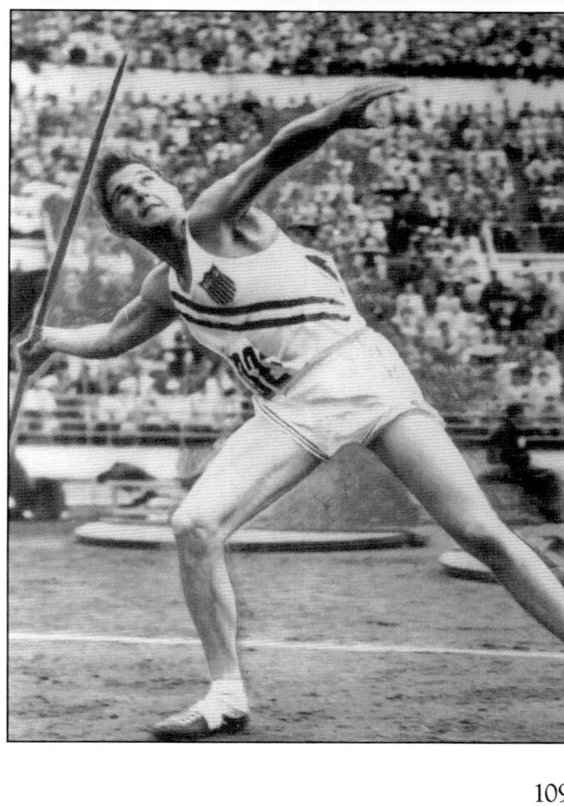

FOOTHILLER OLYMPIAN BUD HELD, 1952. Grossmont grad Franklin "Bud" Held continued the tradition of high-level Foothiller athletics. A high school pole vault champion, Held switched to javelin at Stanford University, became a six-time national champion, and later set American and world records and made the 1952 Olympic team. Such Grossmont athletic success was assisted by many great coaches, including legends Jack Mashin and Marlin Baer.

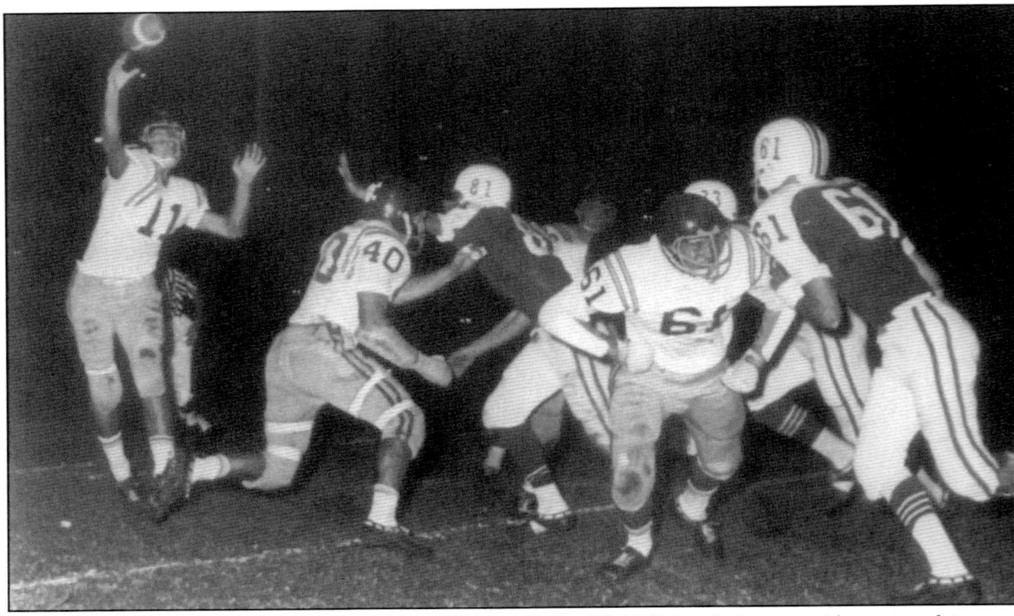

GROSSMONT'S BRIAN SIPE, 1967. Fletcher Hills resident and 1961 Little League Championship team member Brian Sipe, here making a pass, is another of many accomplished Foothiller athletes. Sipe, an All-Grossmont League quarterback, went on to star for San Diego State before an All-Pro career with the Cleveland Browns (1972–1983) of the NFL, earning the Most Valuable Player Award in 1980.

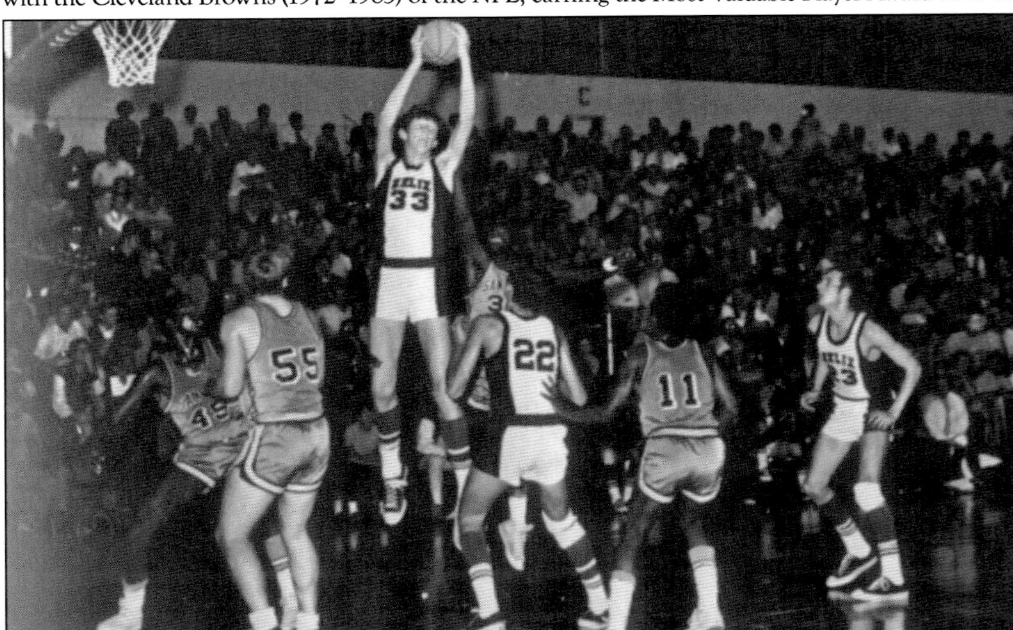

HELIX'S BILL WALTON (NO. 33), 1970. Helix High athletics grew, both literally and figuratively, with the arrival of Ted and Gloria Walton's children. Here basketball star Bill leads the Highlanders to a section championship before legendary hall-of-fame college and professional careers at UCLA and the NBA, following older brother Bruce, another UCLA star and NFL lineman. The Waltons, among many other standouts, instituted decades of Helix athletics excellence.

CORRIDORS FOR DEVELOPMENT, 1956. New automobile corridors would be key infrastructure for La Mesa's expansion. State Routes 94 and 125 freeways, in construction here cutting from lower left up to U.S. 80, would open expansion to the south and east. The U.S. 80 Bypass, along with the recently completed Fletcher Parkway, opened up the now-visible north city (top center) following Lake Murray Boulevard out to Fletcher Hills (top right).

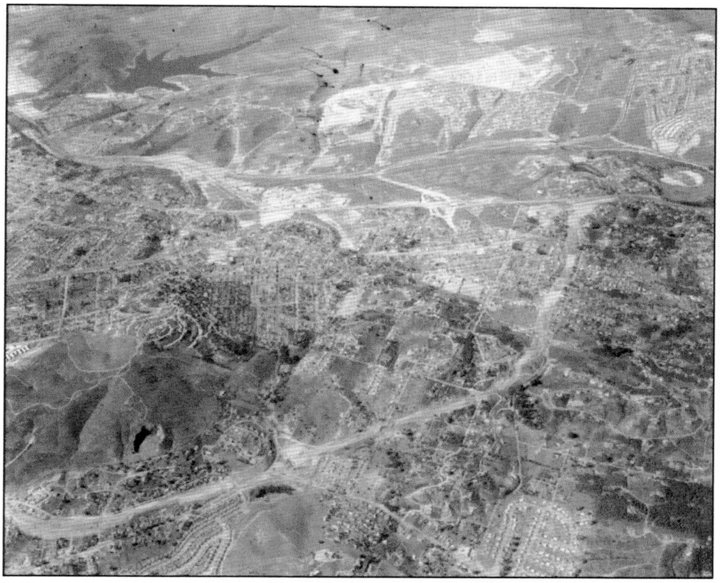

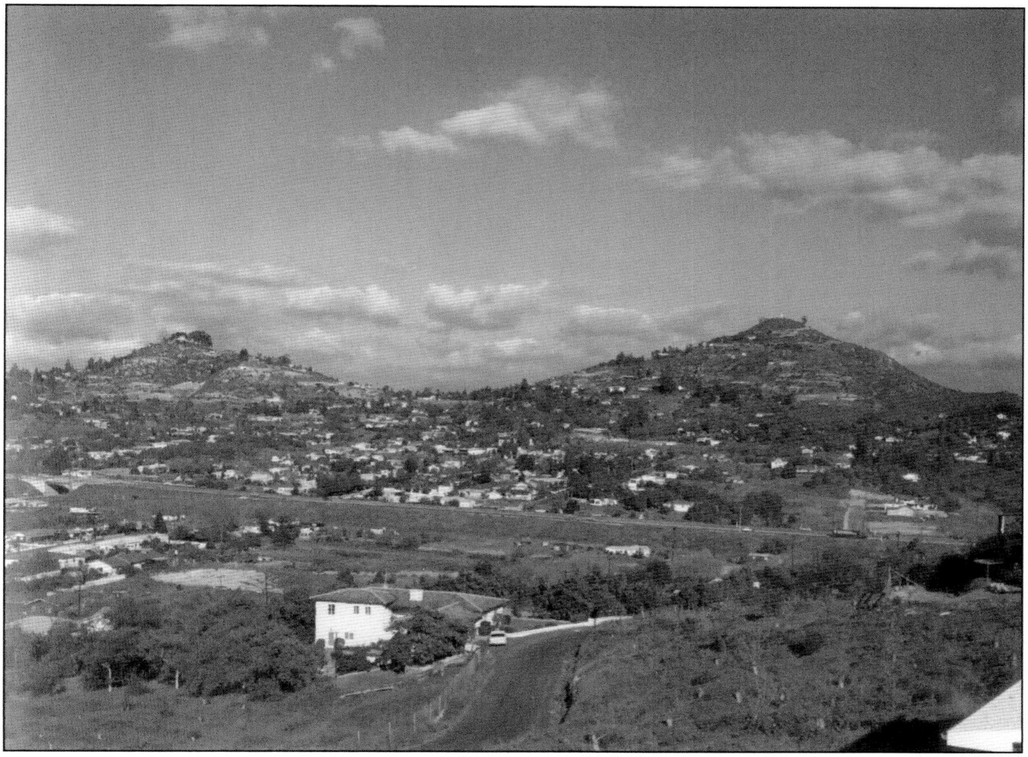

POSTWAR GROSSMONT AND MOUNT HELIX, 1962. The Grossmont and Mount Helix area became known for some of the county's most impressive residential architecture. Developers and homebuilders seeking their own unique versions of the postwar home provided opportunities for some of the region's most noted local modernist architects and designers, including Cliff May, Lloyd Ruocco, R. K. Davis, and Homer Delawie, among others.

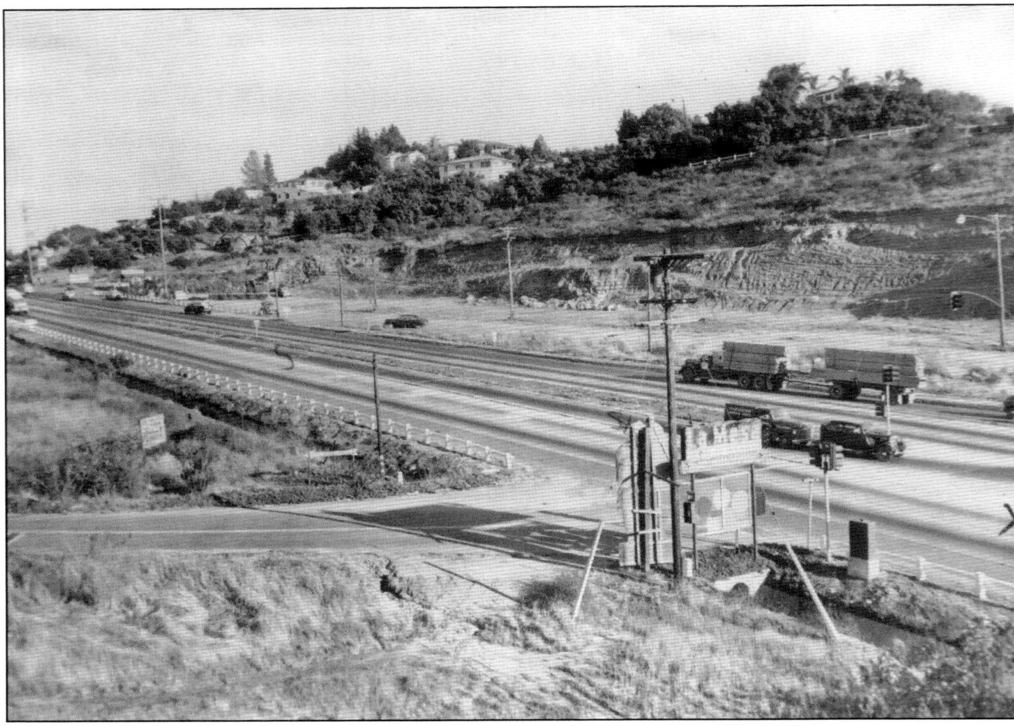

U.S. 80 BYPASS, 1952. The U.S. 80 Bypass, extending the Alvarado Highway from Baltimore Drive through to Grossmont Pass, was key for the city's northern expansion. The new highway, with Porter Hill to the right, became Interstate 8 in the 1970s, about the time that the majority of the city's population resided north of this high-speed east-west corridor.

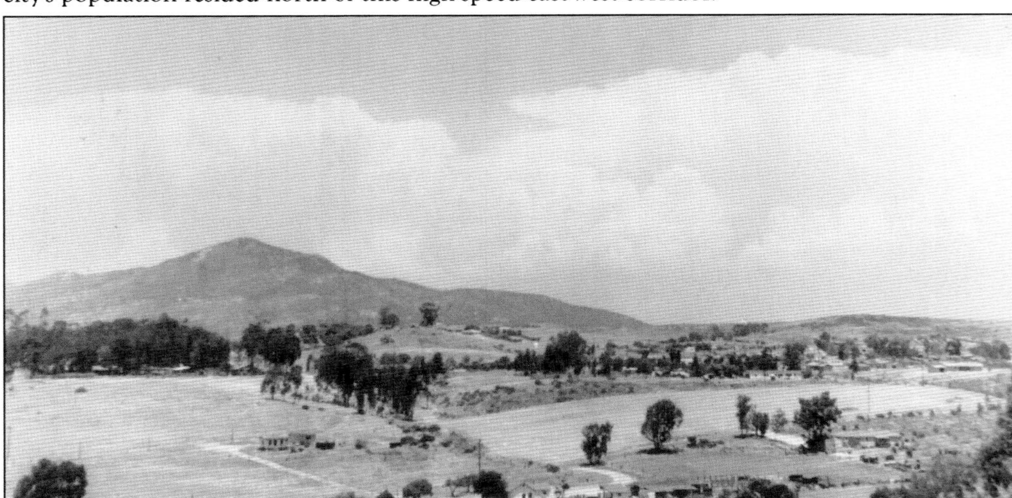

OLD MARYLAND HEIGHTS, 1940S. This land was opened by new 1950s thoroughfares including the paving of the old Lake Murray to Bostonia Boulevard in the former Maryland Heights. The former La Mesa Colony tract lands were known for poultry raising and small ranches and farms through the early 20th century. The most recognizable landmark was nearby San Diego State College's "S" painted annually on Cowles Mountain by the incoming freshman class.

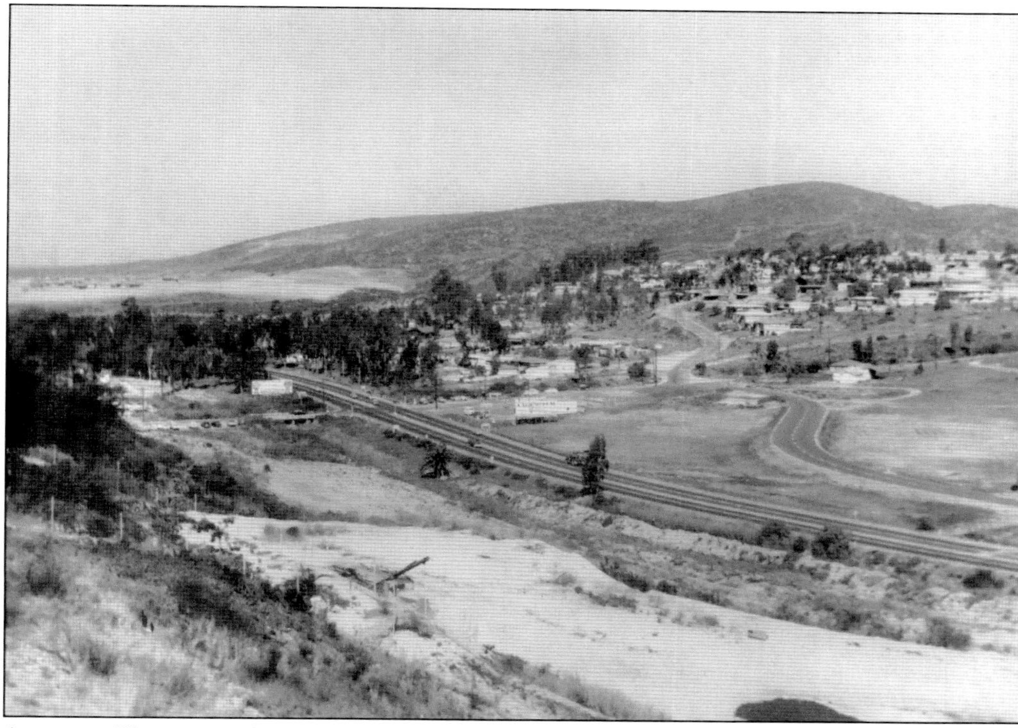

ALVARADO HIGHWAY AT SEVENTIETH STREET/LAKE MURRAY BOULEVARD C. 1955. Alvarado Highway, opened in 1950, provided access to not only Maryland Heights but the north city's San Diego neighbors as well: the old Waring Ranch, now Allied Gardens (1954); Del Cerro (1955, being graded); and San Carlos (1959). The partially developed 1920s Rasonia subdivision on the hill overlooking Murray Dam, shown here at center right with its streets named after states, would eventually be annexed into La Mesa.

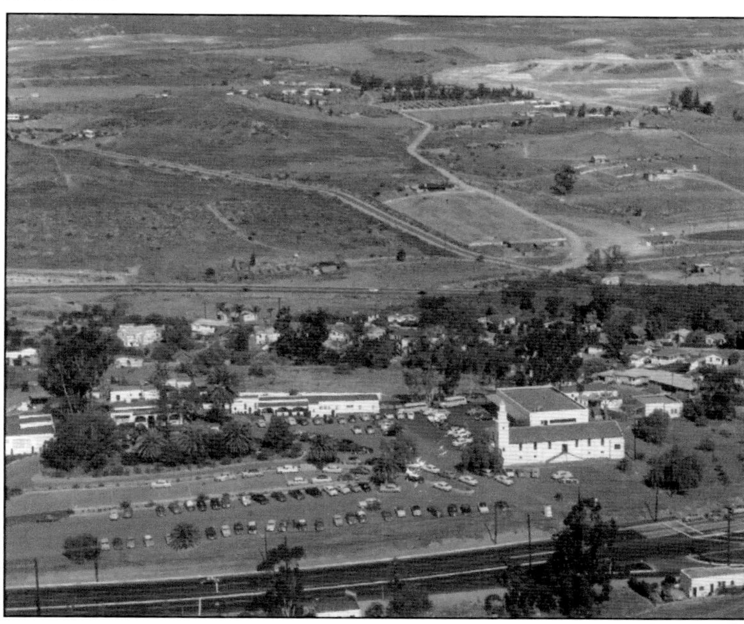

PREPPED FOR DEVELOPMENT, C. 1952. This view from above the relocated and expanded St. Martin's Church and Academy School at El Cajon and La Mesa Boulevards shows what would rapidly become the city's new population center. Baltimore Drive is the paved road heading toward top left. The initial grading for the planned 1,000-home Lake Murray Manor tract is seen at upper right.

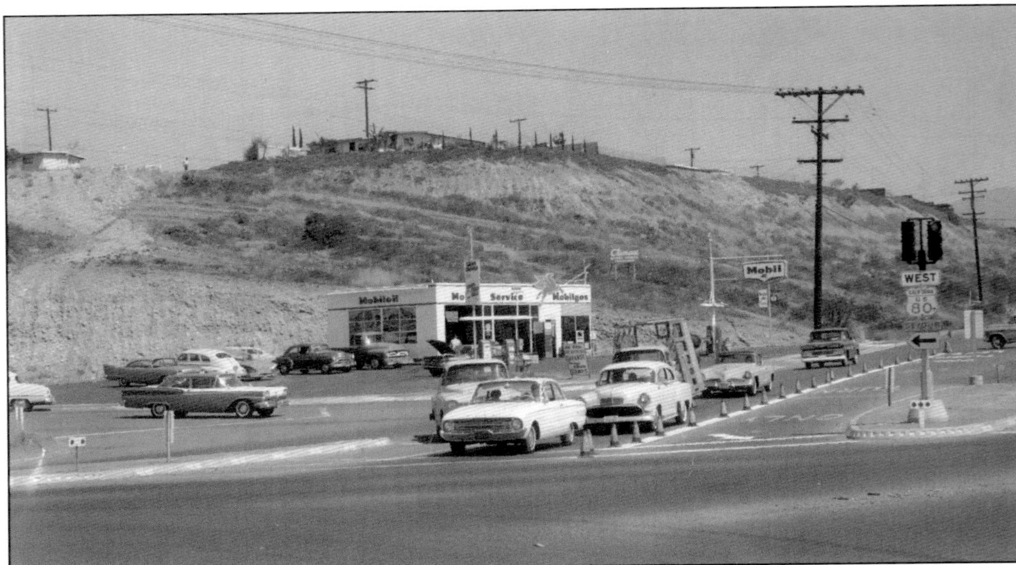

Jackson and Fletcher and Jackson Drive Houses, c. 1959. In early 1951, discussions of developing Texas oilman H. H. Howell's property for up to 2,500 new homes began. Questions of annexation to La Mesa or to San Diego swirled. Developers and contractors already building in other San Diego tracts began to inquire and propose development. La Mesa moved quickly to annex the area within the irrigation district boundary line below old Flume Road and provided access through a Jackson Drive extension. In 1952, developers Bollenbacher and Kelton's Lake Murray Manor tract opened south of Lake Murray Boulevard and east of Marengo Avenue with many Texas-inspired street names per Howell. Marketing to the large entry-level VA/GI loan market, these early tracts featured several models of prebuilt, contemporary-style homes that were quickly filled with new suburbanites.

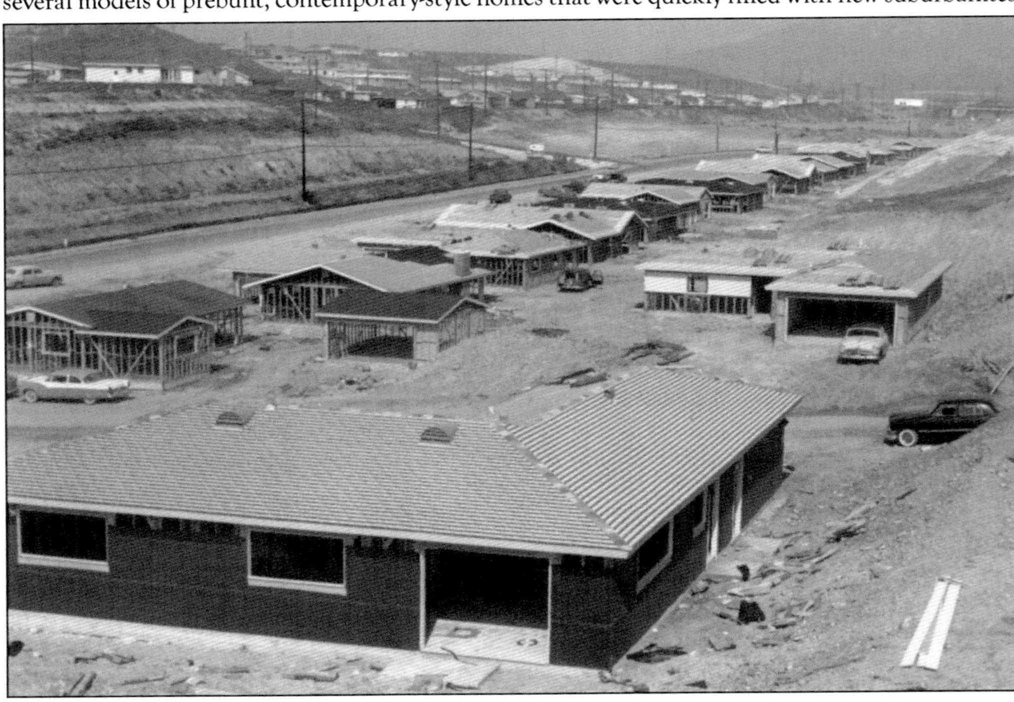

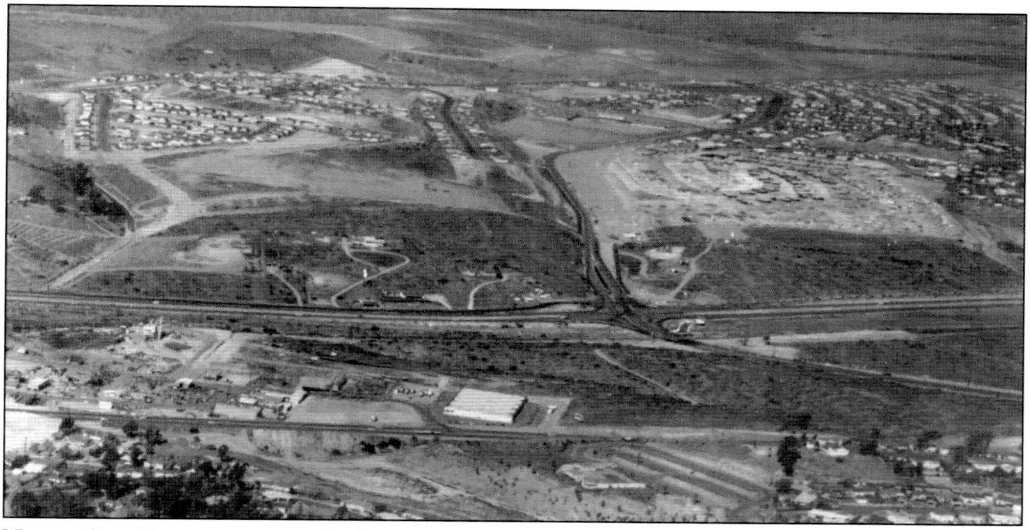

North City Emerges c. 1957. Hobart Home's Lake Murray Village (1955–1959), with homes west of Jackson Drive, was the largest development. The "Village" was preceded by numerous Fletcher Hills/Severin Manor tracts (starting 1946), Lake Murray Manor (1952), and Regal Homes' Parkway Manor (1955) and was followed by McDonald Brothers' Town and Country units (1956), Smith and Kahn's Lake Oaks (1959), Dass Construction's Lake View Estates (1960), and American Housing Guild's College Hill (1963).

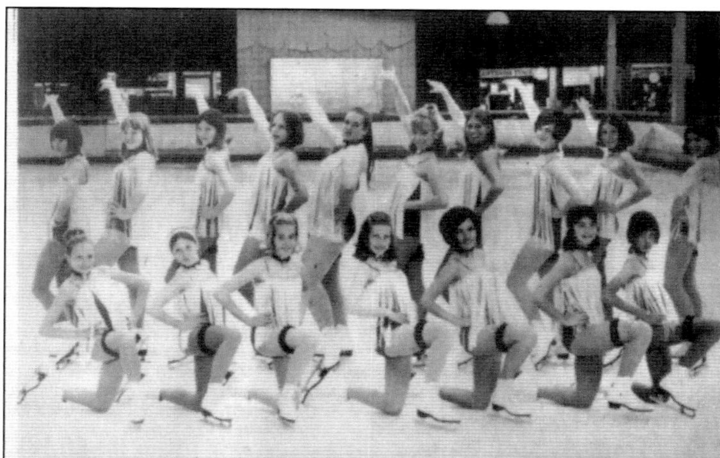

HOUSE OF ICE OPENS — Seven La Mesans are among the "Cabaret" dancers featured in the San Diego Figure Skating Club's revue, "Welcome to the House of Ice," due April 26 and 27, 8 p.m. in the new La Mesa rink. Left to right, back are: Karen Chillo of College Park, Susan Stark of East San Diego, Zane Clark of La Mesa, Bonnie Markle of La Jolla, Lori Stewart of San Carlos, Jan Shinski of Lemon Grove, Valerie Coffield of La Mesa, Christine Knott of Serra Mesa, Janet Tressman of La Mesa and Cathy Chadwick of Point Loma. Left to right, front are: Cathy Evans of Serra Mesa, Pattie Schutte of Allied Gardens, Carrie Riehle of La Mesa, Sharon Ballard of La Mesa, Lisa Kershaw of La Mesa, Linda Lippett of La Jolla, and Karry Eschenburg of La Mesa.

"House of Ice Skaters," 1969. The northern neighborhoods included more than houses and schools. The city added several new parks, including Jackson and Briercrest (1959), La Mesita (1960), Sunset (1962), Northmont (1969), and Aztec (1975). Shopping centers provided groceries and other services, but many fondly remember family entertainment businesses La Mesa Bowl (1963), later Coleman College, and this Lake Murray Boulevard ice skating arena (now a local church).

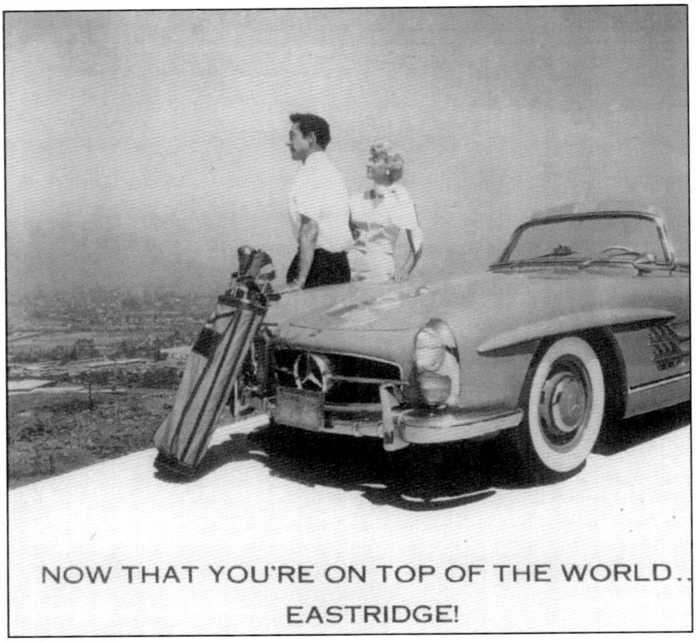

EASTRIDGE ADVERTISEMENT, 1960. Not all La Mesa developments were aimed at the middle-class market. High-end tracts, such as Grossmont Hills off Severin Drive and Eastridge overlooking Helix High, provided homes marketed to professionals, featuring view lots and large custom contemporary-style homes. Notably Eastridge would only be partially built-out in the 1960s, seeing its final development in 2006.

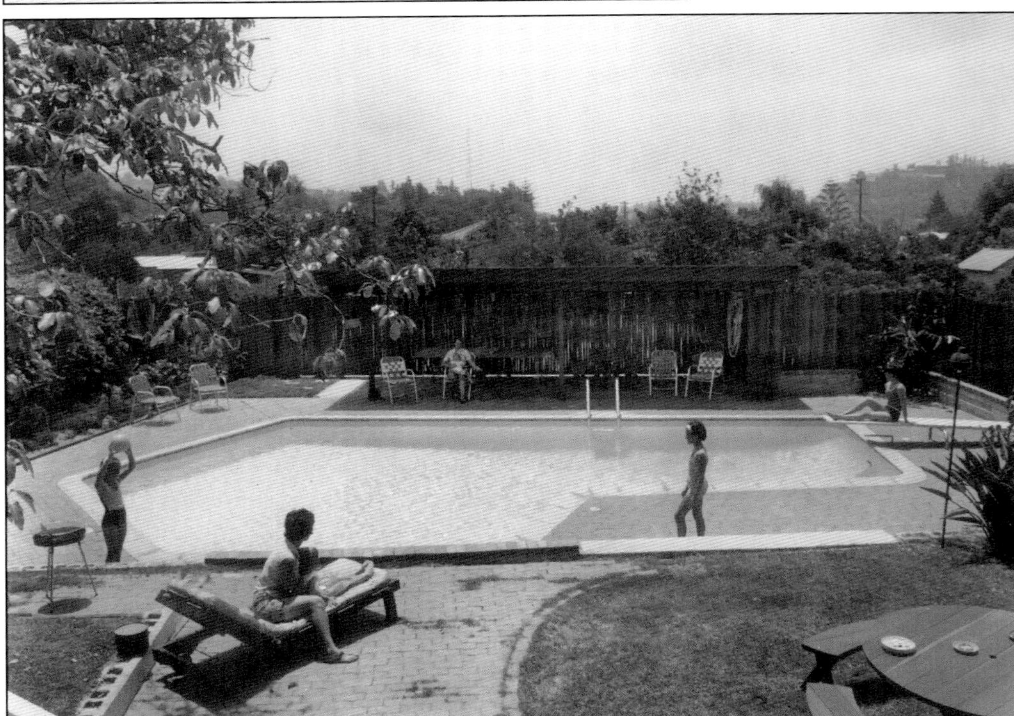

LA MESA SUBURBAN BACKYARD, 1960S. Suburbanites were able to personalize and improve their homes with amenities such as swimming pools, barbecues, rec rooms, and outdoor patios. Postwar La Mesa subsequently became a poster community for the young and vibrant San Diego outdoor suburban lifestyle. Not without problems and growing pains, most postwar residents still recall these vibrant years of growth fondly.

Six

Hometown for the Next Century
1980 to Present

By 1980, La Mesa had completed four straight decades of double-digit population growth, having topped 50,000 residents that year. The 25-percent growth experienced in the 1970s, when the town was led by Mayors J. Robert Helland and Paul Fordem and city managers Donald Wolfer and Gayle Martin, was fueled by increases in apartment and condominium projects (the first dating back to 1964), filling in downtown lots and following the Spring Street extension south, and in the north following auto corridors Baltimore Drive, Parkway Drive, Lake Murray Boulevard, and Fletcher Parkway. In the 1980s, downtown redevelopment plans were implemented west of Spring Street, featuring multistory housing and the La Mesa Springs Shopping Center, all overseen under direction of Mayors George Bailey and Fred Nagel Jr. The revival of the old San Diego and Arizona Railroad line as part of the San Diego trolley system also made La Mesa a prime candidate for new transit-oriented and multiuse developments during the last two decades both downtown and along Fletcher Parkway and Amaya Drive, most of it under the watch of longtime city manager Dave Wear (1990–2002) and the city's longest serving mayor, Art Madrid (1990–present). Although La Mesa's growth has steadied, it continues to be not only a sought-out location for doing business, making a home, and raising a family but also a community that generously welcomes visitors to its historic downtown village to experience the customer-friendly services of its locally owned small businesses and annual and regular community events such as Oktoberfest, Flag Day parades, classic car shows, antique shops, and weekly farmer's markets. As La Mesa enters its next century, its hard-earned reputation as a well-run suburban city with popular and sought-after child-to-senior-friendly recreational programs, tree-lined, walkable streets, and diverse retail and commercial opportunities continues to foster a community proud of its long-standing traditions of first-rate civil servants, merchants, service clubs, schools, parks, neighborhoods, and neighbors—all integral parts of La Mesa's time-honored hometown qualities.

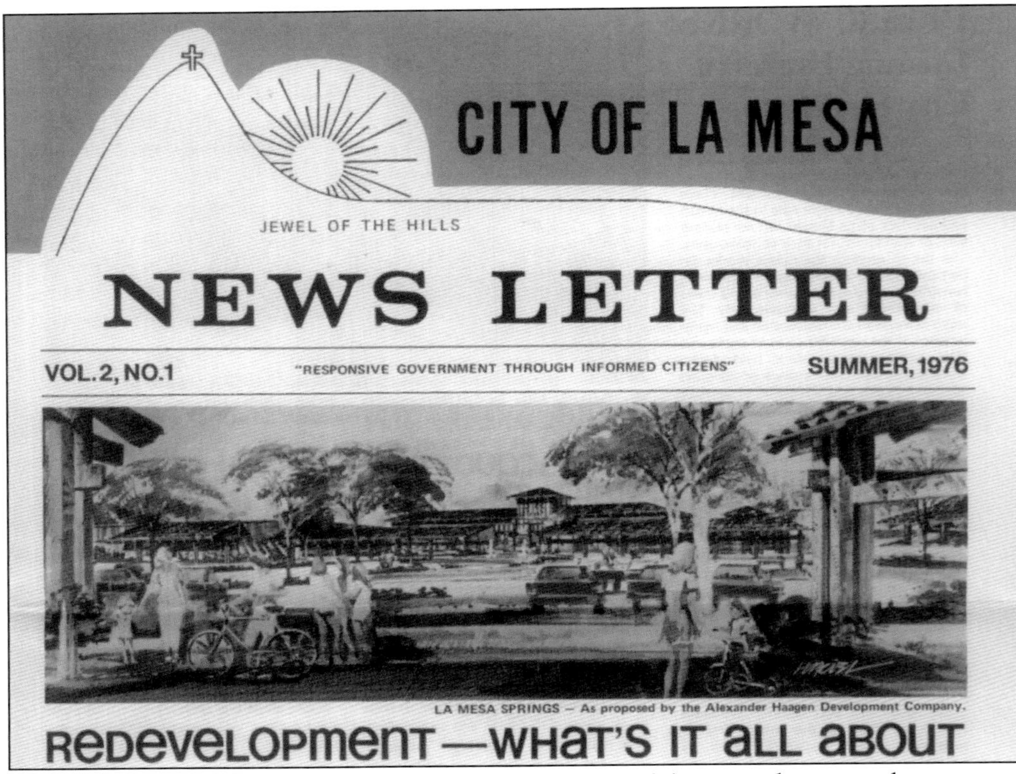

CITY OF LA MESA

JEWEL OF THE HILLS

NEWS LETTER

VOL. 2, NO.1 "RESPONSIVE GOVERNMENT THROUGH INFORMED CITIZENS" SUMMER, 1976

LA MESA SPRINGS – As proposed by the Alexander Haagen Development Company.

REDEVELOPMENT—WHAT'S IT ALL ABOUT

DOWNTOWN REDEVELOPMENT, 1976–1990S. Revitalization of the aging downtown business and residential district had roots in the 1960s. In the late 1970s, the La Mesa Springs Shopping Center was a catalyst redevelopment project, providing a supermarket, new businesses, and ample free parking. It also initiated mandated public participation in city development projects and planning efforts, a direct result of citizen empowerment brought about by the environmental movement.

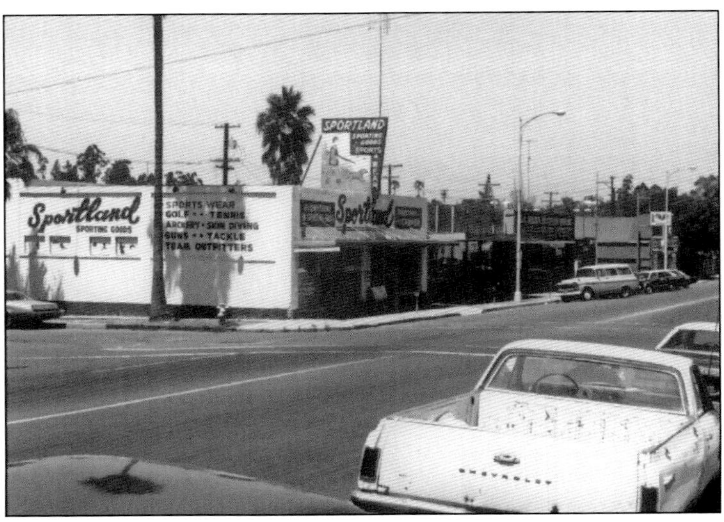

REDEVELOPMENT AREA, LA MESA BOULEVARD, 1980. The greatest changes occurred west of Spring Street and north of La Mesa Boulevard up to Allison Street. Several multistory and multiuse projects replaced aging and obsolete business blocks, resulting in new residential and commercial buildings, closing one block of Date Avenue north of the boulevard, and truncating Orange Avenue.

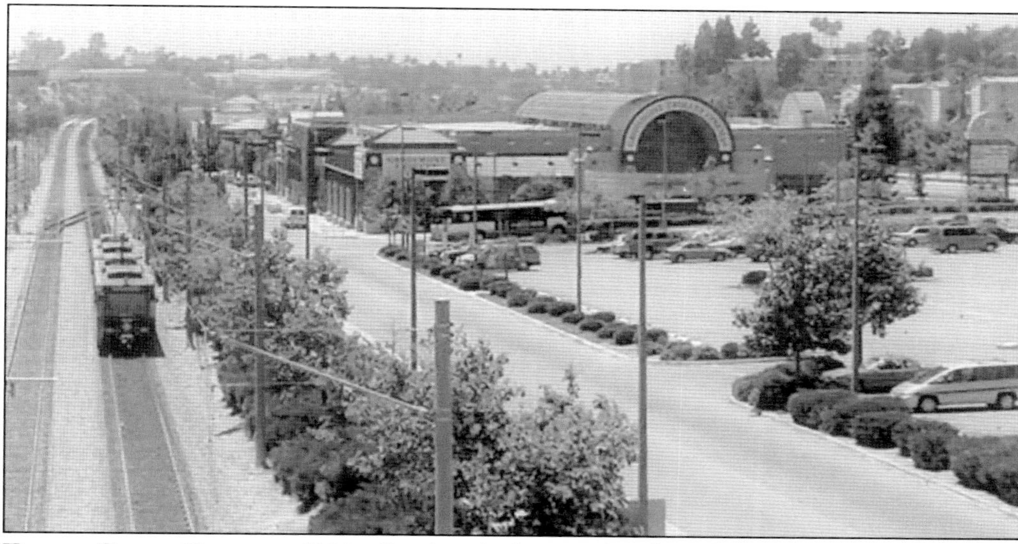

TROLLEY CENTER THEATERS, 1990s. One hundred years after the railroad arrived in La Mesa, rail transit reappeared with the San Diego trolley in 1989. The trolley not only provided an important mass-transit option for La Mesans and visitors, it also triggered additional housing, commercial, and mixed-use projects such as long-planned and award-winning Fletcher Parkway developments.

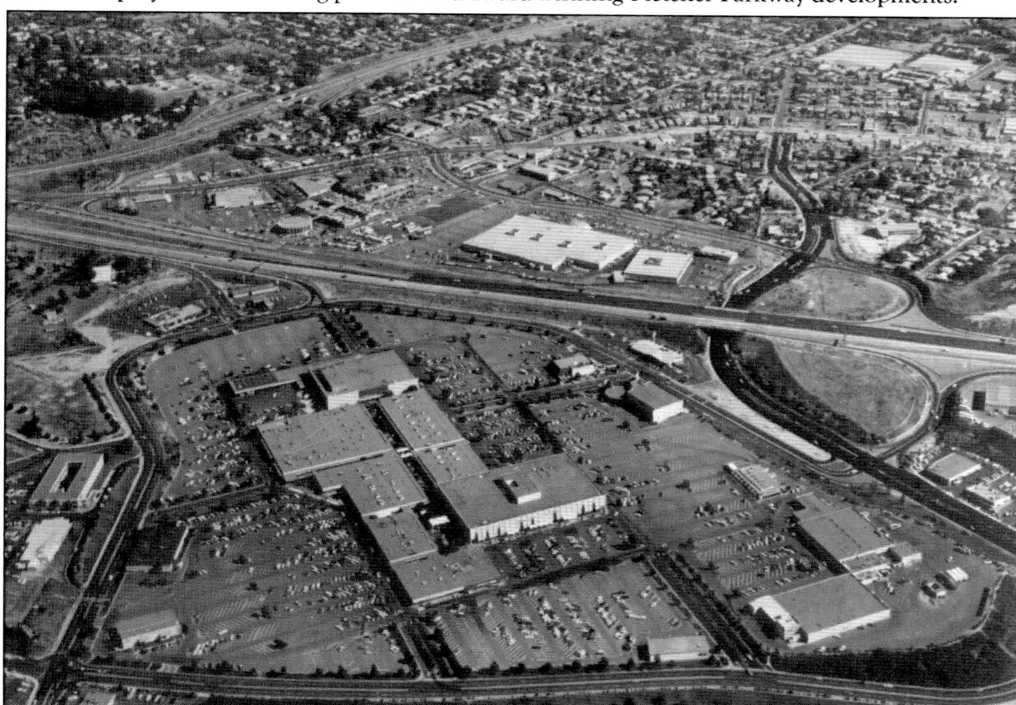

GROSSMONT CENTER, 1980s. With residential development slowed, the city focused on its commercial development. Grossmont Center continued to be an economic mainstay, with anchor retailers, restaurants, and entertainment venues providing employment and revenue. The center also triggered additional commercial projects surrounding and across Interstate 8 along Jackson Drive and Grossmont Boulevard.

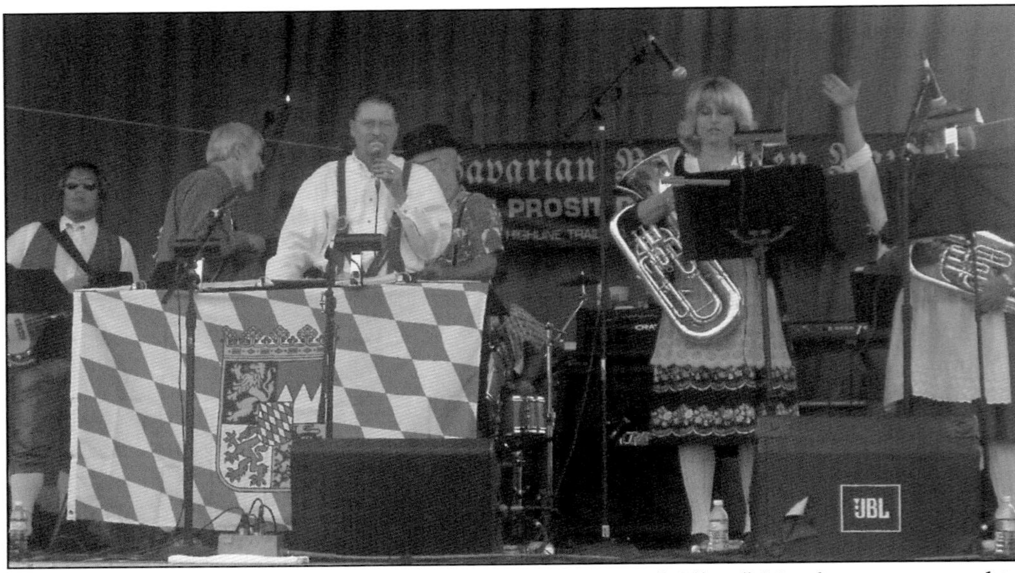

OKTOBERFEST PERFORMERS, **2005.** In 1975, the Downtown "Village" Merchants converted its annual sidewalk sale into the first official Oktoberfest street fair. From a first year attendance of 300, the event grew rapidly, meeting the visitor demand for booths, stages, and beer gardens. Today the Village Merchant Association's annual three-day event features over 300 vendor booths, live entertainment, and attracts an estimated 200,000 attendees. (Eva Hill.)

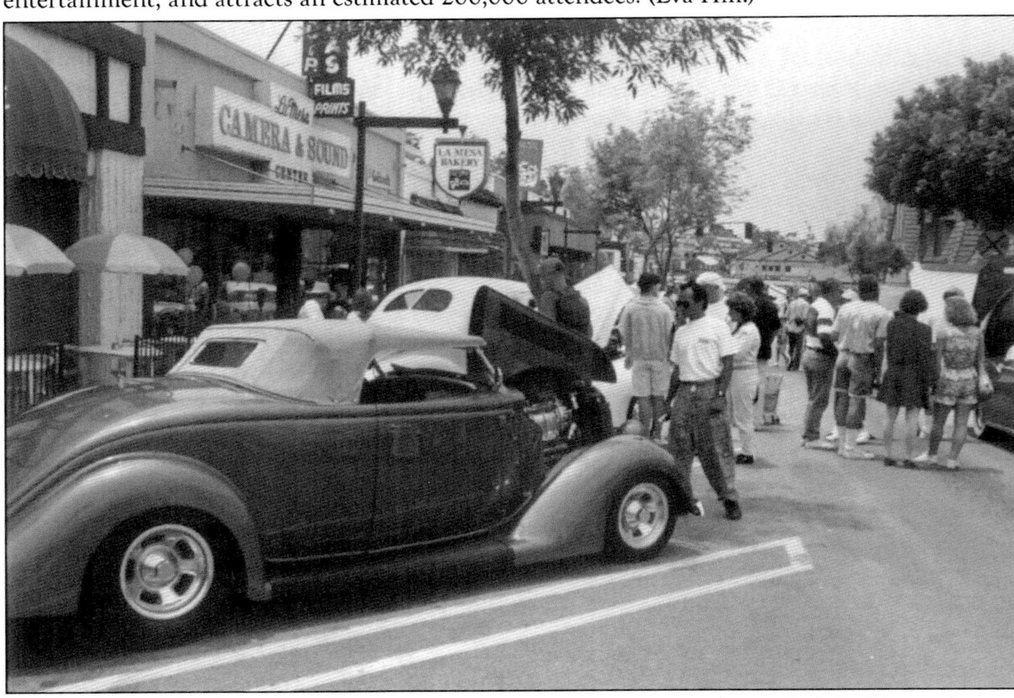

SUMMER CAR SHOW, **1990s.** The success of the Village as an attraction has included additional events and programs. The historic buildings and pedestrian-friendly small-town atmosphere, along with events such as weekly summer classic car shows and year-round farmer's markets, popular restaurants, an array of antique shops and specialty stores, has become an iconic La Mesa community asset.

Flag Day Parade, 2008. The last Fiesta de los Flores parade was in 1958, and although the La Mesa Arts and Crafts show, sponsored by local longtime civic groups such as the Foothills Arts Association, continued, it was not until 1997 that the annual Flag Day Parade reinstituted the tradition of a community-wide display of La Mesa's civic pride.

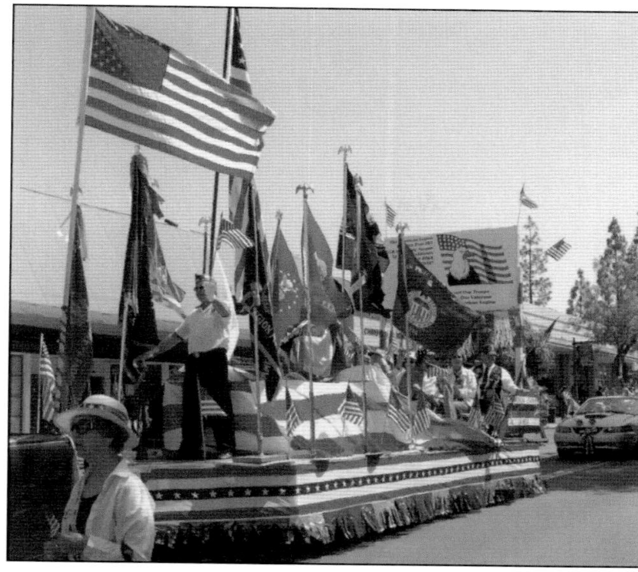

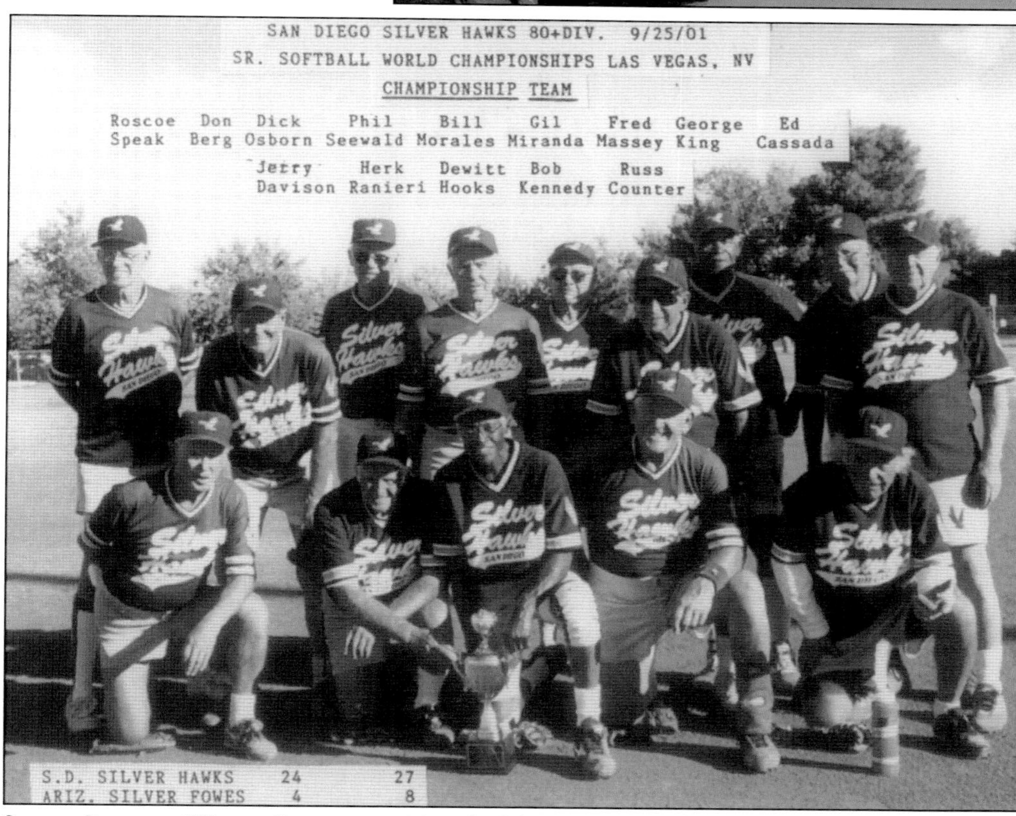

Senior Softball World Champions, 2001. La Mesa is renowned for its wonderful array of youth and senior arts, culture, and recreational programs. Its award-winning Adult Enrichment Center features diverse senior-based programming. Notably the La Mesa–based senior softball league has been another source of community pride, especially during its 1988–2001 run featuring 10 world championships led by Senior Softball Hall of Famer and La Mesan Don Berg.

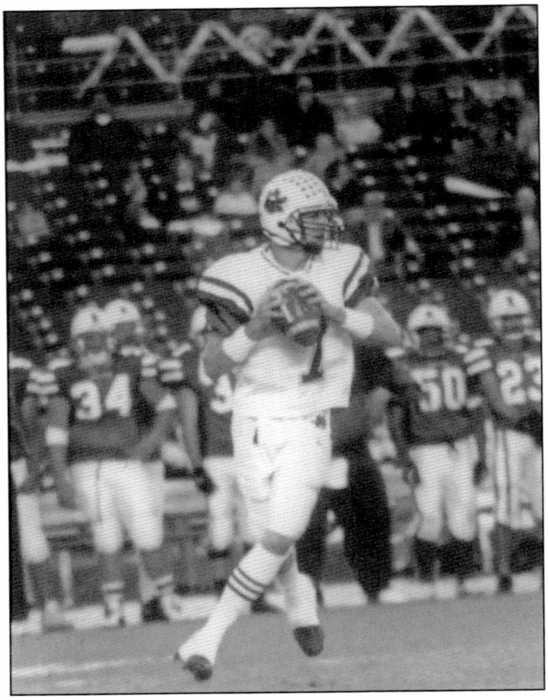

HELIX HIGH'S ALEX SMITH AND REGGIE BUSH, 2001. Helix High athletics has experienced a long run of success, notably in its football program. The record-setting program, led by legendary coaches such as Jim Arnaiz (1973–1999), has produced multiple championships and numerous college and NFL players. Most memorably are the 2000–2001 championship teams that featured quarterback Alex Smith and running back Reggie Bush. Smith later led the University of Utah to an undefeated season in 2004, becoming the first choice in the 2005 NFL draft. Bush went on to star at USC, winning the 2005 Heisman Trophy as the most outstanding college football player, and was the second draft pick in 2006. Both players were Heisman finalists in 2004, the only time a high school had two finalists in the same year.

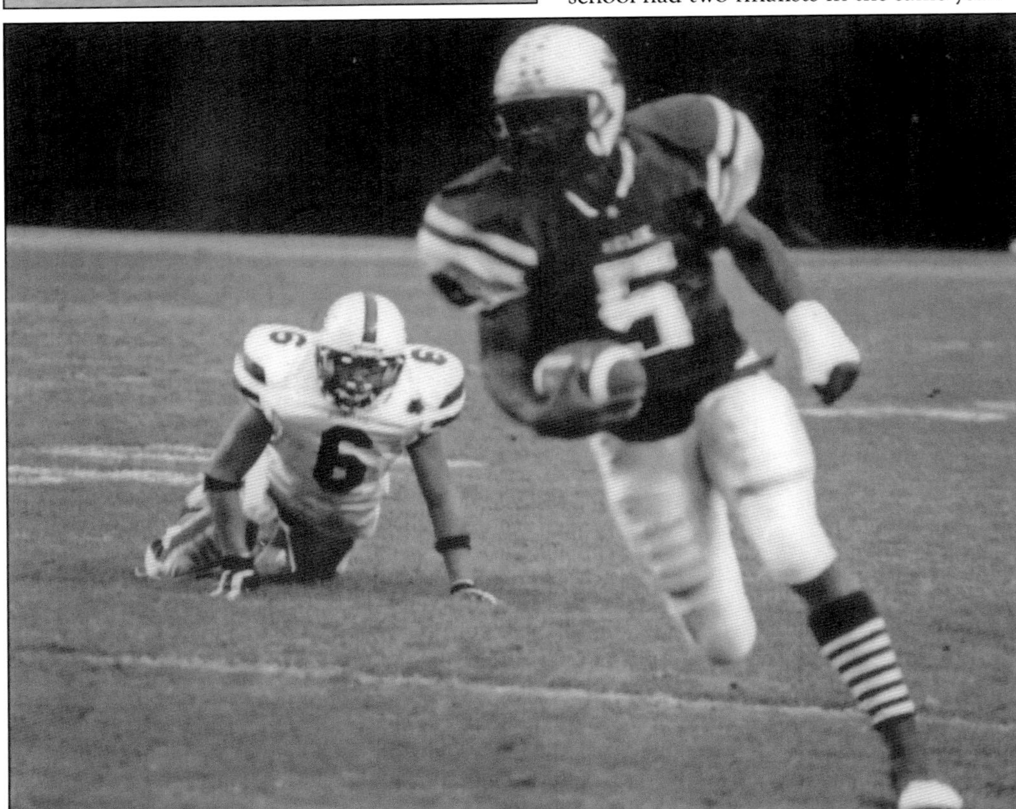

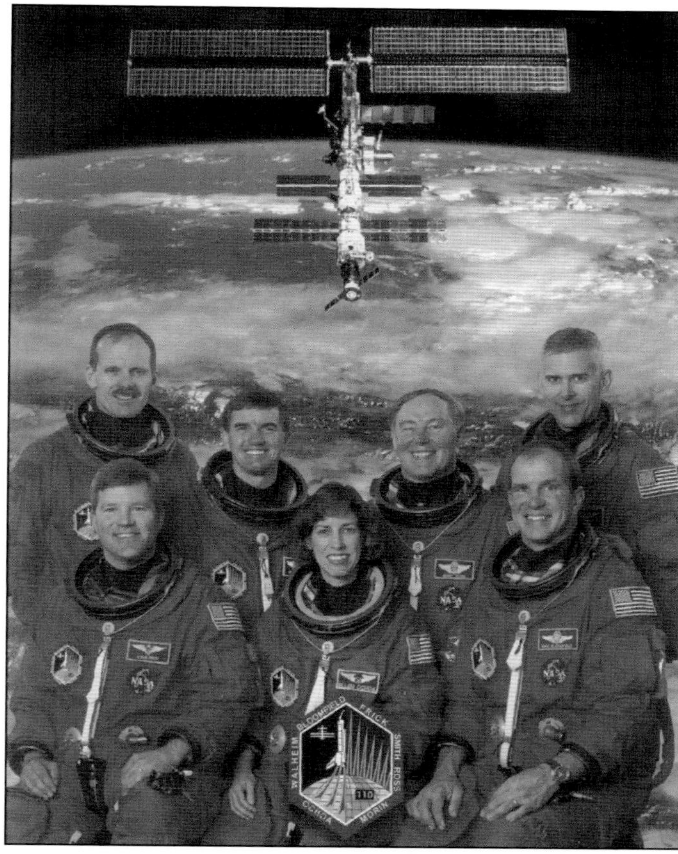

GROSSMONT HIGH ASTRONAUTS ELLEN OCHOA AND RICK STURKOW. While Grossmont High also produced many great athletes, it became renown for being the only public high school having three alumni who were astronauts. Joining Bill Anders were Dr. Ellen Ochoa (right, bottom center), class of 1975, also a graduate of San Diego State University, an optics specialist who logged hundreds of hours in space as member of four space shuttle missions; and Rick Sturkow, class of 1978, seen with his former teachers Fred Helm and Kay Adams. Sturkow was a U.S. Marine Corps pilot, Operation Desert Storm veteran, and two-time shuttle mission pilot. (Both, Grossmont High Museum.)

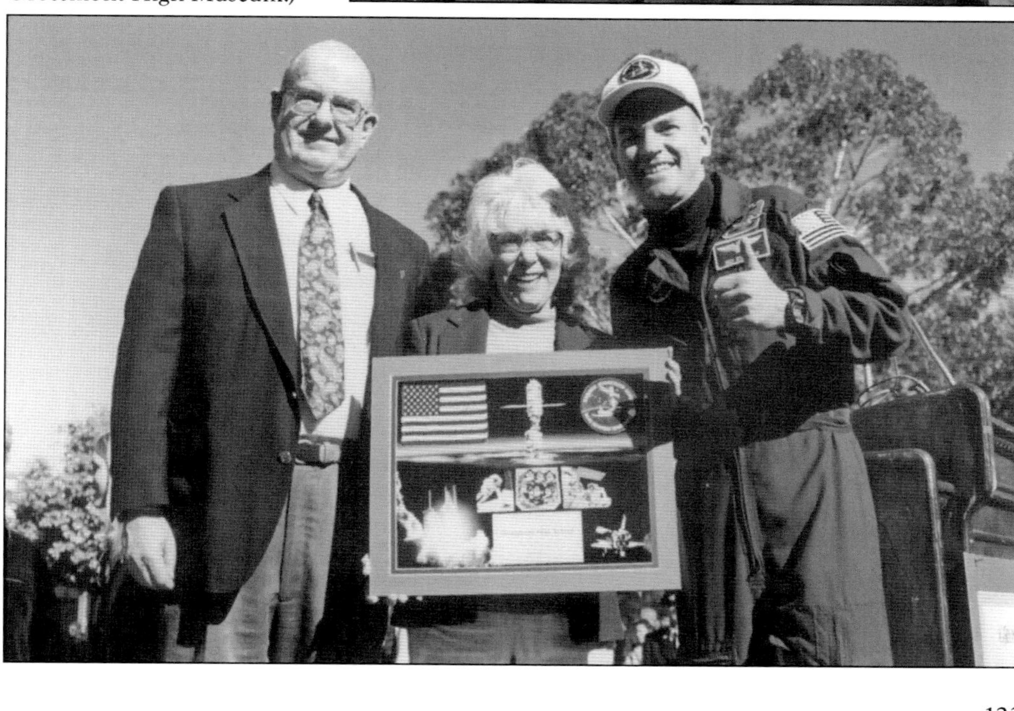

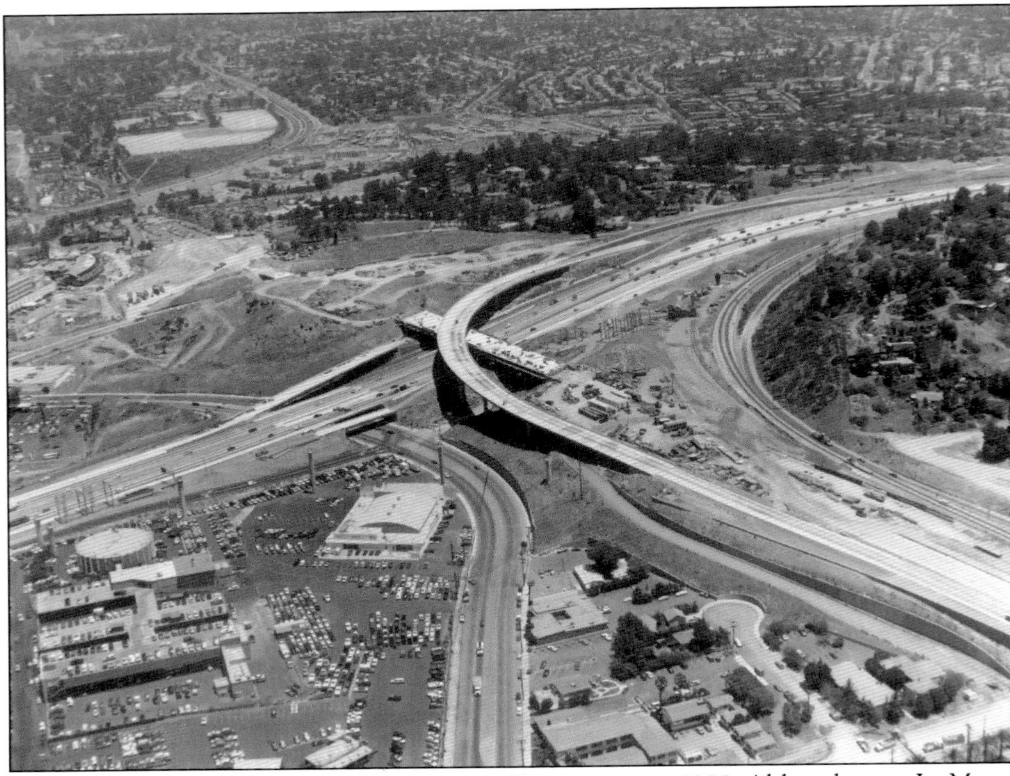

Interstate 8–State Route 125 Interchange Construction, 1988. Although most La Mesans cannot hope to travel to space, they can reach some elevation on this major freeway interchange. Planned for several decades before being funded in the late 1980s, the northern 125 extension through Fletcher Hills provides direct freeway access to Grossmont Junior College and on to Santee. Also shown are the Drew Ford roundhouse showroom and the now-gone Aquarius RollerRink.

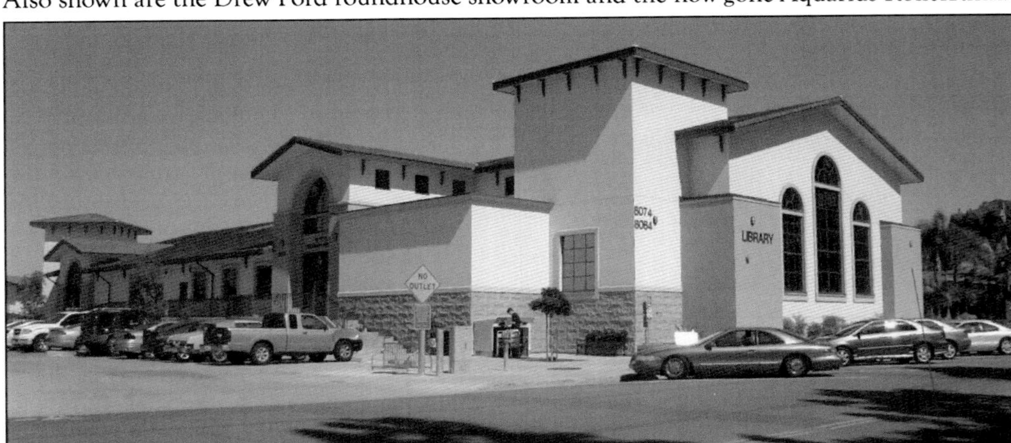

New La Mesa Library, 2008. From the early 1990s, La Mesa had looked to replacing and upgrading its civic center complex. Plans called for a new north-side vehicle entrance, new fire and police stations, and library, post office, and administration building upgrades. The new Fire Station No. 11 (2006), library (2008) and post office (2009) opened first, with the new police station dedication set for 2010.

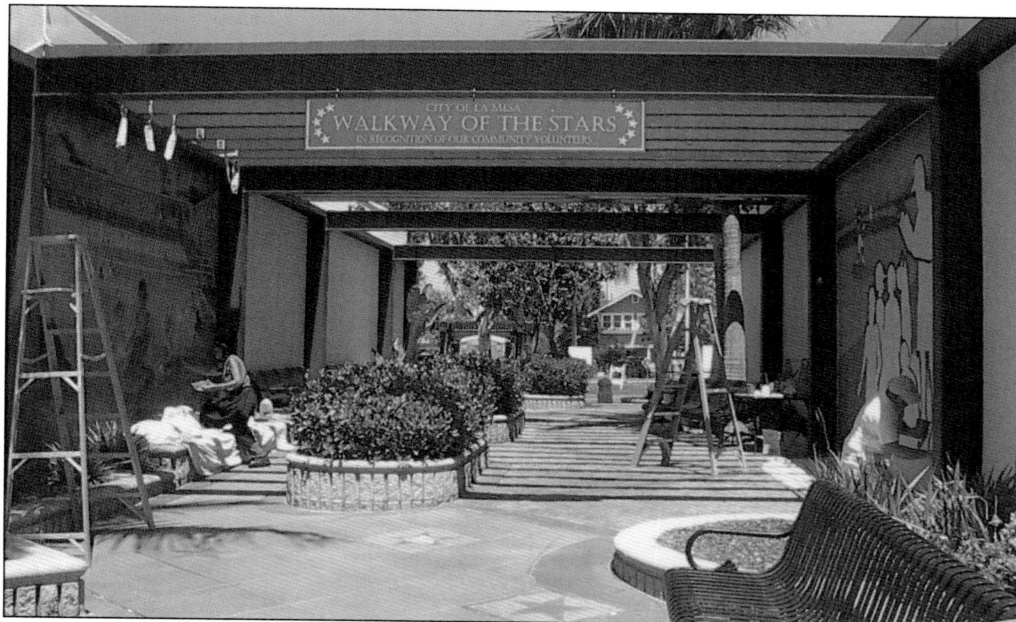

WALKWAY OF THE STARS MURALS, 2004. La Mesa takes pride in its wide range of community services, service clubs, and civic-minded citizens. Longstanding councilmember Ruth Sterling provided the vision for honoring those extraordinary city volunteers who provide over 10,000 hours of service with this downtown urban park. The murals were added in the theme of "People Helping People."

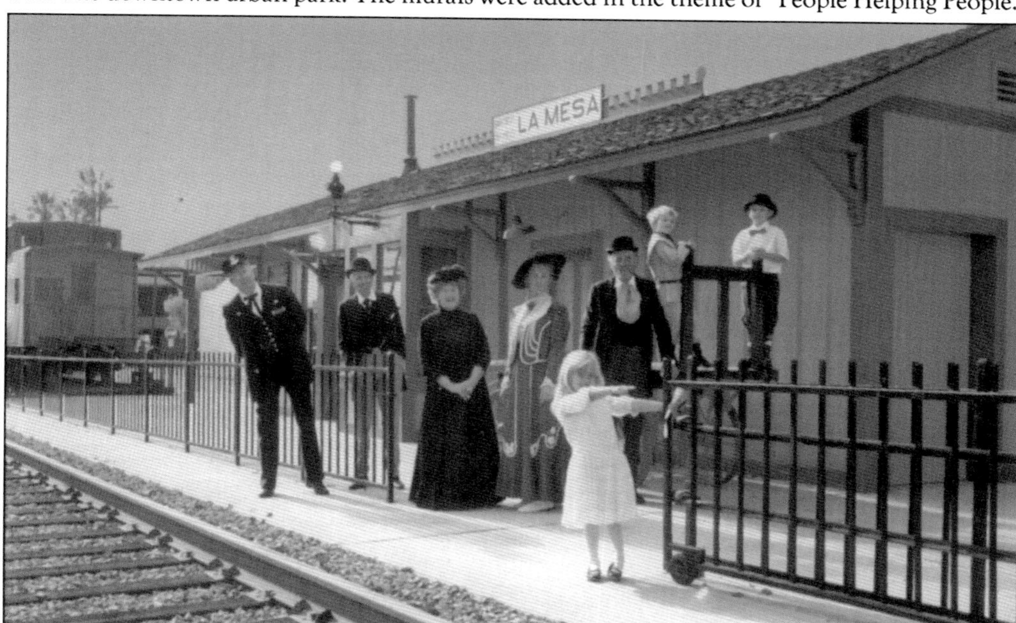

RELIVING LA MESA HISTORY, 1994. San Diego Railroad Museum volunteer and La Mesa architect Larry Rose led the effort to return and restore the historic 1894 La Mesa Depot to its original location in the late 1970s and early 1980s. The project resulted in purchasing the dilapidated building from its relocated site in Lakeside, coordinating for its return to its original location, and completing its historic restoration and furnishing.

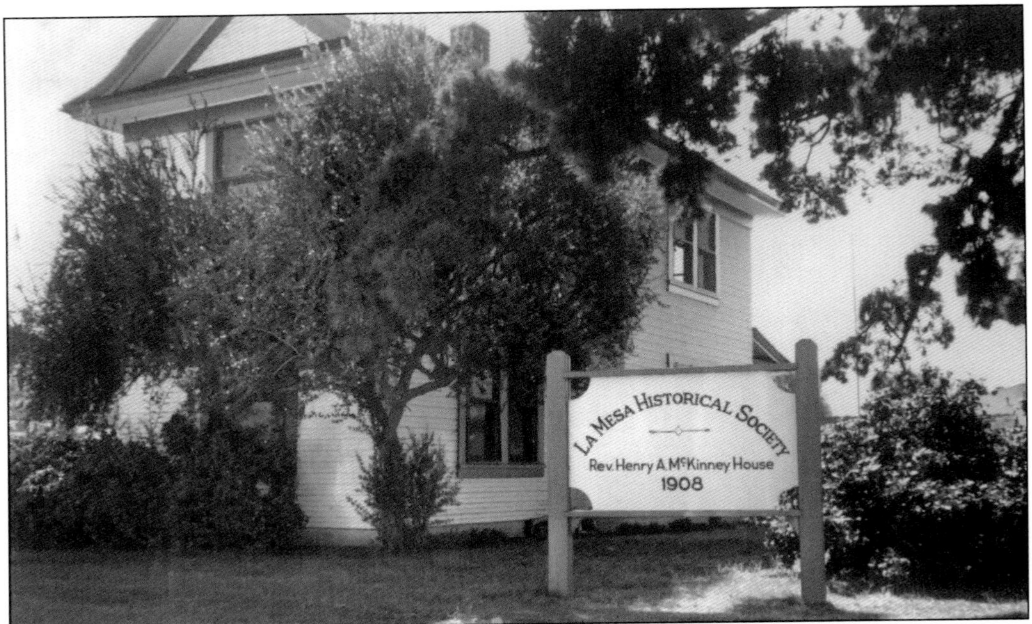

Historical McKinney House 1978 and the Jewel of the Hills 1925. Founded in 1976, the La Mesa Historical Society is a volunteer organization actively engaged in preserving La Mesa's unique heritage for future generations to seek out and enjoy. The society operates the historic H. A. McKinney House Museum at the corner of University Avenue and Pine Street. The society's historical archives provide La Mesa with an invaluable resource for researching and compiling the story of the individuals, buildings, institutions, sites, and events that make up the community's collective past. Society activities include historic home tours, presentations, lectures, exhibits, publications, and documentation and promotion of local historic preservation activities. The society hopes that readers have enjoyed this brief look into the history of La Mesa—in our humble opinion, still the "Jewel of the Hills."

La Mesa - Jewel of the Hills

IF you'd find a quiet haven, far from storm and stress of life,
Where sweet peace and love abideth and no tho't of restless strife,
Seek La Mesa, beauteous suburb, San Diego's child, alone,
Nestled in among the foothills, near the vale of El Cajon.

WHERE the ever watchful mountains as on picket duty stand,
Guarding o'er the cozy dwellings, fairest picture in the land;
When the sun in dying splendor, sheds its glory everywhere,
Tinting all with radiant beauty, happy homes and gardens rare.

THERE the peak of Grossmont riseth dark against the azure sky,
And the stately head of Helix, with old San Miguel close by;
Looking westward in the distance, dimly seen the ocean blue,
With the wondrous mother city lying plainly in the view.

SEEK La Mesa, perfect jewel, in a setting most sublime,
And you'll choose to live your life there in the Southland's gentle clime;
And if from its friendly borders you should ever chance to roam,
In your heart you'll hear it call, calling you to come back home.

WHERE the birds all wish to tarry, far from gale and tempest roar,
And are evermore returning when their wanderings are o'er;
Where the flowers are always blooming 'neath the California sun,
You would love this little city and its people, every one.

Mary D. Garfield.

Bibliography

Adema, Thomas Joseph. *Our Hills and Valleys: A History of the Helix–Spring Valley Region.* San Diego: San Diego Historical Society, 1993.

Bibb, Leland Eugene. *The La Mesa Town Center Project.* M.A. thesis, Public Administration and Urban Studies, California State University, San Diego, 1973.

El Cajon Valley News. Various newspaper articles, 1889–1930. El Cajon Historical Society Archives, El Cajon, CA.

Fletcher Collection. MS81 collection. Including the San Diego Flume Company Archives. University of California, San Diego, Special Collections.

Gilbert, Anna M. *La Mesa Yesterday and Today.* La Mesa: La Mesa Women's Club, 1924, reprint 1975.

Ginn, Donald J. *Grossmont High History.* MS, Grossmont High School Museum Archives, 2006.

Guy, Hubert. *Grossmont: It Isn't Just A Shopping Center, A Comprehensive History of Grossmont, Mount Helix, and the Surrounding Valleys.* El Cajon, CA: privately published, 1993.

La Mesa Historical Society Archives. Photographs, manuscripts, newspapers, maps, clipping files, and primary and secondary source materials. Palermo Building, La Mesa, CA.

La Mesa Scout. Various newspaper articles, 1907–1985. La Mesa Historical Society Archives, La Mesa, CA.

La Mesa Spring Valley School District (LMSVSD) Archives. Photographs, manuscripts, records, maps, drawings, plans, clipping files, and primary and secondary source materials. La Mesa and Spring Valley, CA.

Linke, Howard Charles. *The Evolution of the La Mesa City Government.* M.A. thesis, Public Administration, San Diego State College, 1965.

San Diego Union. Various newspaper articles, 1869–2009. San Diego State University, Love Library.

Strathman, Theodore Andrew. *Dream Of A Big City: Water Politics and San Diego County Growth, 1910–1947.* Ph.D. dissertation, University of California, San Diego, 2005.

West, Norrie, Karna Webster, Pat Kettler, and Carol Lockwood. *La Mesa through the Years.* La Mesa, CA: La Mesa Historical Society, 2001.

Wolin, Rita, et al. *La Mesa–A Brief History, A Bicentennial Salute 1976.* La Mesa, CA: La Mesa Historical Society, 1976.